Hungary: A Decade of Economic Reform

Hungary: A Decade of Economic Reform

Edited by
P. G. HARE, H. K. RADICE
and N. SWAIN

London
GEORGE ALLEN & UNWIN
Boston   Sydney

First published in 1981

GEORGE ALLEN & UNWIN LTD
40 Museum Street, London WC1A 1LU

© P. G. Hare, H. K. Radice and N. Swain, 1981

British Library Cataloguing in Publication Data

Hungary.
  1. Hungary – Economic policy – 1945 –
  I. Hare, P. G.   II. Radice, H. K.
  III. Swain, N.
  330.9439′053   HC300.28   80-42124

  ISBN 0-04-339021-8

Set in 10 on 11 point Times by Red Lion Setters, London
and printed in Great Britain
by Biddles Ltd, Guildford, Surrey

Contents

Preface

The idea of writing this volume first arose in discussions between two of us (Hare and Radice) in 1977. We had previously worked individually on various aspects of the Hungarian economy, our interest being stimulated by the comprehensive reforms of 1968, which introduced what was then called the New Economic Mechanism. Unlike many of the reforms elsewhere in Eastern Europe, the Hungarian reforms, despite some setbacks, survived right through the 1970s. It is this long experience of reformed economic management that makes Hungary such an interesting country to study. This experience both demonstrates that there are viable alternatives to the traditional centralised model of planning of the Soviet type, and may also have some lessons for Western countries seeking to develop new forms of economic regulation and control.

By providing a generous research grant, the Social Science Research Council made it possible to translate rather sketchy ideas for assessing the first decade of Hungary's reformed system of economic management into the reality of a book. Nigel Swain (the third editor) was employed as a research fellow for the project, which culminated in a small research colloquium held at Stirling University at Easter 1979. The papers presented there, now revised and updated, form the main content of this book.

Research on Hungary is facilitated by the volume of good economic literature produced there, including excellent statistical publications. Most of the papers by Western economists presented here were based on individual research visits to Hungary, so they required co-operation and support from a large number of economic institutions and involved interviews with many academic economists, officials and enterprise staff and managers. The fact that such co-operation and assistance were forthcoming on an impressively generous scale is a testimony to the openness of economic debate in Hungary. We have all made good friends too in Hungary; it is a hospitable country, and the restaurants of Budapest are a strong incentive to further research. We thank, on behalf of all the Western contributors to this volume, our many Hungarian colleagues and friends for their support.

We would also like to thank the British Library and the library of the Institute of Soviet and East European Studies, Glasgow University, which proved to be valuable sources of Hungarian literature, and the University of Stirling for hosting our colloquium.

Finally, the revised papers were admirably typed, despite the abundance of unfamiliar Hungarian names, by Mrs E. Bruce, Mrs A. Cowie, Mrs C. McIntosh, Mrs W. Sharp (Stirling University) and Miss A.

Gaskin (Leeds University); their help at all stages of preparing the manuscript was quite invaluable.

PGH (Stirling)   *April 1980*
HKR (Leeds)
NS   (Cambridge)

Note on the authors

The editors

P. G. Hare Senior lecturer in economics, Stirling University. He has a D.Phil. (Oxford) on Hungarian planning techniques and has published several articles on the Hungarian economic reforms, notably in *Soviet Studies* (1976) and the *Cambridge Journal of Economics* (1977).

H. K. Radice Lecturer in economics, Leeds University. He has written several articles on the Hungarian economic mechanism in general and on co-operation agreements between Western and Hungarian firms in particular.

N. Swain Sociologist, completing a Ph.D. thesis on Hungarian agriculture for Cambridge University. He was employed as a research fellow on the project supported by the Social Science Research Council, which led to this volume.

The remaining authors

A. Abonyi Assistant professor of politics, Department of Politics, Queen's University, Kingston, Ontario. He is currently working on a Ph.D. concerning the introduction of new technology by Hungarian enterprises.

I. Gábor and **P. Galasi** Lecturers in economics, Karl Marx University of Economics, Budapest. They have written several articles on the labour market and the second economy in Hungary.

G. Kozma Senior research fellow, Institute of Economic and Market Research, Budapest. In recent years he has mainly studied international factors affecting the Hungarian economy.

P. Marer Associate professor of international business, Indiana University, USA. He has written extensively on Hungary in the past. More recently, his research work has been concerned with international trade in general, but this volume provided him with an opportunity to combine these two themes.

M. Marrese Associate professor of economics, Northwestern University, USA. He recently completed a Ph.D. thesis on investment in Hungary and is now working on wage regulation and other aspects of the Hungarian economic mechanism.

X. Richet   Lecturer in economics, Université de Paris X, Nanterre, France. He has a long-standing interest in general features of the Hungarian economic mechanism and in economic reforms in Eastern Europe.

Hungarian Sources Mentioned in the References

1 Publishers

Akadémiai Kiadó	Academic Press
Kossuth Könyvkiadó	Kossuth Publishing House
Közgazdasági és Jogi Könyvkiadó	Economic and Legal Publishing House
Közoktatásügyi Kiadóvállalat	Educational Publications Enterprise
Szépirodalmi Könyvkiadó	Literary Publishing House
Tancsics Könyvkiadó Vállalat	Tancsics Book-Publishing Enterprise

2 Newspapers and Periodicals

Figyelő	The Observer (weekly economic newspaper)
Gazdálkodás	Farming
Gazdaság	The Economy
Ipargazdaság	Industrial Economics
Ipargazdasági Szemle	Review of Industrial Economics
Közgazdasági Szemle	Economic Review
Külgazdaság	External Economy
Marketing és Piackutatás	Marketing and Market Research
Mezőgazdasági és Élelmiszeripari Értesitő	Bulletin of the Ministry of Agriculture and Food Supply
Népszabadság	National Freedom (main daily newspaper)
Pénzügyi Szemle	Financial Review
Statisztikai Havi Közleményei	Monthly Statistical Bulletin
Statisztikai Szemle	Statistical Review
Valóság	Reality
Vezetéstudomány	Management Science
Világgazdaság	World Economy

3 Other Publications

Agrárgazdasági Kutató Intézet Füzetei	Pamphlets from the Agricultural Economics Research Institute
Beruházási-Epitőipari Adatok	Investment and Construction Industry Data
Ipari Adatok	Industrial Data
Ipari Addattár	Industrial Data Collection
Ipari és Épitőipari Statisztikai Értesitő	Statistical Information on Industry and Construction
Külkereskedelmi Árstatisztikai Adatok	Statistical Data on Foreign Trade Prices

*Külkereskedelmi Statisztikai
Évkönyv*
Magyar Füzetek
Magyar Statisztikai Zsebkönyv
*Mezőgazdasági Statisztikai
Zsebkönyv*
*Mezőgazdasági Szövetkezetek
Gazdálkodása a Számok Tükrében*
Statisztikai Évkönyv
Szövetkezeti Kutató Intézet Évkönyv

Szövetkezeti Kutató Intézet
Közleményei
Termelőszövetkezeti Jogszabályok

*Törvények és Rendeletek Hivatalos
Gyujteménye*

Foreign Trade Statistical Yearbook

Hungarian Reports
Statistical Handbook of Hungary
Statistical Handbook for Agriculture

*The Operation of Agricultural
Co-operatives in Figures*
Statistical Yearbook
*Yearbook of the Co-operative
Research Institute*
Reports of the Co-operative
Research Institute
*Statutory Provisions for Producer
Co-operatives*
*Official Collection of Laws and
Decrees*

4 Other Official Sources

Gazdaságkutató Intézet
Központi Statisztikai Hivatal
Termelőszövetkezetek Országos
Tanácsa

Economic Research Institute
Central Statistical Office
National Council for Producer
Co-operatives

Part One

General Issues

Chapter 1

Introduction

1 The context of economic reform in Hungary

Hungary is one of the smaller countries of Eastern Europe, with a population of only 10 million and an income *per capita* of about £1,000 in 1975; this is close to the average income level in Eastern Europe. But Hungary's relatively modest economic weight does not detract from the importance and interest of its innovations in the sphere of economic policy, which have deservedly attracted worldwide attention and critical discussion. It is these innovations which form the subject matter of the present volume. Of course, Hungary was not alone in Eastern Europe in introducing economic reforms in the 1960s, and it is essential to see the Hungarian reforms against the background of reforms going on elsewhere, as part of a reform movement. Moreover, even within Hungary the comprehensive reforms introduced in 1968, as the New Economic Mechanism, did not simply happen overnight; instead, they were preceded by several attempts to carry out minor reforms, which achieved only limited success, and by two years of impressively careful preparation. In carrying out their reform programme the Hungarians sought to learn from their own past mistakes as well as from the experience of other countries. Since 1968 many details of the original reform package have changed, but enough remains of the reform principles for us to be able to claim that the Hungarian economic mechanism has proved itself to be a viable alternative to the traditional centralised Soviet model of a planned economy. This is not, however, to claim that the performance of the economy has been as satisfactory as the leadership might have wished, as the chapters that follow make abundantly clear.

(a) *Economic management under traditional central planning*
From 1950 until the introduction of the 1968 reforms, Hungary was managed in accordance with the familiar Soviet model of centralised planning (Nove, 1977; Berliner, 1976; Joint Economic Committee, 1976). The principal instrument of economic management was the plan; five-year plans determined the broad framework of economic development in each period, while annual (and often quarterly) plans, disaggregated down to enterprise level, provided the basis for operational management. Enterprises received sales or output targets and

allocations of the major material inputs; in addition the plan specified cost reduction targets and the permitted wages fund for each enterprise. All these targets were based on plan calculations that sought to satisfy a large number of economic balances, taking into account the results achieved in the previous plan period.

Kornai (1975) pointed out that in practice the traditional methods of plan formulation employed in the centralised model do not permit the precise satisfaction of all such balances. This is partly because the information required to construct a detailed national plan cannot be assembled and processed in its entirety; the sheer volume of information is simply too vast. Moreover, all statistical agencies take some time to organise the data that they collect from enterprises and individuals into a form suitable for use in planning exercises. In addition, numerous indicators that enter into planning calculations (e.g. input norms) are at best approximations and with technical progress are likely to change quite rapidly in several branches of the economy. All this produces a situation where the planners are compelled to concentrate attention on a relatively small number of important economic balances while taking others into account only in a very rough and ready fashion. The result is inevitably a plan that is detailed but very approximate – hence the usual need to amend many enterprise plans in the course of their execution. Thus, the centralised model has the appearance but not the reality of precision. The practical inability to formulate reliable detailed plans was one source of pressure in favour of some type of economic reform, both in Hungary and elsewhere in Eastern Europe.

Aside from these problems of plan information, shortcomings of the enterprise-level incentive system added to the pressures for reform. The management of enterprises was rewarded on the basis of its performance in relation to plan. In particular, bonuses were paid for fulfilment of the output plan, whether or not this happened to satisfy the needs of customers. Ideally, of course, the plan itself should take account of the structure and level of demand, given the level of income and the prevailing price system. But there are lags in adjustment, and even the most detailed plans do not give enterprises output targets specified in terms of individual commodities. Instead, these targets were usually stated in value terms for commodity groups. Consequently, enterprises always had some degree of flexibility in varying their product mix towards 'easy' products to ensure fulfilment of the plan, although this meant on occasion producing goods not in demand. Given the short-run character of the enterprise incentive system, with bonuses based on performance in the current year, it is not surprising that enterprises often appeared reluctant to introduce new technology or new products, unless specifically instructed to do so in the plan. Such effects of the incentive system tended to take much of the initiative for innovation away from enterprises, where most of the relevant information was likely to be found, to the higher levels of the planning hierarchy, which had a stronger desire for innovation and technical change but less of the required information.

The incentive system also undermined the quality of plan information; for if enterprises perceive that the output levels that they will be instructed to achieve and the inputs with which they will be supplied to meet the planned levels of output depend on information supplied by themselves, it is clear that enterprises will err on the side of caution. Feasible outputs are likely to be underestimated, while input coefficients are overestimated. In response to such behaviour, the planners tend to operate according to the so-called ratchet principle of planning, whereby the next period's output target is based on the current period's performance plus some average allowance for growth (see Gács and Lackó, 1973). In effect, therefore, the interaction between enterprises and planners creates a rather conservative economic mechanism, with a bias against change in any particular enterprise.

(b) *Arguments for reform*

Now, these failings of the centralised model are not peculiar to Hungary, and very similar observations have been made about all the Eastern European planned economies. Nonetheless, it would be a mistake to conclude that the centralised model of a planned economy is totally inefficient and ineffective, for it has generated impressive growth rates of output and employment, notably during the 1950s and 1960s. However, the nature of the growth process seems to have changed somewhat during the 1960s. In Eastern Europe itself it is now quite conventional to distinguish between extensive and intensive periods of growth; the former refers to growth based on massive increases in inputs of both capital and labour, while the latter involves growth accompanied by rapidly increasing capital intensity. Thus, the 1950s, when savings and therefore investment, rates were rapidly expanding and large numbers of workers were moving out of agriculture into industry, was a decade of extensive growth. More recently, it has become apparent that labour reserves are largely exhausted and that future growth depends crucially on raising the productivity of an almost static labour force. This requires many factories to be re-equipped with better capital, raising the degree of automation or mechanisation throughout the economy in a process of intensive growth. Since the capital intensity of industry has actually been rising ever since 1950, it is hard to discern from the official statistics just where the transition from extensive to intensive growth took place. However, in the perceptions of policy-makers it played an important role in the mid 1960s, when discussion of possible economic reforms reached a peak of intensity almost everywhere in the region. There are two reasons why the transition between the two types of growth should have so seriously troubled the policy-makers and stimulated thoughts of economic reform.

First, much of the earlier period of industrialisation was devoted to the establishment or expansion or a range of basic industries (e.g. steel, heavy engineering, generation of electricity) to the relative neglect of light industry and infrastructure. The traditional centralised techniques of planning seemed to be relatively well adapted to manage such priorities, since each of the industries of interest has a fairly narrow and well-defined product range as well as a reasonably well-tried menu of available technologies. The prospect of entering a more intensive phase of development was bound to call into question many of the technical choices that had been made in these industries, since it was rapidly becoming more important to save labour. The fact that the emphasis of economic policy was also beginning to shift in the consumers' favour also called into question the traditional planning techniques themselves, for their application to Hungarian light industry had already been heavily criticised (Kornai, 1959), and it was soon widely recognised that they could not handle the diverse and rapidly changing product mix and technology in such industries as textiles and pharmaceuticals.

Secondly, the realisation, already noted above, that continued growth would increasingly have to be based on productivity gains was expected to place new demands on the planning apparatus. The types of information that accumulated in the planning system in the course of operating the traditionally centralised model (i.e. material and labour input norms, and achieved output levels for the existing list of goods and services in production) were not necessarily the most useful when it became necessary to change the pattern of production quite drastically rather than merely replicate the existing pattern at a higher level. While the centre could play an important part in promoting technical development (e.g. by organising co-ordinated investment programmes in certain key sectors), much of its contribution was likely to be more passive. Enterprises, and perhaps branch organisations, had the fullest information about market trends, potentially attractive new products and technical changes affecting them, so that, if the centre provided resources and/or organisational help, lower level initiative could then be relied on to do the rest. Indeed, an essential task of economic reform in a number of countries has been to devise means whereby the above type of decentralised decision-making may function well in practice; we have already observed that it does not do so in the centralised model.

In the Hungarian case, probably to a greater extent than elsewhere in Eastern Europe, foreign trade considerations served to strengthen the case for economic reform. Around half of Hungary's national product was and is exported, with just over a third of these exports going to Western (convertible currency) markets and the remainder to other countries of the Council for Mutual Economic Assistance (CMEA); the structure of imports was quite similar to this, of course. Hungary's development was heavily dependent on imported raw materials, the bulk of which have always come from the Soviet Union. But it was very likely that in the future the country would have to obtain increasing supplies from elsewhere, particularly from Western markets. This meant that more exports had to be sold on these markets in order to earn the necessary hard currency, and for this to happen on a significant scale it was clear that the quality of many Hungarian products needed to be dramatically improved. Moreover, many of the large investment projects could only be viable if part of the output could be exported, since the efficient scale of plant was often capable of producing more output than the domestic market alone could absorb. Again, therefore, investment had to be carried out with export prospects in mind right from the start – an approach that seemed to be quite inimical to the balancing procedures that characterised the centralised-planning model, for the latter tended to plan trade by starting from the import requirements of the domestic economy, constructing balances of supply and demand for the major products and then identifying surplus products that could be made available for export. Within such a framework trade flows were unlikely to be very efficient, and any influence of trade prospects on investment decisions was at best very indirect. As Bolthó (1971) pointed out, this approach to trade was already being criticised in the late 1950s, and Hungary (along with·Poland) was one of the first socialist countries to develop export efficiency indicators in an attempt to inject greater rationality into trade flows. However, by the mid 1960s it had come to be believed that only a fairly radical reform of the economic mechanism could significantly improve the country's trade performance.

(c) *General features of reform proposals in Eastern Europe and the USSR*

We have seen that Hungary, as well as its partners in the CMEA, by the early 1960s had several reasons for giving serious consideration to economic reform. While most of the reasons were valid throughout the region, the responses in terms of specific reform proposals, and even more in terms of reforms actually implemented, showed considerable diversity. Since this is not the place for a full account of reforms except in Hungary itself (for reforms elsewhere see Bornstein and Fusfeld, 1974; Bornstein, 1973; Feiwel, 1969; and Nove, 1977), it is appropriate to concentrate on the general features of the Eastern European reforms rather than on their concrete details. The reforms that the region experienced may conveniently be grouped into a number of general categories as follows:

(1)   measures that left the traditional model intact but sought to render it more effective by strengthening central control;

(2)   measures that left the traditional model intact but sought to render it more effective by improving the incentive system; and

(3)   measures that substantially changed the traditional model by eliminating some important central powers and/or conferring new powers on lower-level economic units.

Most countries restricted themselves to measures of types (1) and (2), while the Hungarian reform is especially interesting in that it included several measures of type (3). Even the Hungarian reforms were preceded by a number of partial reforms falling into the first two categories.

Central control can be strengthened in several different ways, although the means most commonly employed in Eastern Europe include organisational changes and attempts to extend the scope or number of compulsory plan indicators imposed on individual enterprises. More recently, automation of some plan calculations and moves towards the computerisation of the plan information system have been seen as a major component of efforts to increase the reliability of central planning, especially in the Soviet Union (Cave, 1980). Hungary's last significant organisational change came quite early in the reform process. This was a comprehensive amalgamation of many small enterprises into trusts and large enterprises, which took place in the early 1960s. As with all such processes the amalgamations, by drastically reducing the number of independent producing units, offered some hope of raising the effectiveness of central control over the economy. At the same time the deliberate creation of monopoly positions in many branches of the economy created obstacles to the more radical reforms that came later, as explained in subsequent chapters of this volume.

Organisational changes were also introduced elsewhere in Eastern Europe. The Soviet Union came first with its abandonment of industrial ministries under Khruschev. From 1957 to 1965 the economy was organised on a regional basis, with regional economic associations forming the key organisational link between the central agencies in Moscow and individual enterprises. This experiment was rather short-lived, because it soon transpired that for planning purposes links between enterprises in the same industry but different regions were more crucial than interindustry links within any given region. However, an element of regionalism still survives in that much of the system for supplying enterprises with intermediate inputs has a regional rather than a sectoral organisational structure.

The other organisational innovation, now introduced almost everywhere in the region, is the association. Like the Hungarian trusts, this is a form of amalgamation of enterprises and has a similar objective, namely, to raise the effectiveness of central planning by reducing the number of separate bodies with which the central agencies have to deal. In addition, it has frequently been argued that associations may be conducive to technical change by linking research and development activity more closely to the production that it is supposed to serve. As with the lower level enterprises themselves, however, it still seems to be difficult to devise an appropriate set of plan indicators for these new bodies. Moreover, in several countries (not including Hungary) their legal status in relation to the enterprises that they comprise is still not clear; it is often unspecified, for example, how far an association may regroup the resources of its member enterprises against the wishes of individual enterprises. Thus in some cases the associations are treated as independent enterprises in their own right, while in other cases their member enterprises continue to be regarded as having substantial powers of their own. The issue is important, because it affects the extent to which the associations can be regarded as the new, lowest level in the planning hierarchy.

Aside from organisational adjustments the traditional Soviet model has seen modifications to its associated system of economic incentives in much of Eastern Europe, in two important respects: price reform, and changes in the number and scope of enterprise-level success indicators. It may be thought that under a centralised-planning system prices are relatively unimportant, serving merely to record transactions and to facilitate aggregation and reporting of the kinds required by planning calculations. But it must be remembered that, even in the smallest economies of the region, we are dealing with a number of distinct commodities so large (of the order of millions) that it could not possibly be planned in every detail. Plans have always been expressed and elaborated in relatively aggregated terms, and even when broken down to enterprise level the output targets and material inputs to be made available to meet the targets are still quite aggregated for the most part. This leaves scope both for detailed negotiations between supplier and customer enterprise to determine the precise specification of individual contracts, as well as for product mix adjustments in response to the prevailing price signals as mediated by the bonus-forming indicators.

Leaving aside the well-known cases where government intervention would be considered desirable, it is a standard conclusion of conventional Western microeconomics that profit-maximising firms responding to market-determined prices will in equilibrium generate an efficient allocation of resources. While there are many reasons for holding reservations about this strikingly powerful conclusion (see, for example, Kornai, 1971), its acceptance for the present discussion has some important implications. In particular, it suggests three reasons why producers' responses to price signals may not be efficient: first, the prices themselves may be inappropriate; secondly, the bonus-forming, or success, indicators may have been poorly chosen or may have unintended side effects; and thirdly, the economic system may for some reason not be in equilibrium. All these reasons have been cited in numerous discussions about the need to reform the incentive system in one or other Eastern European country.

Debates about price reform often took as a premise the centralised character of price formation. In such circumstances the price office had to be supplied with guidelines enabling it to adjust all producer prices at the time of the reform, and it also needed rules for determining the prices of new products that appeared subsequent to the reform. But productivity and demand changes, taking place at very different rates in different branches of the economy, meant that the initially established prices soon came to bear very little relation to whatever cost concept the reform in question had enshrined as 'correct', and in most cases the price office was unable, largely for administrative reasons, to follow these changes by announcing appropriate price revisions from time to time. Consequently, prices and costs tended to deviate from one another to an increasingly illogical degree, while the relative prices between new and established products were also unsatisfactory (see Berliner, 1976). Eventually, of course, the pressures for change would accumulate, and a new price reform would be announced.

Bonus-forming, or success, indicators are measures of enterprise performance or activity that affect the payment of bonuses, either to managers only or to both managers and workers (see Zielinski, 1973). In the traditional planning system each enterprise received a number of targets, often quite a large number, as part of its plan for the year or quarter of interest. In principle, the payment of bonuses would depend on fulfilment of all the plan indicators, but the practice has not always been as strict as this. In addition, some indicators (e.g. the cost reduction indicator) were conditional in the sense that their fulfilment affected only whether or not bonuses would be paid, not the actual amount. The latter usually depended on one or two key indicators (e.g. gross output measured by valuing output at the prevailing producer prices). Clearly, therefore, to the extent that the price system was deficient, so also was this type of indicator.

However, gross output indicators have two further defects, which gradually led to their replacement with better indicators in the reforms of the 1960s. These defects are their incomplete scope and their failure to provide enterprises with any particular interest in the marketing side of their operations. They are incomplete in that they stimulate enterprises to increase measured output without regard to the associated costs. True, there was often a cost reduction target, but, as suggested above, it was never treated as seriously as output. In order to induce enterprise to take costs of production more seriously, many reform proposals suggested the use of such indicators as profits (Hungary), value added (Poland) or rentability (i.e. profits per unit of capital employed; Soviet Union). In order to stimulate an interest in marketing, the output indicator was sometimes replaced by one based on sales, the idea being that an enterprise should no longer be rewarded for producing unsaleable output. A number of countries, including the Soviet Union, adopted such a proposal, but the effects appear to have been minimal. The reason for this seems to be the persistent shortage conditions that the centrally planned economies generate, implying that even relatively unsatisfactory and low quality output can frequently still be sold. This situation points to the need for an analysis of the origins of shortage and the social mechanisms that reproduce it, and perhaps also to the need for more fundamental reforms in order to remove its causes, instead of further tinkering with its superficial manifestations. However, it would be premature, to say the least, to assert that the Hungarian reforms have achieved quite this much.

Hungary is not the only Eastern European country to propose the more radical reforms of type (3), but is certainly the only country to have implemented them to any substantial extent. At various times both Czechoslovakia and Poland have produced radical ideas for reducing the powers of central agencies and granting greater enterprise independence, in the hope of stimulating more rapid improvements in economic efficiency. Indeed, in many respects the Czechoslovakian proposals of 1967 and 1968, associated with the writings of Sik (1967, 1972), are remarkably similar to the New Economic Mechanism that Hungary introduced in 1968. As is well known, however, the Soviet invasion of Czechoslovakia in 1968 eventually led to a reversion to a considerably more centralised form of economic management. It is less clear in the Polish case how far the cautious approach to economic reform may be attributed to pressures from the Soviet Union or to such internal factors as the political weakness of the Polish leadership, making major reform appear far too risky (see Zielinski, 1978). In such countries as East Germany and the Soviet Union such radical ideas as have appeared to date have predominantly been the work of mathematical economists in relatively isolated research institutes; their ideas have provoked debate rather than action. Accordingly, the leadership's confidence in the basic features of the centralised model has not been seriously shaken, so that, even when reforms are on the agenda, careful deliberation results in fairly modest measures of types (1) and (2). In other words, it is recognised that there may be some room for improvement in the traditional centralised model, but the situation is not considered to require any fundamental reform.

Interestingly, precisely this issue arose at the start of the Hungarian debates that preceded the introduction of the New Economic Mechanism. By the mid 1960s Hungary had already introduced several minor reforms, which come into our categories (1) and (2). (For details see Chapter 2 as well as Portes, 1977; and Hare, 1976.) Although these had produced some positive benefits for the economy, the centralised model was exhibiting a strong tendency to reassert itself in the face of such reforms, thereby gradually undermining their effects. This tendency had already been observed by Kornai in the 1950s (Kornai, 1959), but the problem was more widely recognised later. It may be helpful to give an example at this point. In regulating enterprise behaviour in a centralised system, each enterprise is assigned a plan that contains a number of indicators to be fulfilled during the plan period. From time to time this number becomes large, and the resulting system of enterprise-planning becomes increasingly unmanageable. Consequently, one obvious and commonly adopted reform involves reducing the number of compulsory plan indicators imposed on enterprises. For a while this may work, but inevitably new problems arise in economic management, and the natural response of the centralised system always includes the introduction of new indicators. Hence, after a while the original reason for reform becomes valid once again, and pressures for a new reform are likely to mount.

The Hungarians were therefore faced with the question of whether to introduce further minor reforms, accepting that sooner or later the centralised system would reassert itself, or whether to pursue a more radical approach, seeking reforms that would not be reversed so easily and would confer substantial economic benefits over the longer term. After careful consideration of the alternatives before them, they eventually decided in favour of the most comprehensive and fundamental reforms that have yet been introduced in Eastern Europe.

Aside from the specific reform measures that constituted the New Economic Mechanism, discussed in section 2 of this chapter, the Hungarian reform procedure itself was sufficiently unusual to merit separate comment. In particular, rather than introduce the reform gradually over a period of years, it was decided that all components of the reform should be introduced simultaneously. The reform was seen as a coherent package of measures whose individual elements would not accord with the requirements and expectations of the centralised model. For this reason the introduction of individual measures might have undermined the whole reform concept, as seems to have happened to some extent elsewhere, by showing that the early stages of reform did not improve economic performance. Thus, a radical reform had to be comprehensive if it was to have any chance of success at all. Largely because of its comprehensive character many features of the reform have survived through into the 1980s, although often not without some modification.

2   The Hungarian reforms: Introduction to Chapters 2−10

The Hungarian decision in favour of comprehensive economic reform had some important implications, which have affected the conduct of economic policy ever since 1968.

First, the early agreement on the nature of the required reforms, together with widespread political support for them and a favourable economic climate, all facilitated the careful preparation of the reform package.

It must be realised that the Hungarian uprising and Soviet intervention of 1956 had left deep wounds in the economy, in society at large and in the Party. By its Eighth Congress in November 1962, Kádár had consolidated his authority in the Party and restored its shattered morale. He was safe from attack by dogmatic anti-reform elements, his politics of conciliation and moderation had attracted much popular support, and his 'soft policy' regarding collectivisation was also paying dividends. With a pro-reform politician in command, the 1964 Central Committee Plenum could adopt a resolution to investigate the possibility of wholesale reform and instruct Rezső Nyers to carry it out. Unlike in Czechoslovakia, the question as to whether there should actually be a reform was removed from the political arena. (For an account of this period, see Robinson, 1973, esp. chs 3 and 4.)

This consensus allowed the numerous individual measures to be properly co-ordinated, on the basis of detailed study and research by committees and working parties established for the purpose and functioning from 1965 to 1968. Not only did this mean that the New Economic Mechanism had good prospects of success when it came into force on 1 January 1968, but in addition the procedure established a valuable precedent; for although the reform was amended frequently, and in some respects quite substantially, after 1970, almost all such amendments followed the example of the initial reform-preparation period in being well integrated with the rest of the system.

Secondly, the comprehensive character of the reform called for various transitional measures to facilitate the rapid transfer, more or less overnight, from a form of the traditional centralised model to something much more decentralised. These transitional measures took the form of special taxes and subsidies, both on trading activities and in some cases on production itself, designed to ensure that enterprise decisions based on the new price signals would not immediately involve substantial departures from their pre-reform patterns of activity. Such caution is readily understandable, since the planners clearly had no desire to see drastic changes in output or trading patterns that might disrupt market equilibrium in the short run. Over a period of years, it was intended that all these transitional measures should gradually be abolished, but it seems that there was little progress in that direction before new economic problems of the 1970s provided a pretext for doing nothing further, and at times even for introducing new 'temporary' taxes and subsidies.

Thirdly, it must be remembered that the Hungarian reforms in no way changed the basic power relationships operating within Hungarian society. Consequently, although certainly comprehensive in character and scope, the reforms nevertheless represent a compromise between the competing demands of different interest groups. Very generally, enterprise level and financial management gained in power in relation to production managers and the officials in the appropriate branch ministry, although it should be added that not all enterprise management was happy with its new increased responsibility (see Nyers and Tardos, 1979). The particular form of the compromise is quite clear. While the reform could introduce new policy instruments and eliminate others and could confer new powers and rights on enterprises in particular, it was unable to achieve any fundamental organisational or institutional change. For example, modest attempts to break up some large enterprises into smaller units to promote competition had virtually no effect and soon stopped altogether. Also, early proposals to abolish the industrial ministries were defeated in favour of a milder proposal to weaken their authority in certain respects; this was implemented, but began to be reversed in the early 1970s. Consequently, it very often continued to be the case that branch ministries would bargain directly with the oligopolistic or monopolistic enterprises under their jurisdiction. Using the justification of 'the national interest', ministries would request that an enterprise continue to produce a particular good, at whatever cost, because it was the sole domestic supplier. In return the enterprise might be awarded investment funds without being obliged to pay due attention to financial detail. As set out more fully in the chapters that follow, the lack of institutional change in 1968 turned out to constrain quite severely further developments of the reform process in the 1970s.

Let us now turn to the reform itself. Probably its most striking feature was its abolition of the standard Soviet-type procedures of operative annual planning. Enterprises were no longer to receive *any* compulsory indicators from higher levels of the planning hierarchy. Five-year and annual plans were still to be formulated within the central agencies, indeed in very much the same way as before, but annual plans would no longer be implemented by means of direct instructions to enterprises. Instead, plans were implemented indirectly by means of the so-called economic regulators, which influenced the financial environment within which enterprises operated. Enterprises themselves were supposed to respond to market signals, essentially the price system, in order to maximise their profits. To stimulate such behaviour the reform included a major recalculation of producer prices (see Hare, 1976) and a partial decentralisation of the right to adjust prices, subject only to general guidelines established by the price office.

The price reform incorporated into the prices a 5 per cent charge on fixed capital and a 25 per cent charge on the wage bill. The latter comprised social security contributions amounting to 17 per cent of the wage bill and a wage tax of 8 per cent. In addition, profits taxation at enterprise level allowed enterprises to form sharing funds (to pay bonuses to management and workers and to finance wage increases) and development funds (to finance some investment). Effectively, therefore, the reform involved some decentralisation in the areas of wage determination and investment decisions. Finally, foreign exchange rates were rationalised, and some enterprises were accorded rights to engage in foreign trade without the usual requirement that the Ministry of Foreign Trade should serve as intermediary. In sum, the reforms added up to a significant qualitative shift towards a much greater role for market forces in economic life.

However, during the 1970s there were significant modifications, which indicate at least a partial reversal of this shift. In the markets for both labour and investment the release of market forces rapidly led to problems. As early as 1969 the bonus system had to be altered, because managers were benefiting excessively from it in comparison with workers. In 1971 an element of labour direction was introduced to mitigate excessive turnover, and an abrupt credit freeze was imposed to deal with overinvestment. In 1973 fifty large state enterprises were earmarked for special supervision in return for special financial treatment, and increases in wages and in skill differentials were imposed in industry and construction. In 1974 new legislation increased central control over investment plans. In the same year two of the architects of the reform, Rezsö Nyers and Lajos Fehér, lost their positions on the Party's Central Committee. The less liberal tone of the political climate was also signalled in 1973 by the expulsion of some of the so-called 'Budapest school' of philosophy from their jobs.

Similar measures of recentralisation took place in later years, but now mainly in response to the economic effects of the dramatic rise in the price of oil and other raw materials in 1974–5, coupled with the Western recession. These led to a serious deterioration in the terms of trade and the balance of payments, and much of the response involved increased direct intervention in the fields of foreign trade, domestic price formation and investment. However, in subsequent years it became clear that Hungary's economic leaders (typified by the pragmatic János Fekete, Vice President of the Hungarian National Bank) regarded these deviations from the reform direction as temporary expedients, and the 1980 measures discussed below appear to be a coherent attempt to return to the original aims of the reforms.

This brief summary of the reform's essential components and its development since 1968, elaborated considerably in the remainder of this volume, is already enough to indicate why the Hungarian approach to socialist economic policy has attracted so much attention from Western observers in recent years. Some of this attention, however, especially that focusing on the market orientation of the reform, has been substantially misconceived; for while it is certainly true that Hungary's economic policy now makes much greater use of market forces than before 1968, it would be misleading to regard Hungary as an example of Lange's form of market socialism (Lange and Taylor, 1938). On the other hand, reforms of the Hungarian type, dismantling part of the apparatus of centralised planning as they did, are bound to be understood as a concession that central planning has its limitations, and as such they are bound to raise questions in other countries. In fact, perhaps with this kind of consideration in mind it has sometimes been suggested that Hungary is acting as a large scale laboratory for the rest of Eastern Europe. From that point of view, the present volume should be regarded as an interim report on a fascinating experiment.

The chapters that follow are grouped into six sections, covering general issues, labour and wages, investment, transfer of technology, international trade and agriculture.

Apart from this introductory chapter, Part One also introduces discussion on the general nature of the Hungarian economic model. In particular, X. Richet suggests that the Hungarian reforms were not based on a clear and agreed 'model' of the functioning of the economy. While the reform measures introduced in 1968 (and modified subsequently) were both wide-ranging and fairly coherent, specific and branch interests were sufficiently powerful to prevent significant institutional change from occurring. Largely as a result of this initial contradiction the economy continues to reproduce shortage conditions in many branches, and many features of economic behaviour and performance remain surprisingly similar to the pre-reform situation.

Part Two contains two chapters on labour and wages. The first, by I. Gábor and P. Galasi, is a general study of the labour market in Hungary since 1968, while the second, by M. Marrese, focuses somewhat more narrowly on the evolution of wage regulation. Gábor and Galasi study the particular conditions in the labour market that continue to generate labour shortages. The basic problem is that the growth orientation can never be effectively constrained in a socialist economy; in particular, therefore, it is not constrained by profitability considerations, so that enterprises are always striving to expand employment. This chapter also provides some analysis of the so-called second economy, commenting on developments in that sphere since the late 1960s.

Marrese examines the mechanisms that operate within the socialist sector to control wages, raising issues of relevance not only for Eastern Europe but equally for those Western countries which have sought to impose some form of wages or incomes policy. In the Hungarian case policy on wage control is seen as a compromise between the aim of stimulating the efficient use of labour and other important social objectives (e.g. maintaining an acceptable income distribution). The author contends that currently policy-makers would like to place much greater emphasis on the efficiency objective but are constrained from doing so by various features of the institutional and legal system (e.g. job security, the relatively low importance of profits, the inability to establish task-related wages in many areas). In addition to describing the prevailing system of wage regulation, the chapter emphasises that even under socialist conditions it is actually much harder than commonly supposed to devise a form of regulation that both meets social objectives and functions well in practice. Accordingly, Marrese concludes by making some suggestions of his own for revising the wage system, involving profit centres, profit-related bonuses for the managers and the retraining of redundant workers.

The framework of institutional arrangements within which investment is determined under the New Economic Mechanism is described in P. G. Hare's chapter on investment, which alone comprises Part Three of the volume. The chapter also discusses some of the literature seeking to explain the persistence of investment cycles in Hungary and examines several features of the economic mechanism that contribute to inefficiencies in investment. It concludes, however, by noting that any significant improvement in the effectiveness of the investment process would entail a rather fundamental development of the original reform concepts, in the direction of a much greater degree of autonomy for enterprises. This is because a substantial part of the problem with the investment process as it currently operates derives from centre-enterprise relationships that tend to interfere with signals generated by market forces. Since much of such interference is probably desirable, it is difficult to devise operational rules and procedures in the investment sphere that would make central and enterprise responsibilities significantly clearer than at present. Because of this the author does not expect to see great improvements in the investment process in the near future.

The two chapters in Part Four are concerned with East–West industrial co-operation and technology transfer. H. K. Radice discusses Hungarian policy in relation to industrial co-operation and the effects that such co-operation with Western enterprises may have on broader aspects of economic development in Hungary. The chapter argues that the exaggerated expectations of the benefits of industrial co-operation have not been fulfilled, leading to a more cautious and realistic approach by Hungarian enterprises and policy-makers. An important issue has been whether incentives for industrial co-operation, and in general export promotion, can function efficiently without a greater market orientation among large state enterprises.

Hungarian policy on the import of Western technology is considered in the second chapter of this part, by A. Abonyi. The author emphasises the importance of assimilating Western technology in such a way as to improve the innovative potential of Hungarian enterprises. After outlining the role of branch and functional ministries in this process, the chapter surveys progress in some branches of the engineering industry. The problems identified include the segregation of scientific research from industry and the incompatibility between imported technologies and others in use in the same enterprise or sector. The author judges Hungarian policy in this field to be successful in encouraging the assimilation of Western technology but inadequate in increasing the potential for subsequent domestic innovation.

The chapters by P. Marer and G. Kosma, concerned with some international aspects of the Hungarian economic mechanism, occupy Part Five on international issues. Since Hungary has such an open economy, it is only to be expected that its policy on international trade should have major repercussions on domestic economic activity and performance. The converse is also true, in that domestic policy considerations have often constrained the development of foreign trade policies. Given the importance of trade policy, therefore, it is fortunate that Marer provides a detailed account of the instruments and institutions employed to regulate trade under the reformed economic mechanism. He also provides a useful account of foreign trade aspects of the price system. Marer's chapter then proceeds to an analysis of trade performance in recent years, with the emphasis on the convertible currency balance. The recent poor performance and declining terms of trade are not just the result of such exogenous shocks as the massive increases in oil and raw material prices in the early 1970s but also reflect the relatively poor quality and mix of goods offered on the market. Improvements in this situation therefore require a shift in enterprise incentives, so that producers increasingly seek out, and actively compete in, export markets instead of regarding such markets as marginal. Official policy is now striving to push enterprises towards a much stronger export orientation. It must be emphasised that problems in this area have been exacerbated by raw material shortages within the CMEA, which have increasingly obliged Hungary to seek Western sources of supply, thereby expanding imports payable in convertible currency.

A narrower subject, the role of the exchange rate, is Kozma's topic in his chapter. He begins by criticising the 'average' exchange-rate concept introduced in 1968, which is viewed, however, as a natural consequence of the state's insistence on providing enterprises with a stable economic environment, relatively isolated from the vagaries of the market. But such stability involves a considerable loss in efficiency and undermines the role of profit in the economic mechanism. On the other hand, exports of complex manufactured goods to the West did increase very rapidly after 1968, which may be seen as an indicator of success achieved by the reform. Hungarian reaction to increased oil prices and Western inflation has been extremely slow, although the exchange rate began to be adjusted in 1976. Freezing domestic prices for a while certainly delayed any adjustment to the worsened terms of trade. Finally, the exchange rate itself has had little impact on trade flows to date, because its possible effects have so often been offset by various prices and taxes, but in principle it could play a more important role in the economy.

Part Six, which concludes the volume, contains a single chapter on Hungarian agriculture, by N. Swain. Beginning with a general assessment of agricultural performance since 1968, which is only moderately impressive, the chapter goes on to discuss developments in the relationship between the agricultural producer co-operatives and the government. A notable feature of the period has been the spectacular growth of industrial production systems in agriculture, although this seems to have had more to do with their use as a channel for the allocation of capital goods to the sector than with their inherent superiority and efficiency. During the early 1970s there was a wave of mergers of agricultural co-operatives, and this too was motivated in part by non-economic considerations. Finally, the government's attitude to the private sector's contribution to agricultural output, including the output of private household plots, vacillated sharply during the 1970s, although by the end of the decade the private sector clearly had official blessing. Overall, while the face of Hungarian agriculture has changed enormously since 1968, the situation of agriculture in the economy as a whole has not fundamentally changed. In particular, political and social factors continue to play an important role in its development.

3 Future prospects for the Hungarian reforms

The chapters introduced in the previous section each examine a particular field where the economic reforms may be expected to have had some impact, either in the procedure for carrying out certain economic functions or in terms of economic performance or outcomes. It turns out that in several fields changes of procedure and approach associated with the general switch from directive to indirect planning and economic management are substantially easier to identify than concrete effects on performance. This may well reflect the perfectly understandable point that a major reform of the Hungarian type cannot be expected to have dramatic effects on economic activity straightaway; for although such a thoroughgoing reform immediately transforms the environment within which all economic agents – whether they be enterprise-managers, workers, consumers, planners or other public officials – are constrained to act, the agents themselves remain unchanged. Consequently, behaviour patterns more appropriate to the traditional centralised model can be expected to persist for a time, especially if there is initially some doubt about the durability of the reforms, as we emphasise at several points in the following chapters.

There is another important reason for the apparently limited impact of the Hungarian reforms on economic performance. This is the likelihood, referred to frequently in the mid 1960s, that without the reforms performance might have deteriorated substantially. If this view is correct, the reforms must be regarded as extremely successful, since they have enabled the economy to continue along the growth path that one might have expected by simply extrapolating the results achieved in the late 1950s and early 1960s. However, while a complete assessment of the Hungarian reforms would have to allow for this consideration, as stressed more generally by Johansen (1977, ch. 4.8), the information required to do so satisfactorily is not yet available.

Despite the difficulties in assessing the effectiveness of the reforms, it is necessary to point out that, unlike reforms in many other Eastern European countries, the essential features of the New Economic Mechanism have stood the test of time. As indicated in the previous section, however, some recentralising tendencies asserted themselves in the early and mid 1970s, and the reform principles were slowly undermined, although there was little indication that the major element of the reform, namely, the abolition of directive planning of current production, was a candidate for reversal. By the end of the 1970s, therefore, the reform was surviving certainly, but some parts of it had been so seriously weakened that there was reason to doubt its survival into the 1980s.

Rather than retreat further along this centralising path, however, the Hungarians have demonstrated their confidence in their basic approach to economic management by implementing a number of measures on 1 January 1980 that restore many of the original reform concepts. In particular, many of the special taxes and subsidies on domestic production and trade that proliferated during the 1970s have been abolished, and a comprehensive reform of producer prices has come into effect. (For details see Horváth, 1980.) The revised price system envisages that a substantial part of the social net income will once more be realised through the turnover tax, in contrast to the recent situation when for some years the level of producer prices exceeded that of consumer prices. In order to achieve this capital charges have been abolished altogether, and the part of the mark-up on wage costs that was regarded as a wage tax has also been abolished; the only remaining mark-up on wages is for social security contributions. In addition, the tax rate on enterprise profits has been raised to 45 per cent, increasing somewhat the share of social net income that is centralised. However, enterprises remain fairly free to determine for themselves how to divide up their after-tax income between development and sharing funds, and the required reserve fund is now smaller than before. To stimulate improvements in enterprise efficiency, wage fund control based on enterprise productivity indicators will be the predominant form of wage regulation.

The emphasis in these revisions is very much to differentiate between economic organisations on the basis of their relative efficiency, to encourage competitiveness and enforce rapid gains in efficiency wherever possible. With this in mind, much of the new price revision has aimed to bring domestic prices into line with world prices, and it is envisaged that subsequent price adjustment should reflect the trends in these prices. As in 1968, a few taxes and subsidies remain as 'transitory' measures, but according to present intentions they should soon be eliminated. For the most part the regulator system is based on general norms that should be stable or change only slowly; these include enterprise tax rates and wage regulation principles, together with wage rates, exchange rates, prices, and so on, which are expected to adjust more flexibly than in the past. Alongside all these price-type regulators, of course, the plan will still operate as a dominant influence on the course of Hungary's economic development, but its limitations are recognised. Plans can only be revised periodically, and they are only able to capture a subset of essential relationships involving, for example, some of the major investment projects or the main proportions of development. Once these aspects of the growth path have been established, the economic regulators influence the environment within which enterprise decision-making is left to fill in the details. Evidently, the Hungarian system of economic management is still quite far from the traditional centralised model of Soviet type; this distinctiveness is re-emphasised by the revival of the reform process implicit in the 1980 measures. However, it is important to recall that the original reform measures ran into economic and political constraints that led to the measures of recentralisation described earlier. It remains to be seen whether the new measures will in the event succeed or whether they will continue to be undermined by phenomena inherited from the traditions of directive planning or by events beyond the control of Hungary's economic managers.

References: Chapter 1

Berliner, J. (1976, *The Innovation Decision in Soviet Industry* (Cambridge, Mass.: MIT Press).

Bolthó, A. (1971), *Foreign Trade Criteriu in Socialist Economics* (Cambridge: (Cambridge University Press).

Bornstein, M. (ed.) (1973), *Plan and Market* (New Haven, Conn.: Yale University Press).

Bornstein, M., and Fusfeld, D. (eds) (1974), *The Soviet Economy: A Book of Readings*, 4th edn (Homewood, Ill.: Irwin).

Cave, M. (1980), *Computers and Economic Planning: The Soviet Experience* (Cambridge: Cambridge University Press).

Feiwel, G. (ed.) (1969), *New Currents in Soviet-Type Economies* (Scranton, Pa: International Textbook).

Gács, J., and Lackó, M. (1973), 'A study of planning behaviour on the national-economic level', *Economics of Planning*, vol. 13 (1–2), pp. 91–119.

Hare, P. G. (1976), 'Industrial prices in Hungary', *Soviet Studies*, vol. 27 (2 and 3), pp. 189–206 and 362–90.

Horváth, L. (1980), 'Az 1980-as gazdasági szabályozók' (The economic regulators for 1980), *Közgazdasági Szemle*, vol. 27 (1), pp. 1–11.

Johansen, L. (1977), *Lectures on Macroeconomic Planning. Vol. 1: General Aspects* (Amsterdam: North-Holland).

Joint Economic Committee (1976), *The Soviet Economy in a New Perspective* (Washington, DC: US Government Printing Office).

Kornai, J. (1959), *Overcentralisation in Economic Administration* (London: Oxford University Press).

Kornai, J. (1971), *Anti-equilibrium* (Amsterdam: North-Holland).

Kornai, J. (1975), *Mathematical Planning of Structural Decisions*, 2nd ed (Amsterdam: North-Holland).

Lange, O., and Taylor, F. (1938), *On the Economic Theory of Socialism* (Minneapolis, Minn.: University of Minnesota Press).

Nove, A. (1977), *The Soviet Economic System* (London: Allen & Unwin).

Nyers, R., and Tardos, M. (1979), 'What economic development policy should we adopt?', *Acta Oeconomica*, vol. 22 (1–2), pp. 11–31.

Portes, R. (1977), 'Hungary: economic performance, policy and prospects', in Joint Economic Committee, *East European Economies Post-Helsinki* (Washington, DC: US Government Printing Office).

Robinson, W. F. (1973), *The Pattern of Reform in Hungary* (New York: Praeger).

Sik, O. (1967), *Plan and Market under Socialism* (White Plains, New York: International Arts and Sciences Press).

Sik, O. (1972), *Czechoslovakia: The Bureaucratic Economy* (White Plains, New York: International Arts and Sciences Press).

Zielinski, J. (1973), *Economic Reforms in Polish Industry* (London: Oxford University Press).

Zielinski, J. (1978), 'On system remodelling in Poland: a pragmatic approach', *Soviet Studies*, vol. 30 (1), pp. 3–37.

Chapter 2

Is There an 'Hungarian' Model of Planning?

1 Introduction

In a recent article Professor Brus (1979) wondered what has become of the economic reforms in Eastern Europe. According to his analysis, the various reforms that were undertaken both in the Soviet Union itself as well as in the other countries belonging to the Council for Mutual Economic Assistance (CMEA) had only led to the perpetuation, in modified forms, of the old model of planning based on administrative methods of management.

It is my purpose not to contest this claim by Brus, with which I broadly agree, but to investigate the specific features, and some developments over the last ten years, of the reform of the Hungarian system of economic management. More precisely, I shall endeavour to reveal its essential characteristics by examining the behaviour of the planning system and some aspects of economic regulation that have been affected by the reforms.

Before embarking on our analysis of Hungary, it seems important to introduce some general concepts; that is the object of this introductory section. The use of the term 'model' in the title of this chapter may be considered unsatisfactory, since the broader concept of economic system is more frequently employed in analyses dealing with Eastern Europe. Nevertheless, according to Walliser (1977) the concept of system is actually inseparable from the concept of model, when the latter is conceived of as a representation of a concrete system. Indeed, it may be argued that all real systems can only be understood by means of particular models that represent them.

In another connection theoreticians and ideologists from Eastern Europe have resisted the application of the concept of model to their economies, on the grounds that it is far too restrictive a concept to capture the essential features of the dynamic growth processes that characterise them. On the other hand, much of the Western economic literature dealing with this subject seeks generalisations that permit several countries to be treated together; thus, such terms as 'centrally planned economies' or 'Soviet-type economies' are employed. Such usages are frequently quite acceptable, although they do suffer from the significant drawback that they tend to mask the very real differences between the countries belonging to the CMEA. So, although the GDR and Bulgaria, for instance, both belong to the category of Soviet-type economies, there are nevertheless important differences between them in respect of their extent of industrialisation, industrial structure, methods of planning, structure of foreign trade, and so on.

It is this last point which makes employment of the concept of model rather dangerous, for to speak of a Hungarian model of planning means making a distinction that breaks the unity that, theoretically at least, is supposed to exist within the community of the socialist countries, although it does recognise the real specificities of the Hungarian situation. Another difficulty is that most models are based on distinctions that arise naturally in economic theory (e.g. that between centralised and decentralised planning). Models based on this particular distinction have been widely discussed in the literature, and each type is conceived of as a pure form of model behaving according to its own specific logic. But in practice, rather than models of one or other pure form, the models that we are likely to encounter are likely to combine features of both the centralised and the decentralised forms.

Economic reforms involve modifying some components of the economic mechanism, usually in an attempt to improve certain aspects of economic performance. Later on we shall outline the principal features of the economic reforms introduced in Hungary in 1968. In much of the Western economic literature the idea of economic reform is often associated with one or other of the theoretical approaches mentioned above, namely, centralisation or decentralisation. Within the framework of such an approach, it is natural to analyse particular reforms in terms of the deviations between the behaviour of the concrete planning system under examination and, for example, the behaviour of the pure decentralised model. In this field economic theory has produced numerous contributions by such authors as von Hayek, Barone, Mises and Lange, to name but a few. But these works, while often extremely interesting in themselves, are not very helpful for the analysis of particular systems undergoing economic reforms, since the latter always involve a rather complex amalgam of characteristics associated with both the extreme theoretical models, as Kornai (1975) emphasised.

The reform movement in Eastern Europe and the Soviet Union can be regarded as a natural consequence of the forms of economic development established in these countries from the inception of centralised planning. According to the centralised conception of economic management, the dynamic behaviour of the economy is governed by the accumulation process, and this in turn is directed by the central authorities (the government and the central planners) acting through a vertically structured organisational system (branch ministries, directorates or associations, and enterprises). In this system the 'central will' largely displaces horizontal regulation through the market mechanism. The resulting process of development relies on extensive growth of the economy and requires for its operation only fairly rough and ready economic measures and indicators; these will typically take the form of input norms and other quantity-type indicators employed in the construction of economic balances and the elaboration of output and supply plans.

The hierarchically organised socioeconomic structure that characterises the traditional centralised form of economic management in the socialist countries may well be the most appropriate one when the main tasks of economic policy are concerned with the early stages of accumulation – primitive accumulation, laying the basis for rapid growth in the future – and with constructing the so-called material basis for socialism. But this system of economic management seems much less suitable when the economy reaches a certain level of accumulation, with growth rates on a permanently higher plane and a rapidly increasing volume and range of output. A more efficient system of information and control is needed, and this necessitates the modification of some elements of the institutional structure. Moreover, as labour resources, plentiful in all the socialist countries when planning began, come to be in increasingly short supply, the pattern of development becomes more intensive. Such a change requires new and more sophisticated tools of economic regulation, for the real economic situation becomes increasingly complex, with branches growing at very different rates and many new products and processes being introduced. The control system therefore has to provide for different forms of regulation in each branch, corresponding to its respective role in the economy.

Formulating a model of planning involves an analysis of the main elements of which the planning system in question consists. More precisely, a complete system of economic planning includes a number of forms of planning, each with its characteristic modes of regulation and action. It is convenient to employ the typology proposed by Hegedüs (1976), according to which three specific forms of planning and types of economic regulation are distinguished as follows:

(1) The first form is concerned with administrative planning at the level of branches and sectors. Activities are managed and regulated by means of material balances and quantity rather than value-type indicators.

(2) The second form involves *Khozraschet*. This requires production units to cover their own costs and keep separate accounts and

therefore introduces some elements of economic calculation in terms of prices and profitability. This is especially significant when remuneration is related to such financial indicators as profits; in Hungary the introduction of profit-sharing in industry in 1957 represented an important step in the direction of enhancing the role of profit in the economy (Bokor et al, 1957).

(3)   Once economic calculation in terms of financial indicators comes to be widely accepted, it becomes increasingly important that the formation and function of prices depend on economic and market relations. This brings us to the third form of economic planning, namely, the operation of a regulated market within a planning framework that, at least in principle, should permit the highest levels of productivity to be achieved.

   This typology may also be supplemented by the classification suggested by Brus (1975), which focuses greater attention on modifications that may be introduced into the decision system. In the so-called Soviet-type economies there are three kinds of economic decision, corresponding to three levels in the economic hierarchy: the basic macroeconomic decisions, branch or sectoral decisions, and decisions by the lowest level of economic agents (usually assumed to be enterprises, but logically including households also). Usually, attempts to modify the system of control have sought to replace the hierarchical control involving these three levels of decision-making with a functional decision system based on a more direct relationship between the top and bottom of the original hierarchy.

2   The Hungarian reforms

The Central Committee of the Hungarian Socialist Workers' Party (HSWP) took the decision to reform the country's economic management system in 1966, the reform itself being introduced on 1 January 1968. Contrary to what happened in other socialist countries, the reform was preceded neither by major political and ideological discussions nor by a wide-ranging theoretical debate. Of course, there were extensive discussions among economists concerning the practical possibilities for improving the techniques and methods of economic management.

   Initially, critical analysis of the traditional system began with research on the problem of overcentralisation in some branches of industry. Subsequently, the analysis was extended to the whole economy, particularly through the contribution of Péter (1956), which may be considered a pioneering work; it appeared before the ideas of Professor Liberman, which heralded some important changes in Soviet economic thinking, became widely known. Gradually, the notion of a regulated market within the framework of a planned economy was accepted by the economists and then by a majority of the political leadership (Wilcsek, 1967; Csapó, 1966).

On the other hand, the Hungarian debate on the price system, which became extremely vigorous in the mid 1960s, now seems to have been more sophisticated than practically useful (Richet, 1980). One important benefit of the price debate should be noted here, however; this is the realisation that a reform of the price system alone would not be sufficient to bring about a real improvement in the functioning of the planning system. It was not possible to construct a rational price system in the presence of the prevailing administrative techniques of planning. At the same time the empirical rather than theoretical approach to questions of economic reform made possible a more realistic appraisal of the tasks of reform and the steps required to put the reform into practice than was the case in other countries considering reforms. Kornai (1971) emphasised that the reforms were undertaken not on the basis of strictly verified scientific theories but rather from the pressure of various economic difficulties, notably the increasing problems faced by the planners in maintaining and even increasing the economy's growth rate.

Aside from two partial revisions to the producer price system during the 1960s, the reform was also preceded by an agrarian reform, which served to strengthen the support of the regime among the rural population. In the late 1950s prices paid to agricultural producers for compulsory deliveries of produce to the state were substantially increased, and at the beginning of the 1960s compulsory deliveries were suppressed altogether. Instead, a policy of favourable purchase prices for agricultural produce and subsidies on certain agricultural inputs was substituted in order to satisfy the interest of both the rural workers and the state. For the peasants this policy assured them of an increase in income; for the state it was the means of ensuring a regular and stable supply of agricultural products. Another factor contributing to the success of the regime in the countryside was the approach to collectivisation; the early 1960s saw a renewed collectivisation campaign, which brought most of the peasantry into the socialist sector. But unlike the ideologically motivated campaigns of the 1950s, this one appealed to the peasantry's economic interests by promising to make available the resources needed to make the co-operative farms efficient and prosperous (Richet, 1979).

More basically, the 1968 reform can be considered as a delayed response, in the economic sphere, to the violent uprising of 1956, expressing in particular a new orientation to the process and style of accumulation. The classical Stalinist scheme of accumulation giving absolute priority to accumulation in the sphere of heavy industry (i.e. the means of production) was finally abandoned.

The principal aims of the Hungarian economic reforms may be summarised in the following way. First, the reform sought to increase the productivity of factors of production by improving the incentive system. Secondly, there was a general desire to stimulate greater efficiency in all branches of the economy and to improve the country's foreign trade performance. Finally, it was hoped to change the nature of the persistent sellers' market conditions that characterised the traditional system of economic management and to make production more responsive to changes in demand. In order to meet these objectives, the reform itself, called at first the New Economic Mechanism, consisted of a fairly well co-ordinated package of measures covering the areas of planning, pricing and incentives. Bornstein (1977) set out the principal features of the reform as follows:

(1)   The central administrative specification of enterprise production and sales programmes was abandoned, and enterprises were permitted to determine their production patterns on the basis of contracts with customers.

(2)   Central administrative allocation of material inputs was also ended, aside from a few minor exceptions.

(3)   One-year operational plans, disaggregated to enterprise level, were discontinued, and the five-year plans were to become the chief orientation for economic development and the 'steering' of the economy.

(4)   The practice of fixing wage scales centrally came to an end, but average wage levels of enterprises were severely restrained by a new tax on wage increases.

(5)   The predominantly central allocation of resources for investment was changed to a system in which self-financing from profit had a more important role to play, although central supervision of investment activity was to remain strong.

(6)   The chief objective of enterprise activity was to be the pursuit of profit, and incentives for managers and workers were linked to profit, since this was to be the basis for enterprise fund formation. The two main funds were to be the sharing fund (to finance wage increases and bonus payments) and the development fund (to finance enterprise investment).

(7)   Separate foreign-trade multipliers for the CMEA and Western-world market trading areas were introduced to link domestic production and overseas markets. (More precisely, the multipliers were established for convertible and non-convertible currency trade respectively.) These multipliers replaced a much more complex system in which different multipliers were set for individual product groups, making it very difficult to assess efficiency in foreign trade activities. However, the traditional system of

taxes and subsidies on exports and imports, involving price equalisation funds, was retained.

(8) A comprehensive price reform adjusted relative producer prices
and introduced greater flexibility into price formation.

However, this parametric approach to planning the economy did not
abolish all the contraints induced by the traditional vertical and hierarchical structure of economic organisation, since despite the reforms
this structure remained largely intact. Several factors explain this
survival. First, the economic reform was exclusively confined to the
economic sphere and was not at all concerned to seek modifications in
the social and power relations in Hungarian society. Yet, the reforms
did have some implications for relationships within the ruling class, as
recognition of the important role of economic management at enterprise level entailed a considerable increase in the power and status of
people holding management positions. In other words, the leading
politicians transferred part of their economic powers to other social
strata within the ruling groups of society (Rakovski, 1977).

A second factor is Hungary's membership of the CMEA, for
economic relations between the CMEA countries are planned according to the familiar administrative methods. Moreover, none of these
countries has gone so far as to introduce a comprehensive economic
reform of the Hungarian type. Developments following the so-called
Czechoslovakian 'spring' of 1968 – including the strong opposition to
radical reforms, with their associated political risks, to which it gave
rise – have tended to put a very firm brake on any proposals to extend
and deepen economic reform anywhere in Eastern Europe. Aside from
its important relationship with CMEA countries, the Hungarian
economy also benefited from the expansion and relative price stability
of Western world markets in the late 1960s and early 1970s. The end of
the 1960s was still characterised by a steady expansion of the Western
economies, which was a source of increasing demand for Hungarian
products. But it seems likely that Hungary's close involvement in both
Western and CMEA markets, each with its own logic of behaviour,
will soon impose further constraints on the country's development.

The third factor explaining the survival of much of the old administrative structure is the retention of many administrative functions
operating within the new market mechanism. This point can be made
clearer by presenting some examples.

Two important examples concern (1) the role of market prices and
the associated measures of profitability and (2) intervention in the
sphere of investment; for although the reforms did ensure that
personal incomes were linked with enterprise results, and that the size
of investment that an enterprise could undertake would be related to its
profitability, the state nevertheless has held certain prerogatives for

intervention. To a limited extent the state may interfere directly in enterprise management, or it may interfere indirectly by manipulating the price system or some of the other economic regulators. Ostensibly, the justification for such measures of economic policy is to avoid the development of a wage–price inflationary spiral, among other things. Through administrative means the state maintains the old 'financial bridges' between producer and consumer prices in order to keep down the cost of living (Hare, 1976). The lack of flexibility and losses for enterprises that result from the obligation to operate this kind of two-level price system are counterbalanced by subsidies. It seems therefore that a return to, or retention of, old established practices is often easier than trying to develop the principles of the new regulatory system and to put them into practice by means of a really active and consistent price policy.

Moreover, the old methods have negative effects throughout the economy, for they imply that there are multiple criteria for judging the effectiveness of different enterprises. Some will be judged in terms of market-type criteria, whereas others will tend to be regulated by means of administrative tools and hence judged in similar terms. In such branches as clothing, agriculture, services and the food industry, most of whose products are heavily subsidised, indicators of profit measured in official producer prices are not very relevant in assessing performance. On the other hand, a policy of subsidies may be more defensible in the most capital-intensive sectors or branches, where the funds required for capital investment could not be generated through normal market relationships; infrastructural branches are clear examples of this situation.

The investment sphere in general soon gave rise to severe problems when it came to implementing the reform principles, for the freedom allowed to enterprises to make their own investment decisions led to bouts of overinvestment, which in turn induced the central authorities to intervene with restrictions on new investments. Brakes were imposed in an effort to restore unity to the whole process of investment; this actually meant that the managers of the economy were determined to preserve their macroeconomic prerogatives by regulating decisions at microeconomic level. The reformers did not dare to introduce a really effective capital market through which enterprises would have been able to finance their investment projects under competitive conditions, for in such a situation credit policy would necessarily have had to be based on uniform principles that could tolerate very few exceptions. Instead of this rational measure the centre preferred to introduce a complex system for allocating investment resources, combining macro-economic criteria and microeconomic motivations. Thus, the centre determines the major investments on the basis of calculations of plan balances at national level and provides the finance for them; in addition, it seeks to influence enterprise decisions by encouraging them to link their own projects with developments favoured by the centre.

Given this approach adopted by the central authorities, the optimal strategy for an enterprise may well not accord with the centre's wishes, for the enterprise's interest is to minimise its own contribution to the costs of any investment that it undertakes, by getting as much support as possible from the state. At the inception of the reform of the economic mechanism, many enterprises sought credits and subsidies for investment projects, some of which state support was quite unnecessary, since the enterprises concerned already had adequate resources. The result was overinvestment – the counterpart of freedom of decision at enterprise level in a situation where investment seemed almost costless. These tensions in the investment markets provided a pretext for the state to impose a partial recentralisation of decision-making, especially in the fields of income distribution and investment. The partial recentralisation at the beginning of the 1970s was presented as a response to the disfunctioning of the investment system, but it also provided some politicians and managers with an opportunity to try to restore some of the old principles of administrative management.

3   Disfunctioning of the New Economic Mechanism

Let us now consider some of the factors that contribute to the disfunctioning of the New Economic Mechanism in a number of fields. An important contradiction arises from the conflict between the high degree of concentration of production into a very small number of enterprises and the role ascribed to the market in the reformed system of economic management. The degree of monopolisation of the economy has actually remained fairly stable since the last major rearrangement of the productive system, which took place in 1963. This involved a process of horizontal unification, with the effect that most large enterprises have become extremely diversified; indeed, Schweitzer (1978) suggested that large enterprises are not really large enterprises at all, for their product diversity is such that they are basically conglomerates made up of a number of small plants. Yet, the question of breaking up these conglomerates in order to create the smaller units required to promote effective competition did not occur to the reformers, except perhaps as a rather minor side issue. Before the reforms the large enterprises were managed through sectoral institutions, namely, the branch ministries, and in that context their large size and small number were undoubtedly convenient. It seems paradoxical, however, that the downgrading of the role of the sectoral institutions in the reforms, which removed the main justification for the large enterprises, was not accompanied by any real organisational changes. Not only that, but the survival of the old industrial structure facilitated survival of the types of managerial behaviour that characterised the pre-reform period. Moreover, the monopolistic position of certain large enterprises gave them the opportunity to get what resources they needed directly from the centre and effectively to impose their own choices on the planning office, in line with their own particular interests (Bauer, 1975).

At the same time many of the old functions of the branch ministries were gradually restored, until they have now recovered the greater part of their former privileges. Even in 1968 the ministries retained the important right to appoint and dismiss enterprise-managers, but 'advisers' concerned with the affairs of individual branches have subsequently assumed substantial influence over such areas as investment decisions, choice of production, marketing, and so on, mainly owing to the passive and cautious attitudes of many enterprise-managers.

It should be borne in mind at this point that a reform of economic management, with the introduction and generalisation of the profit motive, is not by itself sufficient to transform the leaders of state enterprise into a kind of 'Schumpeterian' manager. For many years managers were trained in the spirit of, and became familiar with, the requirements of the administrative management system; even in the framework of the new management system, it must often seem easier to follow the old practices. Also, the know-how and experience possessed by the leadership and staff in the branch ministries can often provide managers with facilities for organising the supply of inputs and the distribution of their output; this can only serve to reinforce the traditional relationships.

At the higher levels of the administrative hierarchy, this new situation has made it possible for the branch ministries to direct their powers against the functional ministries and the planning office. The result is a bargaining process with the centre in which the ministries strive for more favourable positions in the allocation of investment resources. The juxtaposition of the institutional structure left over from the centralised model with that of the New Economic Mechanism based on market relations was bound to create some tensions in the system, investment decisions being an obvious example of such problems. In the investment sphere we can distinguish three distinct levels and centres of decision (Bauer, 1974; Deák, 1978; Hare, 1976); these concern economy-wide, branch and enterprise aspects of investment. Thus, the centre establishes the general orientation of investment policy and tries to secure higher efficiency by minimising costs, reducing construction periods and maximising output. On the other hand, for the branch ministries, the main aim is the expansion of production in physical terms, while enterprises are primarily concerned to achieve an optimal financing position: that is, a situation in which they are assured of the maximum amounts of 'free' money (i.e. subsidies) for the realisation of their projects before they approach the banks or commit their own resources. These conflicting goals ensured that the kind of financial control by means of the regulators and through the banks envisaged after the reforms simply could not operate in practice.

In order to avoid the development of erratic movements in prices, and to stabilise economic policy, the centre has used a variety of direct and indirect tools, including close central supervision of the fifty largest enterprises after 1971 and a series of centrally organised price revisions following the explosion of raw material prices in the period 1972–4. This experience indicates that the centre, when faced with difficulties, typically prefers to employ administrative tools of control instead of trying to modify the causes of the disfunctioning and promoting an extension of the conditions for real market regulation.

An additional constraint on the development of the reform results from the double insertion of the Hungarian economy in the international division of labour. The importance of foreign trade in the formation of national income has already been mentioned; participation in both the socialist and non-socialist world markets is involved, but each market has its own principles of operation. In the last few years the terms of trade have moved in a direction unfavourable for Hungary's products, but the fact remains that the New Economic Mechanism offered the country a real opportunity to improve its foreign trade performance. But accepting the principle of an open economy would have entailed a much closer linkage of domestic prices to movements in world prices. In addition, it seemed that the policy-makers had to protect the level of domestic prices in order to maintain internal equilibrium, and a certain gap was needed between external and domestic prices in order to secure the competitiveness of Hungarian products.

As in other fields, so in that of international trade. It turned out that enterprises were not sufficiently motivated to find external markets for their products; interestingly, their propensity to expand imports was much stronger. Here too, enterprises seek state support and subsidies for increasing both exports and imports. In the former case enterprises that are exporting, and that are working within the semi-administrative framework of the domestic price system, often need subsidies to develop exports in order to reduce the level of domestic prices down to, or below, that of the corresponding world market prices. In the latter case, enterprises wishing to import should, at least theoretically, be able to finance them themselves; in practice, however, they try to obtain subsidies when external prices are higher than domestic prices in order not to disturb domestic equilibrium. It is clear from all this that the state's control of foreign trade by means of subsidies and quotas maintains a screen between internal and external prices, which tends to preserve the traditional production structure and inhibit economic change.

In the face of these problems of adapting to fluctuations in Western world markets, we may ask whether Hungary's membership of the CMEA can be considered as an antidote to such erratic movements. It is certainly true that the planned exchanges of commodities between socialist countries do ensure some degree of regularity in the foreign exchanges. In some circumstances, CMEA partners can absorb unintended excess supplies, which may result, for example, when the volume of demand for Hungarian exports falls on Western markets; this can result from general recession or restrictive trade agreements within the European Economic Community (EEC). On the other hand, as Tardos (1978) demonstrated, the policy of specialisation among the socialist countries can often reduce the available range of choice both on the demand and supply sides of many markets. In addition, a certain lack of flexibility results from the planning of exchange within each branch, often on a bilateral basis. In this field the old method of establishing the quantities to be exchanged is still widely used; this involves the construction of plans in physical units, with an attempt to secure balanced exchange. At the early stages of the negotiations, enterprises are excluded, but later they receive direct orders from the ministries to execute the agreed plan targets. This situation means that an enterprise whose production is oriented towards CMEA markets is not greatly affected by the reforms, since its major production decisions, on both prices and quantities, are decided not at enterprise level but directly by agreement between the branch ministries of the different socialist countries.

At this stage of the analysis, we may ask what remains of the New Economic Mechanism. Having described the main features of the reforms and the problems that arose in implementing it, it is also interesting to consider whether the Hungarian experience has given rise to a specific model of planning. In fact, the specificity of the Hungarian model of planning may be traced to the existence and manifestations of several phenomena. First, we may refer to the existence of a large sphere of activities outside the scope of the planned economy, which form the so-called 'second' economy – the spontaneous economic activity that escapes direct control by state institutions. In the Soviet-type economies there have always existed some manifestations of such market forms (or 'coloured' markets, as they are sometimes referred to), and generally the state has tended to condemn them and resist their development. But at the same time these phenomena are immanent to the planned economy, in the sense that they represent a resurgence of the kind of individual initiative often discouraged in a rather rigid central-planning system and fulfil functions that a centralised system is actually unable to perform effectively. In Hungary the second economy has spread to various sectors of the economy, especially agriculture, construction and some services. Within its own limited sphere private initiative is now accepted and recognised in Hungary. This acceptance gives specificity to the Hungarian reforms; these economic practices are explicit and in some sectors even encouraged by the state, and there is a real symbiosis with the so-called 'first' economy.

But the first economy itself cannot any longer be considered as a homogeneous system. Within the sector a complex bargaining process is developing among the different groups, institutions, and branch and functional ministries. De facto lobbies, not yet institutionalised, are at work, and the five-year plans increasingly take on the appearance of a fairly loose co-ordination of separate interests as opposed to the expression of a central will or the materialisation of a clear central policy. In parallel to this, economic policy has tended to become more autonomous in relation to the central-planning process, and the role of short-term economic regulation has become more important. Thus, the reforms have tended to downgrade formal planning over the medium term in favour of short-run policy interventions.

Given these developments, could the economic situation of the country be improved by either a restoration of the traditional centralised system or a fundamental extension of the reforms? In all probability recentralisation would not change the reality of the situation that has arisen since the reforms. In a sense, a return to branch management might even be worse than retaining the present 'semi-reform', because of the modifications to equilibrium positions and the dynamic of economic growth induced by the economic reforms. On the other hand, further development of the reform would necessitate major changes in the institutional structure in order to make it more appropriate to the requirements of a market structure. From the point of view of the political leadership, this would have inconvenient implications, for it would entail a significant transfer of power and initiative to enterprise leaders, thereby reducing the powers of branch ministries. It would also require the elaboration of adequate tools for the operation of market-regulated planning, such as a reformed price system, an active capital market and a more rational taxation system.

Nevertheless, it seems that the real choice at present is not that between these two alternative modes of development. Instead, it is most likely that the objective constraints that impinge on the economy, the present political equilibrium between the various social groups and organisations within the country, and the empirical attitude of the leadership will contribute to maintain many of the characteristic features of the Hungarian system of economic management as they have emerged in the years since 1968. I do not expect to see major reorientations of the economic system in the near future.

References: Chapter 2

Bauer, T. (1974), 'Over-investment, growth cycles and economic reform in some CMEA countries', discussion paper presented to the bilateral colloquium on investment of the Institutes of Economics in Belgrade and Budapest (mimeo.).

Bauer, T. (1975) 'A vállalatok ellentmondásos helyzete a magyar gazdasági mechanizmusban' (The contradictory position of the enterprise in the Hungarian economic mechanism), *Közgazdasági Szemle*, vol. 22 (6), pp. 725–35.

Bokor-Gadó-Kürthy-Meitner-Sárosiné-Wilcsek (1957), 'Javaslat az ipar gazdasági irányitásának új rendszerére' (A proposal for a new system of economic management in industry), *Közgazdasági Szemle*, vol. 4 (4), pp. 371–92.

Bornstein, M. (1977), 'Price policy in Hungary', in A. Abouchar (ed.), *The Socialist Price Mechanism* (Durham, NC: Duke University Press).

Bródy, A. (1965), 'Three types of price systems', *Economics of Planning*, vol. 5 (3), pp. 58–66.

Brus, W. (1975), *The Economics and Politics of Socialism* (London: Routledge & Kegan Paul).

Brus, W. (1979), 'The Eastern European reforms: what happened to them?', *Soviet Studies*, vol. 31 (2), pp. 257–67.

Csapó, L. (1966), 'Central planning in a guided market model', *Acta Oeconomica*, vol. 1 (3–4), pp. 237–54.

Csikós-Nagy, B. (1966), 'Two stages of the Hungarian debate on prices', *Acta Oeconomica*, vol. 1 (3–4), pp. 255–66.

Deák, A. (1978), 'Vállalati beruházási döntések és a gazdaságosság' (Enterprise investment decisions and efficiency), *Gazdaság*, vol. 12 (1), pp. 17–36.

Hare, P. G. (1976), 'Industrial prices in Hungary', *Soviet Studies*, vol. 28 (2 and 3), pp. 189–206 and 362–90.

Hegedüs, A. (1976), *Socialism and Bureaucracy* (London: Allison & Busby).

Kornai, J. (1959), *Overcentralisation in Economic Administration* (London: Oxford University Press).

Kornai, J. (1971), 'Economic systems theory and general equilibrium theory', *Acta Oeconomica*, vol. 6 (4), pp. 297–318.

Kornai, J. (1975), *Mathematical Planning of Structural Decisions*, 2nd edn (Amsterdam: North-Holland).

Neuberger, E., and Duffy, W. (1976), *Comparative Economic Systems: A Decision-Making Approach* (Boston, Mass.: Allyn & Bacon).

Péter, G. (1956), *A Gazdaságosság es Jövedelmeőség Jelentösége a Tervgazdálkodásban* (The role of Efficiency and Profitability in a Planned Economy) Budapest: Kögazdasági és Jogi Könyvkiadó).

Portes, R. (1971), 'Decentralised planning procedures and centrally planned economies', *American Economic Review: Papers and Proceedings*, vol. 61 (2), pp. 422–9.

Rakovski, M. (1977), *Le Marxisme face aux pays de l'Est* (Paris: Savelli).

Richet, A. (1978), 'Processus de planification et de régulation de l'économie socialiste', in M. Lavigne (ed.), *Economie politique de la planification en système socialiste* (Paris: Economica).

Richet, A. (1979), 'La Question agraire dans le socialisme: l'expérience hongroise' (mimeo.).

Richet, A. (1980), 'Régulation dans la planification décentralisée: le cas de la Hongrie', doctorate dissertation, Université de Paris X, Paris.

Schweitzer, I. (1978), 'Választék és vállalatnagyság' (Choice and enterprise size), *Figyelő*, vol. 22 (12), p. 3.

Tardos, M. (1978), 'L'adaptation de la Hongrie à l'évolution du marché mondial', in F. Renversez and M. Lavigne (eds), *Régulation et division internationale du travail: l'expérience hongroise* (Paris: Economica).

Walliser, B. (1977, *Systèmes et modèles: introduction critique à l'analyse de systèmes* (Paris: Sevil).

Wilcsek, J. (1967), 'The role of profit in the management of enterprises', *Acta Oeconomica*, vol. 2 (1−2), pp. 63−76.

Part Two

Labour and Wages

Chapter 3

The Labour Market in Hungary
since 1968

1   Introduction

There is no unanimity among Western writers about even the most
fundamental questions of the nature of the labour market in socialist
countries. Some treat the labour market in socialist countries as identical to the corresponding institution in developed capitalist countries;
others think that employees in socialist countries work in bureaucratic
organisations for a fixed wage and that laws restrict their free choice of
workplace. Some consider full employment to be the essence of the
labour market in socialist countries; others show how in these economies too there is unemployment. As far as the regulation of the labour
market is concerned, Western writers sometimes put the emphasis on
central planning and sometimes on the economic regulation of the
market.[1]

   In this chapter, based on an analysis of the Hungarian experience
since 1968, we shall express our own views rather than counterpose the
various conceptions that can be found in the literature. First, we
examine the most important features of the labour market in the
Hungarian economy. Next, we consider the most important trends in its
operation. Finally, we briefly sketch out the measures that have been
used until now to regulate labour demand and allocation and consider
how effective they have been.[2]

   Let us begin our exposition with an outline model of the Hungarian
economy. Initially, we shall suppose that the economy has a single
sector. We shall then claim that, in parallel to the socialist sphere, there
exists the so-called 'second economy' (i.e. the non-socialised economy
sphere) in which extensive earning activity takes place. The existence of
the second economy naturally does not alter the fundamental features
of the model, although it does modify them to a certain extent.

   What, then, are the main features of the outline model? There are
three essential aspects from which all the other important characteristics of the economy can be deduced:

(1)   The means of production are under social ownership. There is
      therefore no private appropriation. As a result entrepreneurial

profit (which is the engine of reproduction in the capitalist economy) and, associated with this, the self-regulating system linking commodity and factor markets, institutions that fundamentally regulate the operation of the economy, are abolished. The centre of economic administration integrates the economy. Its functions are: to create and abolish economic units; to determine the surplus product; to decide what proportion of it is to be assigned to development ends and what proportion is to be distributed; and to regulate the hierarchical relations of subordination within the institutional system of the economy.

(2)   At the same time the socialist economy is a commodity-producing economy. Separate units offer products for sale. Thus, in addition to the system of taxes and reimbursements there exists a centrally regulated market in which, at this micro-level, the participants are obliged to act on the basis of economic rationality.

(3)   A socialist economy reproduces itself on an increasing scale; that is, it is growth-oriented. The reproduction of its basic features is both the precondition for, and the necessary result of, extended reproduction.

Remaining at an abstract level of analysis, we can distinguish three elements in this economy: employees, enterprises and the centre that integrates the economy. The most important characteristics of these elements are the following:

(1)   In a commodity-producing economy free from private appropriation, the means of subsistence can be acquired for the most part on the commodity market. In the absence of any alternative source of income, this means that, in order to earn a living, the individual has to sell his labour power. As a result labour power is a commodity, and workers are obliged to husband their limited labour-power inputs. This husbanding of resources presupposes rational behaviour, namely, an attempt to maximise relative net advantage. The core of workers' behaviour and actions is consumer behaviour. In essence, this means that individuals strive for ever greater consumption and accumulation. The aspirations of consumer behaviour can be understood in terms of the individual's desire to maintain a certain standard of living. In addition, the desire to keep pace with rises in the general standard of living also functions as a macro-social norm.

(2)   Enterprises also act rationally, but this rationality must be understood in the context of the given economic model. Crucially, enterprises do not operate with their own equipment. They are therefore less interested in minimising costs, when compared to capitalist entrepreneurs. They are oriented towards growth and

development; and given this, domestic economic factors restrict their endeavours only to a very limited extent, since the price level is artificial and the market does not determine the allocation of the means of development. As a result enterprises create a constantly growing tendency towards excessive demand for all factors of production. Since one function of the centre in economic organisation is to determine the profile (i.e. production level and structure) of enterprises (consequently necessitating restrictions in the capital market), enterprises strive for the maximum possible growth within the approved framework. In this sense we can say that the enterprise in a socialist economy is not just less cost-sensitive than the capitalist entrepreneur. In the prevailing restrictive conditions one of its aims is actually to increase one element of production costs, namely, wages.

(3) In addition to determining enterprise profiles, the organising centre of the economy also creates and abolishes enterprises. It establishes a balance between the enterprise profits and losses that result from the relatively artificial price system. The centre also determines the wage fund for a given period and tries to influence both the basic wage that individual groups of workers are able to receive and the overall allocation of labour.

2 Features of the labour market

From these fundamental features every essential characteristic of the Hungarian labour market can be deduced. These characteristics determine each sector's sphere of action, including the amount of autonomy that central economic management is able to enjoy. Subsequent analysis is based on the five points that are presented below:

(1) It is a further consequence of the fact that the economy is growth-oriented and commodity-producing, and that its workers calculate rationally with their labour power, that the economy can only be conceived of as operating on the basis of material incentives; that is, it must use some system of individual rewards. The standardisation of living standards, by which we mean the desire of families to keep their consumption in line with the general rise in the level of consumption, is directly linked with the money income that workers are able to achieve.

(2) It follows from the preceding point that individual wages cannot be fixed. The centre of economic management can only regulate the total wage bill.

(3) Individual incentives and unfixed wages can only guarantee relatively disturbance-free reproduction of the economy if minimum

wages enable workers or their families to reproduce their living standard at a socially acceptable low level. As a consequence minimum wages must at least be at a level where it becomes advantageous for the worker to retain his status as an employee (i.e. to continue in his place of work).

(4) Since workers' wages are not fixed, and since workers are not administratively tied to their place of work, they are in a position to try to maximise relative net advantage. They have the means to:
  (a) achieve an increase in their wages within the enterprise, by directly regulating their work intensity and by restricting performance;
  (b) achieve promotion; and
  (c) change workplace in search of higher wages.
  Enterprises are unable to counter this behaviour, for two reasons: first, wages are downwardly inelastic; and secondly, enterprises are growth-oriented. One of the most important characteristics of enterprise behaviour in relation to growth is to retain labour and therefore to try to increase personal incomes.

(5) In the absence of alternative sources of income, and given the population's high degree of willingness to take on work in an era of full employment, the activity rate of the population (i.e. the ratio of employees in the socialised sector to the potential working population) is very high. Full employment does not, of course, mean that every individual of working age is employed in the socialised sector; it simply means that everyone who wants work can find it.[3]

On the Hungarian labour market, therefore, the activity rate and willingness to work are high, wages are not fixed and are downwardly inelastic, and the individual is free to take on work. In addition, there is a constant excess demand for labour, and this is manifest in the labour market, once reserves of labour have been exhausted, in the form of a continual labour shortage. This naturally reproduces the high activity rate and puts workers and those who take on work in a position of power. This in turn affects the efficient use of labour and its balanced allocation throughout the economy. The frequent attempts to regulate the functioning of the labour market have focused on neutralising or eliminating the consequences of this continual excess demand. The so-called labour shortage stands at the centre of both official regulations and of public opinion. It is fruitful, therefore, to show in more detail how restricted the possibilities are for controlling excess demand in the economic model described above.

3 Excess demand in the labour market

The causes of excess demand for labour are ultimately macroeconomic.

However, the concrete mechanism behind this can be studied in the micro-sphere. If we examine the Hungarian economy from the point of view of the excess demand for labour, it is clear that economic growth is not limited by the level of profits, as it is under private ownership of the means of production. For labour demand this means that, while in capitalist economies the introduction and maintenance of reserves of labour can be rational only while they produce a profit in excess of the product necessary for the reproduction of labour power, in socialist countries there is no such constraint. On a national economic level it seems rational to continue bringing labour reserves into production as long as the wages paid for that labour power produce some new value, no matter how small it is. The activity rate is thus almost always close to its theoretical maximum; that is, there is no mobilisable surplus of labour. Excess demand for labour at the enterprise level (their orientation towards growth expressing itself in attempts to increase the labour force) is an expression of this macroeconomically determined situation.

The growth orientation of economic units can be explained by numerous factors. Some of these clearly follow directly from the model; others appear to be related only to particular forms of the many possible means of economic regulation that are known and have already been tried. Of the former, the first that should be mentioned is the dependence of economic units on the centre or on the centrally regulated market. Next comes another important impetus for growth, namely, the attempt to escape from the effects of even a centrally regulated market by means of closer links with the organs that run the economy. From the point of view of the enterprise, we must remember that the controlled market (compared with the ideal-type market) is a source of uncertainty and cannot be perfectly understood. In addition, we should mention prestige, importance and defensiveness, which increase with enterprise size, and the greater prestige, security and comfort that result from the near-monopoly position of many enterprises. These phenomena are also manifest in the capitalist economic model. In the Hungarian context it is natural that bigger enterprises find it easier to establish close links with the centre. The degree of an enterprise's influence on the centre's actions in relation to the conditions of economic activity is above all a function of its size, and this gives a clear impetus for growth.

In addition to these organisational causes, a growth orientation is also founded on some effects that emanate from within the system of economic regulation. It is usual to consider that attitudes favouring growth in the economic mechanism are simply related to a subset of the many possible types of regulatory system within the given socialist model. We consider this assumption to be not only unprovable but also mistaken. Even if it were true that the efficiency of enterprise activity could be criticised without also criticising other factors that condition its sphere of operation, there would still be a problem. It is theoretically impossible to set in operation an automatic regulatory mechanism that puts enterprise efficiency (i.e. the ability to produce surplus product) instead of growth at the centre of enterprise interest and yet, at the same time, gives preferences to some enterprises and discriminates against others from the point of view of their potential for development and for increasing personal income.

Given that the enterprise profile is administratively restricted and that the reallocation of capital between enterprises (which is essentially the same thing in the long run) is narrowly limited or prohibited, the use of the bulk of developmental resources formed at enterprise level must be decided on centrally. Otherwise, enterprises would use them for their own development and thereby preserve the existing structure of the economy. In this way, as far as the allocation of developmental resources is concerned, the impulses of the market mechanism mediated by the autonomous decisions of enterprises are narrowly restricted.

This undoubtedly has economically irrational consequences, which in the micro-sphere manifest themselves in terms of rigidity in adapting to needs and a 'hunger' for central resources. In these circumstances it is inevitable that a number of factors should be important in affecting the chances of individual enterprises' securing developmental resources. In addition to centrally determined criteria of the economic mechanism, there are criteria of economic power, such as the nature of the relationship with the organs of economic management, personal factors, and the degree of enterprise influence as determined by its size. Finally, it is also economically irrational in Hungary that the relatively modest funds that do remain with enterprises (calculated to allow for the 'dynamic maintenance of a given output level') can be used within the given enterprise profile, even if stagnation or reduction of activity within this profile may be desirable on the national economic level.

However, an end to profile regulation and an expansion of inter-enterprise capital reallocation cannot be permanent elements of policy for a socialist economy. Under capitalism production units of the most varied profiles can be integrated within a single enterprise on the basis of capital ownership. This is one way of diminishing the risk associated with a narrow profile, and as such it can undoubtedly be seen as rational for the capital-owning entrepreneur. Under socialism the 'capital-owner' cannot play an integrating role like this, because enterprises do not operate with their own equipment. Thus, a capital market cannot operate either. As a consequence individual enterprise profiles can only be justified in terms of wider or narrower interpretations of technical and economic requirements of the production process. Decisions of this sort clearly cannot be entrusted to units in the micro-sphere, and they must therefore be decided centrally.

In the above model, then, units in the micro-sphere strive for permanent expansion within restricted production profiles. This is their natural condition. Occasional stagnation or a decrease in size either is the result of central pressure on the economic unit or is deviant enterprise behaviour. If an enterprise were of its own accord to set itself the aim of stagnation or of a decrease in its size in its development plan, we would undoubtedly have to consider it pathological.

The route to long-term economic growth for an enterprise is to expand capital equipment and the labour force. The stock of capital equipment that may be used for expansion, however (including the investor's and the contractor's physical capacity), is always just as restricted on a national economic level as the labour force. In a socialist economy where, in principle, growth is only ultimately restricted by the quantity of production factors available, actual developmental resources are generally scarce in comparison with the desired growth. There is therefore insufficient of all factors of production. In this respect the labour shortage is in no way different from the shortage of other elements necessary for development. It is merely one of the manifestations, in its own particular sphere, of the general shortage of factors of production (i.e. development).

These two elements in the shortage of production factors each create (i.e. make possible) their own allocation mechanisms, and these have different economic results. In order to understand this, we must describe the different ways in which enterprises treat these two sorts of production factor in their economic (i.e. development) decisions. As far as the equipment necessary for development is concerned, enterprises depend on central decisions for the majority of the investment goods that they need for expansion. Their own capacity to meet investment demand (i.e. their financial funds) are scarcely adequate. On the other hand, the enterprise's financial situation does not put any limits on its demand for labour. Moreover, the labour market is a rather specific market whose mode of operation differs in many ways from both the commodity and investment markets (if indeed we can talk of an investment market at all).

In theory, labour can be acquired (i.e. found employment or redistributed to the enterprise's advantage) even if there is very little of it numerically; that is, it can be utilised advantageously even if there are no reserves of labour to be used up. (That not every enterprise is able to get enough labour in a situation of excess demand is a different problem.) The enterprise, however, can scarcely forgo the possibility of acquiring more labour, since, as we have shown, its very nature is to accumulate. Abstention is only possible if the enterprise is compensated by the centre's investment funds, allowing it to introduce mechanisation to replace labour. However, even in this case the enterprise only ceases to acquire labour temporarily.

Even if an enterprise, guided by self-restraint and conscious of the general labour shortage, does not expand its labour force, it is still forced to compete with rival enterprises for labour and to win state help in this. If enterprises do not compete, they will lose their existing labour force. Competition on the labour market is always keen, because success is only just beyond one's grasp. This is in contra-distinction to the market for investment goods, where permanent readiness of this type is unnecessary, because, once acquired, capital equipment cannot be 'lured away'. In addition, the way to get more capital equipment is not via the market but through struggles with the central authorities, in which the larger enterprises for the most part have an advantage. Precisely because the more acute the labour short-age, the less possible it is for an enterprise to abandon its attempts to increase the labour force, the labour shortage becomes a permanent feature of our model.

4   The second economy

In our presentation so far we have treated the Hungarian economy as if it consists of a single (socialised) sector. It is common knowledge, how-ever, that beyond the socialised sector there is an extensive private sector, which has a considerable influence on the conditions in, and regulation of, the labour market. What are the most important features of this 'second' economy, and how can they have a fundamen-tal effect on the state of the labour market?

Before answering this question we must briefly consider the concept of the second economy, since both its dimensions and its functions differ significantly from similarly defined institutions in capitalist economies. The Hungarian second economy differs fundamentally from the petty commodity sphere of capitalist countries in that it is primarily the locus of income-earning, or income-saving, activity by those who are already employed in the socialist economy or by those who are statistically considered 'inactive'. While the number of those whose principal occupation is in petty commodity production is only 200,000–250,000, there are, for example, 1·8 million small-scale (part-time) agricultural plots with which half of the country's population, over 5 million people, is associated. The individuals belonging to these households perform the equivalent of 750,000–800,000 people's yearly worktime. Within this total pensioners work a daily average of 4·4 hours, those who work within the household complete 4·3 hours per day, and those who are employed in the socialised sector work a further 3 hours daily at home. The population builds annually roughly 40,000 dwellings using its own resources. This is equivalent to the annual worktime of 120,000 people. The great majority of these 40,000 private dwellings are built by workers employed in the socialised sector, working at weekends, on holidays or while ostensibly on sick leave. They even become temporarily unemployed in order to do it. This means that a worktime equivalent to that of about 1 million people is spent in second-economy activities in agriculture and dwelling construction alone; this may be compared with the published figure for the total economically-active population of 5·2 million.

The enormous extent of the second economy, or at least of its use of labour, is apparent from these approximate and incomplete data. The second economy is of primary significance for the labour market, because it increases the possibility of workers employed in the socialised sector but also active in the second economy to regulate their performance and effort in their official workplace. In this way it tends to increase both the existing excess demand for labour (i.e. the labour shortage) and the trends towards increasing wages.

In summary, we can state that the existence of the second economy does not diminish the amount of labour power sold in the socialised sector. However, it does diminish the effective volume of that labour power, measured in terms of actual capacity to work. We should note as well that this has consequences for the continuity of employment in the socialised sector. In one of our studies, workers with their principal occupation in the socialised sector spent 10 per cent of their worktime employed outside that sector. (In this study we were considering only periods spent in between jobs in the socialised sector.)

The existence of the second economy makes both the fixing of wages and the restriction of labour mobility even more unrealistic. At the same time it decreases the possible effectiveness of wage-based incentives within the socialised sector.

5 Labour market regulation

In the light of these characteristics of the Hungarian labour market, we can comprehend the measures taken by the economic administration to regulate it. We can also draw some conclusions about the limitations of those regulations. It is important for economic management to moderate the demand for labour, to neutralise the harmful consequences of overdemand and to prevent effective employment in the second economy. These are necessary to combat the trends of worsening labour discipline and increasingly higher wages. The economic administration considers that its most important task is to decrease the 'labour hunger' of enterprises and, related to this, on a national level to promote the efficient allocation of labour.

However, as one of the functionaries of the Ministry of Labour wrote: 'Central organs are not in a position to combat unjustified claims with substantial arguments. They cannot prove that, on a national level, the required labour is more necessary somewhere else.' In addition, as a result of the organisational structure labour-planning 'can only be realised on the basis of co-operation between enterprises and councils (local area administrations). Councils alone cannot perform this function.' There is constant pressure on the economic administration and on the local and regional administrative organs. Both enterprises and ministries expect those organs dealing with labour to solve the labour problems. The organs cannot avoid this pressure, since that is their job. This is especially obvious when new investments are brought on stream. Without central intervention new investments would often not even begin to operate. In consequence, the role of central and regional intervention in the allocation of labour has increased in recent years.

In the concluding part of this section of the chapter, we examine briefly the nature and effects of the recent measures aimed at directing labour supply. The measures were of four main types:

(1)   the direction of careers for certain skilled groups (specialists);
(2)   restrictions on administrative and clerical staff;
(3)   the general direction of labour; and
(4)   regulations on the size of the enterprise labour force.

These measures had two aims: the regulation of employment or changes of employment, and the limitation of the size of the labour force in various groups of enterprise.

The first measure was aimed at alleviating the great shortage of doctors and teachers in certain provincial areas, which was preventing the provision of basic services to the population. To this end newly qualified teachers were to be compulsorily placed at the beginning of their careers, with the obligation to choose a post from a centrally published list and to spend a minimum of three years there. Similar regulations covered the employment of newly qualified doctors.

The implementation of this prescriptive measure has been facilitated by three factors: a relatively small number of people are concerned; the possible posts can easily be counted; and the regulations can easily be tied to those with a given level of education. On the other hand, it is clear that, precisely because it has affected only immediate school-leavers, the measure can have had only a very restricted impact in decreasing regional inequalities in labour supply.

A further measure was directed at restricting the number of workers in administrative and clerical jobs, since their number was considered excessively high. The essence of the measure was to block additional employment in such posts in 1977. Further employment in these fields was simply not allowed. The reasoning behind the measure was that it would solve the problems of labour supply in productive areas. However, either enterprises defended themselves by reclassifying their administrative and clerical workers as manual workers ('labour concealment'), or they used every possible excuse to gain exemption from it. The measure was withdrawn two years after its introduction.

Unlike the above-mentioned measures of a centralised nature, the direction of labour and the introduction and extension of enterprise categorisation were initiated by local and regional administrative organs. Both measures began initially in a single county and were then gradually extended to the whole country. The direction of labour, the essence of which has been that it is only permissible to change jobs via the local council's labour office, served to restrict the mobility of labour. It was considered 'exaggerated' to introduce it at a national level. In addition, the new system had the role of organising in a planned manner the jobs that people were changing to. The need was felt to direct labour to places of work that were more efficient, more productive and more important from the standpoint of the national economy. The compulsory direction of labour was thus linked to prescriptions about the pattern of labour force development. Enterprises were divided into categories depending on their importance in the national economy. The first category contained enterprises that were permitted to take on new workers without restriction. This could include labour sent from the local labour office, and in addition the labour offices were under an obligation to direct to these enterprises workers who did seek to change jobs. The second category contained enterprises that were permitted to maintain the size of their labour force and could therefore replace any labour that left. The third category was made up of enterprises that were not even allowed to take on workers to replace those who left.

As may be expected in the light of the discussion so far, this last measure has not borne the expected fruit. One of the many reasons for this is that it has proved impossible to find adequate efficiency criteria by which to classify enterprises. Enterprise size and the degree of its local power have been primarily decisive in this classification. Only a few enterprises with a small labour force have been put into the third category, and a long-term reduction in the labour force of such enterprises has not helped the overall problems of labour supply very much.

In addition, it is questionable whether the compulsory direction of labour is effective as a way of rationally allocating labour to efficient employment. This is because the majority of those who change jobs are unstable, unskilled and even untrainable workers. It is significant that, in the area covered by one of our studies, in a given six-month period 85 per cent of those changing jobs or taking on work had no formal qualifications and more than 50 per cent of them found unskilled jobs. Since the cost for the economy as a whole of in-service training in new jobs is practically zero, it is of little consequence where this group of workers is placed. The compulsory direction of (this unskilled) labour therefore cannot have a significant influence on the more efficient allocation of labour.

In the light of this examination of the attempts made to regulate the labour market, we can establish that the economic administration's autonomy of action in this regard has been fairly limited. Enterprises' continual excessive demand for labour, the attempts of workers as takers of jobs rationally to husband their labour power, the existence of the means necessary to realise these attempts and weaknesses in the self-regulating market mechanism all have played a primary role in this. As a result the Hungarian labour market today operates essentially in a 'market manner' without central intervention. It also has the characteristics described above: wages are not fixed, but they are inelastic downwards; there is continual overdemand; there is freedom to choose and change jobs; and the second economy also plays a role. The economic administration influences market forces by limiting the size of the wage fund, by establishing, merging and abolishing enterprises, and by regular or occasional increases in the wages of certain groups of workers. We can say of the latest measures that they follow market forces rather than change them, in that it is generally groups of workers whose wages have fallen behind that now receive the largest increases.

Studying the labour market in the light of the history of economic management since 1968, we must conclude that, when further developments of the reform of economic management came to an end (by the early 1970s), this was accompanied by apparently drastic, yet essentially unsuccessful, direct and temporary intervention in the operations of the labour market.

Depending on the success of the principles of the economic strategy for the 1980s and of the comprehensive and carefully thought-out extensions to the reform, we can expect some advantageous changes in the labour market, especially concerning the creation of equilibrium conditions and the improvement of possibilities and methods for the regulation of the market.

Notes: Chapter 3

1   By way of example we point to just three essentially differing examples from this extensive literature. Nuti (1976), for example, considering the Czechoslovakian economy as a model, wrote of a *perfectly free* labour market, where wages fluctuate and the state only regulates; the means of production are enterprise property. Marczewski (1978) thought that in a socialist economy the state fixes wages and the economic administration strives above all for the maintenance of *full employment*. Bornstein (1978)

claimed that it can be demonstrated that in socialist economies there exists 'seasonal, frictional and structural unemployment'.

2   We do not want to deal separately with the questions of the regulation of wages and incomes.

3   The population's great readiness to work is a natural consequence of the process by which, with the increase of the activity rate, the ability of wages to support the population decreases. The ratio of wages to living standards is reduced, and as a result the supply of labour reproduces itself extensively, until there are no reserves of inactive population capable of work.

References: Chapter 3

Bornstein, M. (1978), 'Unemployment in capitalist regulated market economies and socialist centrally planned economies', *American Economic Review: Papers and Proceedings*, vol. 68 (2), pp. 38–43.

Marczewski, J. (1978), *Emploi, salaires et productivité dans les sociétés industrielles* (Paris: Presses Universitaires de France).

Nuti, M. (1976), 'Capitalisme, socialisme et croissance de l'état stable', in G. Grellet, *Nouvelle Critique de l'économie politique* (Paris: Calman-Levy).

Chapter 4

The Evolution of Wage Regulation in Hungary

1 Introduction

Wage regulation, if it is undertaken, is generally recognised to be one of the most difficult macroeconomic tasks of any government. Hungarian experience further demonstrates that the 'correct' system of wage regulation is highly dependent both on the style of economic management and on the goals and constraints facing the economy.

This chapter seeks to discuss the current Hungarian debate on the reform of wage regulation in terms of the lessons learned during the evolution of wage regulation in Hungary. Section 2 is concerned with the construction of an overall framework within which Hungarian wage regulation can be discussed. The third section of the chapter describes the evolution of Hungary's wage regulation system. Section 4 presents statistics relevant in evaluating the effects of wage regulation. Section 5 reviews the current debate, which focuses on the appropriate wage-regulation system to become operative during 1981–5, while section 6 contains my analysis of the debate and my own conception of an appropriate system of wage regulation.

2 A framework for analysis

Figure 4.1 outlines the relationship of the wage regulation system to other parts of the economy. Central to the understanding of Figure 4.1 is the distinction between 'type A labour' services and 'type B labour' services. Unfortunately, it is too misleading a simplification to identify type A labour services with the state- and co-operative-operated organisations of the economy and type B labour services with the private, semi-legal and illegal sectors of the economy. Rather, as we shall see below, it is more convenient to think of type A labour services as being conducted in the first economy and type B labour services as being conducted in the second economy.

The first economy represents the state- or co-operative-regulated aspects of activity within the state- and co-operative-operated organisations. Thus, the remainder, the second economy, includes the

Figure 4.1 *Relationship of the Wage Regulation System to the Entire Economy*

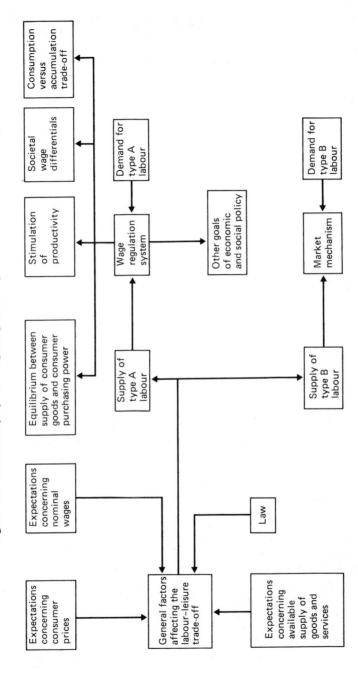

non-regulated aspects of activity within state- and co-operative-operated organisations and all forms of private, semi-legal and illegal activity. Gábor (1979) provided a categorisation of the second-economy labour activity, which appears below in a somewhat modified form:

(1) The legal private sector. This encompasses all private-plot agricultural production, a large portion of residential construction and some retail trade.

(2) 'Not officially registered' activity in the private sector. People in this second category generally have a full-time job in the first economy, which satisfies the legal requirement of 'registered occupation' and enables them to provide part-time services without being registered as a member of the private sector and to receive income that is not taxed. Included in this second category are: the professional services of doctors, lawyers, teachers and architects; the personal services of housekeepers, cooks, seamstresses and tailors; and the repair services of mechanics, painters, plumbers, electricians and carpenters.

(3) Those employees in the service sector of the first economy whose earnings depend substantially on tips, 'thank-you' money and bribes. Those who provide direct medical, dental and eye care, automobile repair and maintenance services, home maintenance services, machinery repair services, moving services and personal services (e.g. sports instructors, hairdressers, barbers) fall into this category.

(4) Those who clandestinely utilise state-owned property or steal state-owned raw materials, spare parts and finished products for their own benefit and those who engage in other types of illegal financial and trade transactions. These people generally have full-time jobs in the first economy.

The left side of Figure 4.1 suggests that individuals have substantial freedom with respect to their labour–leisure trade-off. Expectations concerning nominal wages, consumer prices and the available supply of goods and services combine with laws (i.e. mandatory full-employment regulations and laws concerning the nature of the private sector) to form general factors affecting the labour–leisure choice. Individuals react to these general factors and then provide some combination of type A and type B labour services. A multicoloured market mechanism[1] handles the interaction of the supply of, and demand for, type B labour services, whereas the wage regulation system deals with the supply of, and demand for, type A labour services.

The fact that individuals have a great amount of freedom in choosing the combination of type A and type B labour services that they provide implies that the wage regulation system of the first economy and the market mechanism of the second economy together influence the final distribution of labour services. The importance of this interdependence may be understood partly by noting the size of the second economy, as discussed in the previous chapter.

Before we discuss the exact nature of this interdependence, let us examine why the second economy has been important. The second economy's importance at any point of time may be attributed to four factors: (1) shortages of certain consumer goods and services in the first economy; (2) shortcomings in the distribution of these scarce goods and services; (3) dissatisfaction with the quality of certain goods and services in the first economy; and (4) the inability to live reasonably well from the wages of a single full-time job in the first economy.

Central authorities, conscious of the relationship between standard of living and societal stability, have chosen to allow the private sector (i.e. category 1 of the second economy) to supply agricultural products, housing, clothing, furniture and services instead of choosing to channel the necessary amount of first-economy investments into these areas or to set market-clearing prices. The presence of a legal private sector is preferable to a slower rate of industrial growth and/or measurable inflation.

However, central authorities have generally not encouraged the development of co-operation between the first economy and the private sector, except for the successful example of such co-operation found in agriculture. In particular, the inability to obtain raw materials and spare parts as a member of the private economy has encouraged individuals to opt for category (4) of the second economy. Full-time jobs in the first economy 'allow' these individuals to utilise without cost socially owned raw materials, spare parts and capital in a parallel second-economy job without their having to cover overhead costs or pay taxes. Moreover, such first-economy jobs often give workers access to 'would-be first-economy customers', who are willing to pay first-economy prices for quick higher-quality service. A conflict of interests is certainly present here. For example, a repairman will receive approximately 20–30 per cent of the official labour charge if he works as a first-economy employee, but 100 per cent of the official labour charge plus the official price of 'stolen' spare parts if he works as a member of the second economy. A customer realises the dilemma of the repairman and generally acts in one of two ways in the belief that he will receive quicker or better service. Either a tip is offered to the repairman (i.e. category 3 of the second economy) in his capacity of a first-economy employee, or the work will be completed by the repairman 'privately'. Of course, such pilfering of first-economy time, resources and customers is risky. For one thing, a repairman must be careful to maintain a reasonable flow of first-economy 'production'.

Unfortunately, all of this is not measurable by available statistical data.

Demand for the labour services of the second economy's category (2) have flourished because of shortcomings in the distribution of scarce goods and services and concern about their quality (along with the force of tradition). For instance, tips are offered to medical personnel in a direct attempt to secure higher-quality medical services.

Now that we have argued that there has been demand for all four categories of labour services in the second economy, we can turn to the supply of such labour. For the majority of working people, it is virtually impossible to live reasonably well on the official wage of a single full-time job in the first economy. This is the principal reason why the majority of working people seek a second job. While a person can hold two jobs that do not include the supply of type B labour services, the higher wages in the second economy prove to be very attractive. For example, in early 1979 official statistics indicated that the national average net hourly wage including all monetary bonus payments, based on a 200 hour work month, was approximately 19 forints, whereas a collection of estimates from economists and from a wide variety of members of categories (1) and (2) of the second economy suggest that the average gross (before taxes) hourly wages of those categories was approximately 100 forints.

The degree of wage disequilibrium that appears to exist between the first economy and the second economy is exaggerated because it is inappropriate to analyse the hourly wage of either economy in isolation. In particular, engagement in one job activity may provide not only wages but also an opportunity to engage in another activity. For instance, most members of co-operative farms and state farms are entitled to receive a 'household plot'. This is a great incentive for at least one person in the family to work on a state farm or a co-operative farm. Similarly, a private electrician, carpenter or other craftsman may be drawn to the private sector not only because of the after-tax income that he will receive from his reported activity, but also because of the opportunity to engage in unreported activity, which yields an even higher hourly wage. This is also the case for many service personnel employed in the first economy. Their first-economy job provides them with an official status, which appears on all forms of personal identification and gives them access to state-owned buildings, machinery, spare parts and raw materials, which they can then utilise for their own gain.

A difference in the social recognition accorded to first-economy and second-economy work is another factor that makes a direct comparison of hourly wages somewhat hazardous. The prestige of official full-time employment in the socialist sector seems to be much greater than that of official full-time employment in the private sector. Lying behind this difference is a social perception of four types of irregularity. First, those in the private sector disregard business laws that regulate their activity.[2] Secondly, licences to operate private businesses are in short supply, and many people believe that they may only be obtained through well-placed bribes and/or connections. Thirdly, an initial amount of capital is generally required to start up a private business. This initial capital is often more than an amount that an 'average person' would possess. Hence, many people perceive that only the wealthier have access to official full-time employment in the private sector. Finally, the private sector is considered not to be competitive.

These irregularities might not be interpreted as reasons for animosity towards those engaged in official full-time employment in the private sector were it not for the belief that disproportionately high income is the norm among private sector entrepreneurs.

Consequently, this animosity is responsible for the lower prestige accorded to full-time private-sector entrepreneurs. Furthermore, the presence of full-time entrepreneurs in the second-economy labour force tends to increase the relative wage in the second economy, since these private entrepreneurs are being compensated for their lower prestige in the community.

Other factors that may explain the wage disequilibrium between the two economies are the riskiness of second-economy activity and work intensity. Riskiness is higher in the second economy due to the relatively higher probability that second-economy regulations and the strictness of their enforcement will fluctuate over time. Also, individuals may be encouraged to work harder in the second economy. At this point we may be getting ahead of ourselves, so let us begin to explore the nature of the interdependence between the wage regulation system of the first economy and the multicoloured market system of the second economy.

On the positive side, the second economy has produced many consumer goods and services. This aspect of the second economy frees the first economy from providing these goods and services and generally assists in keeping the population satisfied. For instance, the policies of distributing household plots among agricultural workers and of permitting ownership of weekend houses (which most often feature a garden) take advantage of the expertise of the population, allow the agricultural co-operatives and state farms to concentrate on production geared to large-scale methods and supplement the national food supply.

The inability to regulate certain aspects of second-economy activity and the relative insensitivity of firms to profit maximisation (a failure in the regulatory system of the first economy) have produced two negative effects: (1) individuals have held back effort during first-economy

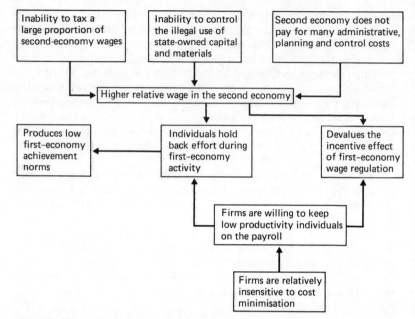

Figure 4.2   *Negative Effects of the Second Economy on the First Economy*

labour activity; and (2) the incentive effects of first-economy wage regulation have been devalued. Figure 4.2 depicts this interaction. On the one hand, the inability to tax a large proportion of second-economy wages, the inability to control illegal free use of state-owned capital and materials, and the fact that second-economy activity often avoids covering overhead costs combine to produce higher relative wages in the second economy. Thus, individuals have an incentive to concentrate their efforts on second-economy activity. On the other hand, firms are willing to keep low productivity workers, because the incentive system of the first economy has failed to create a very strong interest in profit maximisation. Thus, individuals are effectively permitted to hold back effort in the first economy, which in turn produces low official achievement norms throughout the first economy (Gábor, 1979, pp. 26–8).

Now that we have discussed the interaction between the first economy and the second economy, we can return to the entire economy as depicted in Figure 4.1. The task of the multicoloured market mechanism of the second economy is to balance the supply of, and demand for, type B labour services. The wage regulation system of the first economy has a more diverse set of goals, including: mediation between the supply of consumer goods and consumer purchasing power; stimulation of productivity; creation of the desired consumption

Figure 4.3   *Detailed View of the Wage Regulation System*

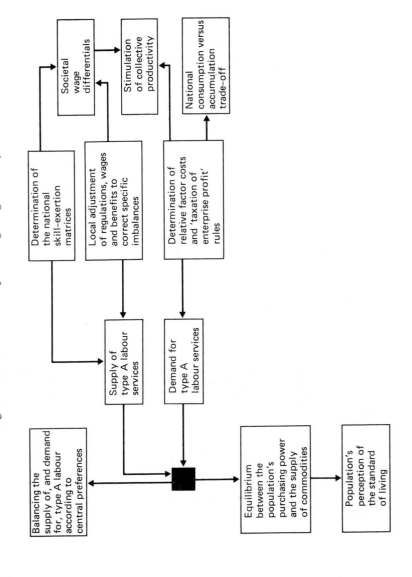

versus accumulation proportion; and control of wage differentials among the different strata of society. One crucial problem that the wage regulation system faces centres on the inadequate number of government policy instruments available to attain all these goals.

Figure 4.3 provides a detailed view of how the post-1967 wage regulation system has responded to its main responsibilities. Wage regulation comprises three categories of policy: determination of the national skill–exertion matrices; local adjustment of regulations, wages and benefits; and determination of relative factor costs and 'taxation of enterprise profit' rules. While these three categories of policy have specific roles, they also interact to determine the degree of equilibrium between the supply of consumer goods and consumer purchasing power. This degree of equilibrium directly feeds into the population's perception of the standard of living – a topic towards which decision-makers are particularly sensitive. Moreover, these three factors together account for the influence of the wage regulation system on the distribution of type A labour services between branches.

Each national skill–exertion matrix contains a skill dimension and a 'difficulty of working conditions' dimension for a particular occupation. Each matrix entry contains an upper and a lower bound, which limits either the salary or the wage for a skill–exertion category of the particular occupation under consideration. The band determined by the upper and lower bounds permits an enterprise to differentiate on the basis of experience, seniority and ability.

The local adjustment of regulations, wages and benefits corrects specific defects that the other categories of policy have been unable to eliminate. Thus, this policy group incorporates the more detailed reactions of central authorities.

Determination of relative factor costs and 'taxation of enterprise profit' rules are designed to stimulate collective productivity[3] through the creation of incentives aimed at encouraging each enterprise to pay serious attention to profit. This area of policy also plays an important role in the national 'consumption versus accumulation' trade-off. Relative factor costs and tax regulations strongly influence the amount of investment resources available to the centre and to enterprises, as well as influencing the amount of available wages.

Stimulation of collective productivity plus the resulting balance between the supply of, and demand for, type A labour services influence the other goals of economic and social policy. Conversely, these other goals, at an earlier point in time, affected the formation of wage regulations.

Figure 4.3 illustrates that the wage regulation system makes no effort to stimulate individual productivity through the threat of dismissal. However, not evident from Figure 4.3 is the fact that the wage regulation system is constrained in its effort to stimulate individual productivity due to the relatively small wage differences associated with 'quality and quantity performance' considerations. Also absent from the figure is any notion that enterprises can avoid the spirit of the national skill−exertion matrices simply by reclassifying an employee. Reclassification is utilised in an effort to retain valued employees and occurs often enough that it weakens the centre's ability to regulate societal wage differentials.

3 Historical experience

To reflect major shifts in the mode of regulating wages, we shall divide the period 1950−78 into five subperiods: 1950−6, 1957−67, 1968−70, 1971−5 and 1976−8. However, this division is not meant to hide the existence of adjustments that occurred annually. Frequent changes in any form of regulation leave an impression that the present form of regulation is temporary. In such a case an enterprise's reaction to that regulation will tend to be different from its reaction if that regulation is viewed as permanent.

The most notable feature of the 1950−6 period was the widespread use of task-related wages dependent on fulfilment relative to norms.[4] While this system contributed to the substantial increase in the quantity of production, Hungarian experience indicated that the task rate wage: (1) did not have an advantageous influence on quality nor on efficient utilisation of inputs; (2) did not encourage the adoption of new technology; (3) had a damaging influence on the formation of income proportions within each strata of society; and (4) alienated many workers. In particular, piece rate wages, characteristic of wide areas in the economy, were held responsible for the degree to which quality was sacrificed for quantity and thus became regarded as economically harmful rather than useful. Hungarian experience during this period has left a deep distaste for the use of piece rate wages as a means of stimulating individual productivity. In fact, the use of a task-rate wage system was no longer a centrally controlled policy option after 1956, when it became an enterprise policy option.

With respect to the wage regulation system followed during 1957−67, central authorities replaced the goal of growth of production with: growth of productivity; balance between the supply of consumer goods and consumer purchasing power; efficient utilisation of labour; and maintenance of the variation of personal incomes within reasonable limits.[5]

Originally, the new wage system was to be based on automatic increases in the wage funds of those enterprises which overfulfilled the gross output plan. Yet, due to inflationary pressure this automatic scheme faded away, and the National Planning Office was given the responsibility of determining the overall wage fund and then distributing this fund among branch ministries. The initial funds that the ministries received were not to be supplemented in the case of overfulfilment of the gross output target. Yet, some decentralisation occurred, as the bands between the upper and lower bounds of the national skill—exertion matrices were widened.

However, the most noticeable event of this period was the change in the thinking of the Planning Office with respect to using incentives in gross output as a measure of productivity. The unadjusted value of an enterprise's gross output was found to be an inadequate measure of productivity; moreover, enterprise gross production could not be used to assess the relative responsibility for performance of selective sections of an enterprise. Thus, during the 1957–67 period other indices (e.g. sales, profits) began to replace gross production as the cornerstone for wage increases.

The introduction of the New Economic Mechanism in 1968 explicitly set forth the complex set of goals and constraints shown in Figure 4.3.[6] The level of profits (in contrast to the previous practice based on increases in profit or in sales) became the key for wage increases. Profit was divided into four parts: (1) profit taxes, which secured revenues for the state budget and thus gave central authorities funds to finance goals of economic and social policy; (2) a sharing fund to be used to augment base wages and designed to encourage collective productivity; (3) a development fund applicable to enterprise investment projects and to the expansion of working assets; and (4) a reserve fund providing some protection against risks, particularly against the risk of fluctuating wage increases and the risk of losses associated with unsuccessful investments.

Let us review the 1968–9 process of the distribution of profit for the simple case in which an enterprise's average wage remains at its 1967 level:

Define

V = value of sales
C = costs of materials and transportation
A = gross value of fixed and working assets engaged
W = annual wage bill
P = annual taxable profit
a = wage multiplier designed to offset differences in capital intensity
t = average tax rate assessed against sharing fund profit; calculated on the basis of a progressive marginal tax schedule with respect to (N_S/W)
N_S = before-tax profit increment for sharing fund
N_D = before-tax profit increment for development fund
S = unadjusted after-tax profit increment for sharing fund

D = unadjusted after-tax profit increment for development fund
R = increment to the reserve fund

Step 1: Determination of annual taxable profit:
$$P = V - C - 0.05A - 1.25W$$

where 0.05 is the charge on the gross average annual value of fixed and circulating assets and 0.25 is the tax on wages.

Step 2: Distribution of profits:

$$N_S = P \left(\frac{aW}{aW + A}\right) \qquad N_D = P \left(\frac{A}{aW + A}\right)$$

This step, designed to promote the desired proportions between accumulation and consumption, distributes profits according to adjusted factor shares of the adjusted value of productive factors. Adjustment occurs through the use of the wage multiplier, which for 1968–70 generally equalled 2, but varied from a low of 0.5 for foreign-trade marketing firms to a high of 8 for public trains, trams and other city transportation. This rigid 'objective' rule was adopted as a compromise between those who did not want central authorities to distribute profit and those who distrusted decentralisation's ability to combat inflationary pressure and income inequalities that might result from enterprise control over profit distribution.

Step 3: Payment of profit tax:

$$S = (1 - t) N_S$$

Table 4.1 indicates that for industry t equalled 0.576 in 1968, 0.581 in 1969 and 0.588 in 1970.
$$D = (1 - 0.6) N_D$$
The linear tax rate of 0.6 held for much of the economy, although trade had a tax rate of 0.7 and agriculture a tax rate of 0.45.

Step 4: Augmenting the reserve fund:

$$R = 0.1(S + D)$$

This holds up to the point where the reserve fund reaches the combined sum of 8% of W and 1.5% of A.

Of particular interest is the role of the sharing fund in this scheme. As an incentive against inflationary wage increases, the sharing fund covered any increase in an enterprise's average 'base wage' (not including bonuses) over the enterprise's 1967 base wage. As a means of stimulating collective labour productivity, three categories of profit shares taken from the sharing fund could augment the base wage. For the highest enterprise executives their actual salary (i.e. base wage plus profit share) could range from 75 to 180 per cent of the base wage; for lower level executives the range was 85–150 per cent, and for workers and others the range was 100–115 per cent.

While the 1968 wage regulation system is an impressive example of the detailed concern that Hungarians have generally shown for economic reform, several problems arose, which prompted the authorities to modify the system in 1970 and 1971.[7] First, since all increases in an enterprise's average base wage above the 1967 average base wage were charged against the sharing fund, enterprises tended to hire workers whose base wages were below the 1967 enterprise average, so that the base wages of more established employees could be increased. Such behaviour exacerbated the shortage of labour and was responsible for the low productivity growth of 1968 and 1969 (see Table 4.2). So, the parameter values utilised in the method of distributing profit were altered, and certain other modifications were adopted. However, the 'adjusted factor share' method of distributing profit between its sharing component and its development component remained intact despite the acknowledgement that this system was too rigid and complicated (Ferge and Antal, 1972, p. 60).

Another response to the excessive hiring of low wage workers was the experimentation in the food-processing and railway branches with wage bill regulation rather than wage level regulation. We shall discuss wage bill regulation later.

Secondly, a strong reaction by workers against the three categories of profit-sharing ended the sharp asymmetry between the profit-sharing possibilities of managers and of workers.

Thirdly, more general issues focused on the inability to use the price system to measure opportunity costs and on the oligopolistic nature of the production structure, which gave enterprises the opportunity to complain of unfair treatment. Thus, certain increases in average base wage were allowed to occur due to preferential considerations that were independent of profit and due to direct subsidisation. Moreover, the introduction of a wage development index (to be explained later) permitted enterprises to raise base wages independently of the level of profits in those instances when decreases in the size of staff occurred.

Thus, initial experience indicated that, even though the 1968 wage regulation system was quite complicated, it could not attain all its goals for a wide variety of reasons. Hence, the role of profit in the wage regulation system was reduced, and a thorough rethinking of wage regulation was initiated.[8]

While dissatisfaction with the wage regulation system was evident in 1971, any major revamping of the style of economic management via reform takes two to five years. So it was not until 1975 and 1976 that substantial modifications occurred. However, starting in 1971, new concepts concerning wage regulation were introduced in an experimental sample of enterprises.

The restructuring of the wage regulation system involved: the partial producer-price revisions of 1975 and 1976; the decline in the charge on assets in 1975; the increase in the wage tax in 1976; elimination of the compulsory 'adjusted factor share' method of distributing profit; temporary levelling of profits; lowering of the marginal tax rate on profit; the 1975 experimental application and the 1976 institutionalisation of four forms of wage control; lessening the dependence of wage increases on higher profits; and restricting possible deviations in profit-sharing practices of enterprises.[9]

Comparing 1974 and 1975 industry data (see Table 4.1), the partial producer-price revisions, the change in the profit taxation rules, the increase in the wage tax from 25 to 35 per cent, and the application of the 5 per cent charge on assets to their net value rather than to their gross value produced significant decreases in the average profit tax, in the portion of profit that increases the sharing fund, in the average charge for the usage of capital, in the ratio of the 'profit increment to the sharing fund' over gross wage income, and in profit's share of net income (i.e. gross revenue minus the costs of material and transport). Moreover, these changes caused increases in the 'profit increment to the development and sharing funds' as a percentage of profit and in the ratio of wage charges to gross wage income.

The shift in the relative taxes on wages and assets was implemented so as to alter the relative factor prices in a manner that would encourage efficient utilisation of labour. The partial producer-price revisions have created relative prices that better reflect opportunity costs; thus, profit differentials better reflect differences in efficiency. Despite this improvement the role of profit in stimulating collective productivity has been restricted through a highly progressive tax structure on annual profit-sharing, which generally means that firms face a lower profit-sharing bound of 6 days of wages per average employee and an upper profit-sharing bound of 36−42 days of wages per employee. Furthermore, to ensure that all firms start from a relatively equal position, profits were set at a relatively uniform low level for all enterprises through the use of differential turnover taxes.

The abolition of the 'adjusted factor share' method of distributing profit between sharing and development funds was necessary because technological changes were continually altering the relative value of assets to wages at different rates for different branches of the economy and because future demand patterns also varied among branches. Profit was henceforth to be taxed at a rate of 42 per cent (36 per cent is a direct profits tax, and 6 per cent is the municipal development contribution), which was lower than previous rates, in an attempt to stimulate profit sensitivity.

Generally, the utilisation of the after-tax profit fund has taken the following form. First, 15 per cent of the fund is put into a separate reserve account, then current investment-related credit obligations must be covered, and finally the enterprise may choose to partition the remainder between profit-sharing and further investment. Of course, the enterprise is constrained in this final decision by the taxes on the sharing fund contributions.

The exact nature of the tax structure's influence on an enterprise depends on the mode of wage regulation that the enterprise follows.[10] Regulation of the average wage of an enterprise is known as *relative wage-level regulation*. Since 1975 it has been employed in enterprises in which increasing employment is a policy goal. Under relative wage-level regulation the permissible increase in the average wage for an enterprise has depended on: (1) any 'guaranteed rise' that the centre wishes to grant (1·5 per cent during 1976–8); (2) performance of the wage development indicator, defined as 'wage plus profit' divided by average staff; and (3) a national target, known as the average wage brake (6 per cent during 1976–8), above which enterprises face high marginal tax rates. An enterprise subject to relative wage-level regulation may increase its average wage up to the guaranteed rise without paying a tax levy. An enterprise may increase, tax free, its average wage above the guaranteed rise to a degree determined by the wage development indicator, but at most to a total increase of 6 per cent (the average wage brake). Any increase in the average wage above 6 per cent is subject to a linear tax levy. Any increase of the average wage above the combined guaranteed rise plus the amount indicated by the wage development index is subject to a progressive tax levy.

Relative wage-bill regulation initially governs the permissible amount of wages and then governs the wage level. The permissible amount of wages generally depends on: (1) any 'guaranteed rise' that the centre wishes to grant (1·5 per cent during 1976–8); (2) performance of the value-added index; and (3) a national target, known as the average wage brake (6 per cent during 1976–8), above which enterprises face high marginal tax rates. Any enterprise subject to relative wage-bill regulation may increase its total amount of wages up to the guaranteed rise without paying a tax levy. An enterprise may increase, tax free, its total amount of wages above the guaranteed rise to a degree determined by the value-added indicator, but at most to a total increase of the average wage (notice that this is not in terms of the total amount of wages) of 6 per cent. Any increase in the average wage above 6 per cent is subject to a progressive tax levy. Any increase in the total amount of wages above the combined guaranteed rise plus the amount indicated by the value-added index is subject to another progressive tax levy.

Relative wage-bill regulation provides the strongest incentive for rational utilisation of labour, because any decrease in staff translates into a greater opportunity for higher wages for the remaining workers.

The essence of central regulation of the wage level or the wage bill is that the tax-free upper bound for the annual increase of wages is centrally determined in the annual plan as a percentage of the wage level or the wage bill respectively. For central wage-level regulation any increase of the wage level above the centrally determined upper bound is taxed progressively. For central wage-bill regulation any increase in the wage bill above the centrally determined upper bound, or any increase of the wage level beyond the 6 per cent average wage brake, is taxed progressively.

In practice, all four forms of wage regulation have guarded against increases in an enterprise's average wage above the average wage brake as a mode of combating inflation. The narrow difference between the guaranteed rise of 1·5 per cent and the average wage brake of 6 per cent has reflected the desire to regulate societal wage differentials. The tying of wage increases to profit increases in the relative wage-level and wage-bill forms of regulation has served as a means of stimulating collective productivity. Finally, the tax parameters, the value of the guaranteed rise and the value of the average wage brake have taken into consideration the desired national consumption versus accumulation trade-off.

4 Statistical trends

The four tables in this section contain statistical information that will be useful for the discussions in sections 5 and 6. Table 4.1 reviews trends in profit and its components for industry. Column A indicates that the average profit tax moved upwards from its 1968–70 level to its 1971–5 level, then decreased starting in 1975. Column B illustrates the downward trend in the 'sharing fund's portion of profits', yet column E indicates that the ratio of the 'sharing-fund profit increment' to gross wage income exhibited more variability. Of most interest in column E is the significant decrease in profit-sharing potential after 1975 due to the levelling of profits and to the restrictive nature of taxes on profit-sharing.

Columns D and F indicate that the relative factor costs between labour and assets altered in 1975 and in 1976. In each instance labour became relatively more expensive. Column G portrays the rather wide fluctuations in the ratio of profit to net income.

Table 4.2 presents labour productivity data for industry. The practice of hiring low-paid workers in 1968 and in 1969 is reflected in the productivity figures, whereas the post-1969 figures exhibit a much healthier growth rate. While it has been shown that no contemporaneous

Table 4.1   *Profit and its components for all of industry, 1968–78.*

Year	A	B	C	D	E	F	G
1968	0·576	0·098	0·326	0·211	0·086	0·109	0·362
1969	0·581	0·082	0·337	0·214	0·070	0·109	0·347
1970	0·588	0·065	0·347	0·214	0·059	0·109	0·363
1971	0·628	0·071	0·301	0·215	0·069	0·112	0·385
1972	0·622	0·071	0·307	0·215	0·074	0·113	0·391
1973	0·616	0·076	0·308	0·215	0·081	0·112	0·406
1974	0·616	0·070	0·314	0·214	0·082	0·115	0·444
1975	0·627	0·067	0·305	0·214	0·083	0·083	0·413
1976	0·500	0·053	0·447	0·292	0·053	0·079	0·346
1977	0·518	0·049	0·433	0·290	0·054	0·071	0·377
1978[a]	0·506	0·043	0·451	—	0·047	—	0·360

A = ratio of profit taxes to profit
B = profit increment to the sharing fund divided by profit
C = profit increment to the development and reserve funds divided by profit
D = ratio of wage charges to the wage bill
E = ratio of the profit increment to the sharing fund over gross wage income
F = ratio of capital charges over the net average value of fixed capital evaluated at current prices
G = share of profit in net income (i.e. gross revenue minus material and transport costs)

[a]1978 estimates are based on data for socialist industry (*Statisztikai Évkönyv*, 1978, pp. 191–3).

Data sources: Statisztikai Évkönyv (1970), pp. 80–1; (1971), pp. 76–7; (1972), pp. 78–9; (1973), pp. 80–1; (1974), pp. 80–1; (1975), pp. 62–3; (1976), pp. 60–1; (1977), pp. 89–9; and (1978), pp. 92–3.

macro-level relationship has existed in Hungary between the rise in real wages and the growth in productivity,[11] a detailed examination explaining both increases in base wages and fluctuations in profit-sharing is required before concrete conclusions can be made concerning the wage regulation's net effect on productivity.

Table 4.2   *Labour productivity in industry as measured by a production-per-employee index, 1961–78.*

Year	Index	Year	Index	Year	Index
1961	8·0	1967	3·8	1973	5·6
1962	4·6	1968	0·9	1974	6·2
1963	3·5	1969	0·3	1975	4·5
1964	4·3	1970	6·7	1976	5·6
1965	3·3	1971	5·3	1977	5·3
1966	4·6	1972	4·2	1978	5·3

Annual growth: 1960–7 = 4·6%; 1968–78 = 4·5%.
Data sources: Statisztikai Évkönyv (1974), p. 124 and (1978) p. 142.

Table 4.3   *Four forms of wage regulation, 1968–78.*

Regulation form	% of workers in the socialist sector, according to the form of wage regulation					
	1968	*1971*	*1973*	*1976*	*1977*	*1978*
Relative wage level	93	82	75	34	29	15
Relative wage bill	7	9	12	35	40	55
Central wage level	—	3	7	21	21	15
Central wage bill	—	6	6	10	10	15

Data Source: Lökkös (1978), p. 178.

Table 4.3 focuses on the utilisation of the four types of wage regulation.[12] The 1976–8 figures for central wage regulation indicate that central authorities feel that about 30 per cent of workers in socialist industry should receive wage increases that are independent of productivity increases. The significant utilisation of central wage control and the 1976 decrease in profit-sharing potential demonstrate the reluctance of decision-makers to use profit-related performance to stimulate greater labour productivity. Table 4.3 also documents the steadily increasing reliance on wage bill rather than wage level regulation; the efficient utilisation of labour has become a more pressing concern over time.

Table 4.4   *Percentage of task-rate employee hours in overall employee hours, 1965 and 1970–75.*

Year	A	B	C	D	E
1965	60·0	63·7	64·8	50·6	60·0
1970	56·7	61·3	68·7	50·8	57·4
1971	56·8	61·0	63·4	51·0	57·2
1972	56·7	60·1	65·8	51·7	57·1
1973	55·3	59·8	62·7	50·9	56·0
1974	57·0	59·5	63·4	51·1	57·0
1975	56·3	58·6	64·0	51·1	56·4

A = heavy industry
B = light industry
C = other industry
D = food-processing industry
E = state industry, total

Data sources: Ipari Adattár (1972), Vol. 2, p. 202 and (1978), pp. 311–12.

Table 4.4 only roughly demonstrates the decreasing importance of task-rate wage payments as a stimulus to individual labour productivity, since it contains no information concerning changes in either the composition or the parameters of the task-rate wage payment. None-theless, the decline in hours spent under the task rate system in heavy and light industry give some support to the general impression that task rate incentives are slowly becoming less important. This may be due to technological changes rather than conscious decision-making.

5   The current debate

During the last few years a debate has unfolded concerning the system of wage regulation to be implemented for the 1981–5 plan period. This debate is particularly important since Hungary is facing a situation of negligible growth in its labour force. In this section we shall review contributions to this debate by Lökkös (1978),[12] Balázsy (1978)[13] and Révész (1978). While these authors disagreed on the degree to which the system of wage regulation maintains work discipline and encourages productivity increases, each recognised the success of the wage regulation system in establishing a balance between the supply of consumer goods and consumer purchasing power and in preventing disproportionate wage differentials.

(1) János Lökkös based his views on the idea that, although wage level regulation was appropriate for the extensive stage of development, wage bill regulation is appropriate for the intensive stage of development currently in progress in Hungary.

Lökkös claimed that the wage bill form of regulation, towards which Hungary has been steadily moving (see Table 4.3), stimulates the rational utilisation of labour and rewards differentials in individual performance. For 1976 Lökkös noted that growth of labour in socialist industry, according to the form of wage regulation, demonstrated that wage level regulation did not encourage firms to save labour. In particular, firms under relative wage-level regulation experienced 0·3 per cent labour growth; those under absolute wage-level regulation 1·4 per cent; those under relative wage-bill regulation − 1·3 per cent; and those under absolute wage-bill regulation − 0·4 per cent. Lökkös concluded that a completely new system of wage regulation is not necessary; rather, wage fund regulation must be modified to stimulate efficiency more strongly.

However, Lökkös failed to point out that enterprises were given their choice of either wage level or wage bill regulation. So, enterprises that expected their labour force to increase chose wage level regulation, and those which expected a decrease chose wage bill regulation. Consequently, the results are quite biased.

(2) Sándor Balázsy was much more critical of the present forms of

wage regulation. His criticisms centre on the half-hearted utilisation of the profit motive, the complicated and prohibitively restrictive character of the tax structure, and the failure to subject all enterprises to the same set of incentives.

The presence of narrowly separated, lower and upper, profit-sharing bounds is the core of Balázsy's analysis. First, guaranteed wage increases (generally 1·5 per cent during 1976−8) are not connected to profit sensitivity. Secondly, performance indicators only have significant influence in determining wage increases as long as wage increases remain within the average wage brake (generally 6 per cent since 1976). Above the average wage brake marginal tax rates have been designed to prohibit further wage increases and thus to end any connection between enterprise performance and wages.

Balázsy also pointed out that efficiency requirements dictate that the total costs of all firms should be based on the same set of regulations. In this sense the separate regulation of various types of enterprise with respect to wage regulation has been a step backwards from one of the basic principles of the 1968 reform.

Balázsy's solution to this problem rests on the belief that wage increases must be connected to increases in the level of profit for each individual enterprise. He proposed to simplify the system of taxation, so that it will be neither prohibitive nor complicated but will combine the positive characteristics of the various wage-regulation systems.

Concretely, Balázsy's proposals consist of three parts. First, in order to smooth out the influence of cyclical fluctuations, the enterprise profit base is to be defined as the average profit earned by the enterprise during the last three years. The rule would apply to all productive enterprises and would thus eliminate the use of firm-specific base indices.

Secondly, incentives for the improvement in productivity and for the efficient utilisation of inputs would be derived from a two-stage taxation system. Let $\bar{P}$ = profit base, P = actual profit and T = total tax bill. For $P > \bar{P}$,

$$T = t_1 \bar{P} + t_2 (P - \bar{P})$$

where $t_2 < t_1$. The tax rate on the profit base, t_1, would be much higher than the tax rate on the increment to the profit base, t_2. Also, t_1 would be allowed to vary among enterprises to reflect different environmental circumstances, while t_2 would be constant for all enterprises.

The third part of Balázsy's proposal is that additional profit would be the main source of bonuses and development funds. Regulations similar to those presently in force would govern the formation of development and reserve funds, whereas a progressive tax structure on wage increases, although less progressive than the present one, would be constructed so as to ensure that income differentials would not become too wide.

(3) Gábor Révész also expressed dissatisfaction with the present stage of wage regulation, but for reasons diametrically opposed to those of Balázsy. Révész maintained that it is not possible to connect wage increases automatically to any single performance indicator, given the deficiencies in the price system, the oligopolistic nature of the production structure, and the importance that preferential considerations play in the formation of profits. He disagreed with Balázsy's proposal, since he believed that enterprise-specific bargaining would develop over t_1 and that it would not be possible to maintain a uniform t_2 for all productive enterprises.

Révész stressed the need for continued administrative regulation of wages, especially since wage costs are treated as a 'special' cost. He supported the utilisation of a centrally co-ordinated wage-level regulation system that would force firms to eliminate unnecessary jobs. This system would also feature equal wages for people doing the same job, irrespective of the profit positions of different firms (it is in this sense that wage costs are a special cost). Thus, Révész stressed the need for a wage regulation system that will provide approximately equal opportunities across enterprises to increase wages. Otherwise, Révész believed that there will arise great conflicts within the bureaucratic hierarchy.

 ## 6   Personal comments

Hungary's economic performance during the 1970s, especially its continual accumulation of foreign trade deficits, and a change in the environment, namely, diminishing prospects for high rates of borrowing convertible currencies, have caused central decision-makers to re-evaluate their ordering of the relevant set of goals and constraints. In particular, the goal of efficient utilisation of labour has been elevated in importance. Two concepts are encompassed by the term 'efficient utilisation of labour'. On the one hand, central decision-makers want to eliminate lax undisciplined work practices that essentially create hidden enterprise-level unemployment. On the other hand, central decision-makers want to motivate managers to end their practice of hoarding superfluous labour.

Why hasn't more progress been made in attaining these aims? With respect to the first aim, management must battle against formal legal regulations, formal juridical supervision, and the influence of enterprise-level labour-union and Party organisations if a worker is to be dismissed. Moreover, profit does not reflect actual productivity, partly due to the oligopolistic structure of industry and partly due to the complex price−tax−subsidy system. Thus, profit has not been used to measure a worker's productivity.

With respect to the second aim, managerial interest in profitability has been undermined by the elimination of the generous profit-sharing possibilities for management in the early 1970s (see section 3) and by the non-uniform character and almost annual adjustment of the wage regulation system. Given the lukewarm attitude towards profits, the uncertainty of the regulatory environment and the national labour shortage, managers tend to hold a reserve stock of the scarce commodity, in this case labour itself.

The idea that profit has not been relied upon heavily (due to the complexity of the price−tax−subsidy system) has been blamed for much of the disappointment with the wage regulation system. While a significant price reform is planned for 1980, I contend that, without a reform of the wage regulation system, the goal of efficient utilisation of labour will still be severely hampered.

Figure 4.3 is helpful in presenting this point of view. For any enterprise there is no centrally controlled policy instrument that stimulates individual productivity. Moreover, only profit-sharing possibilities, themselves constrained by the accepted set of societal wage differentials, contribute to the stimulation of collective labour productivity. Table 4.4 shows that task-related wages are diminishing in importance, probably because enterprises realise that they are not appropriate for many technologically sophisticated products nor for certain services and because they are unpopular among workers. Finally, no army of unemployed propagates fear-related labour productivity.

With respect to collective productivity, I doubt that by 1981−5 the Hungarian production system will become significantly less oligopolistic and that the policy of equal pay for equal work will be removed from the consciousness of society. Therefore, constraints on the ability to stimulate collective productivity, which are related to the inability to measure collective productivity at all adequately, will still exist.

My proposal concerning the reform of the wage regulation system will respect the above-mentioned constraints yet will focus on stimulating responsibility. It consists of eight points and is based upon the assumption that the Hungarian price reforms proposed for 1980−1 will succeed in creating reasonably satisfactory measures of scarcity.

First, the key to the end of enterprise-specific bargaining is that the performance of enterprises should not be allowed to influence to a high degree the wage-earnings of non-managerial employees (not more than 5 per cent). Thus, the principle of equal pay for equal work would be respected, and firms would have less reason to demand preferential treatment. However, non-regular benefits (e.g. bonuses), as Révész

(1978) suggested, could be dependent on profit in a manner similar to present practice.

Secondly, the key to stimulating worker interest is to retrain those groups of workers who are not 'technologically able to work efficiently'. This part of the proposal necessitates the establishment within enterprises of factory-specific and/or product-line-specific profit centres. Each profit centre would be connected to a specific collective of workers within the firm. Managers would have the right to increase or decrease the size of these collectives according to profitability conditions. Workers being dismissed under this scheme would not incur any stigma of individual inefficiency, because such action would have been motivated by changing prices or by the degree of industriousness of the other members of the collective.

The 'profit centre' notion is used throughout the world to maintain accountability for the actions of a technologically distinct group within an enterprise. For instance, the different automotive divisions of General Motors are rather large-scale profit centres. This proposal suggests the creation of small-scale profit centres within which it would be possible to stimulate a collective incentive to work. An alternative to small-scale profit centres would be small firms, but the inevitable bureaucratic opposition to such a structural transformation indicates that this alternative is not feasible. Another alternative would be Yugoslavian-type worker-managed enterprises, but political considerations eliminate this option.

This leads us to the third point. The power of enterprise-level labour-union and Party organisations would have to be greatly reduced in order for managers to be able to decrease the size of an enterprise's labour force. Managers should not be faced with inordinate bureaucratic opposition.

Fourthly, employees dismissed from their current posts would have the option either of attending a centrally controlled retraining school or of finding an alternative job in six weeks. The existence of centrally controlled retraining schools would give decision-makers on the highest level of the hierarchy greater control over the distribution of labour while respecting income distribution constraints. Anyone attending the retraining schools would receive wages equal to 75 per cent of the national wage.

Fifthly, the salaries of managers would vary from 80 to 120 per cent of their base salary depending upon the profit-related performance of their particular profit centres. Ministries would still possess the authority to dismiss top level management, while top level management would be able to dismiss lower level management.

Sixthly, the market would replace the restrictions embodied in the national skill−exertion matrices. Presently, these restrictions are rather ineffective, since managers tend to shift 'sought-after' employees from lower-paying categories to higher-paying categories (subject to wage level or wage bill regulation). In fact, the presence of national skill–exertion matrices may work against the goal of equal pay for equal work, since they create a false impression of fairness and obstruct the dissemination of actual wage information. An individual's wage can very well depend on his knowledge of job alternatives (distorted by the lack of actual wage information) and/or the willingness of his boss to bend the spirit of national skill–exertion matrices. Furthermore, the presence of retraining schools would give individuals an opportunity to react to market-induced wage changes, thus lessening the tension that these wage shifts might otherwise entail.

Seventhly, the negative effects of the second economy would be reduced by increasing the sensitivity of enterprises to profits (see Figure 4.2). However, other measures should also be implemented. Regulations for the second economy that essentially force individuals to conceal the extent of their legal second-economy activity should be abandoned, and a progressive enforceable tax system should be developed.[14] Inventory control should be tightened in order to discourage the illegal use of state-owned capital and materials. Finally, co-operation between the large firms of the first economy and the legal entrepreneurs of the second economy should be encouraged.

Often the rationalisation behind wage level or wage bill regulation has focused on the goal of controlling inflation. However, inflation could be controlled via the determination of relative factor costs and 'uniform' profit-taxation rules.[15] In fact, the major reason for the existence of wage level or wage bill regulation is that the centre wishes to influence the enterprises' use of profit. The last point of my proposal deals with the issue of utilising profit and eliminates the need for the complications introduced by wage level and wage bill regulation.

Why is the use of profit by enterprises a problem? Since an enterprise in Hungary is not allowed to start or purchase another enterprise, profit available to an enterprise must be either reinvested in enterprise expansion or used to supplement wages. The centre does not wish that enterprises control their expansion, since such expansion might not reflect future demand and supply considerations. Profit reflects past success, which may not correspond to future possibilities. Likewise, the centre does not wish an enterprise to have the option of supplementing wages to a high degree, because this might create social tension.

On the other hand, unless an enterprise can retain a sizeable portion of profit as a source for bonus income, welfare benefits and some degree of expansion, the goal of enterprise profit maximisation will never be reached.

Up to now the profit-sharing opportunities of employees have not been too great. Column E of Table 4.1 indicates that the profit-sharing of those employed in industry has been approximately 5 per cent of gross wage income from 1976 onwards. So, I doubt whether the maintenance of this low level of profit-sharing (as suggested in the first point of this proposal) would produce social upheaval. Similarly, I doubt whether the degree of profit-sharing for managers suggested in the fifth point would cause great unrest. Yet, the question remains: what should be done with any 'excess profit', given that the wages of workers are determined in the market place, the wages of managers are determined and constrained by the centre, and significant expansion of an enterprise is the responsibility of the centre? As the eighth and final point of my proposal, therefore, excess profit should be designated as the primary indicator according to which managers of a profit centre are evaluated for promotion, where excess profit is defined as after-tax profit minus profit-sharing bonuses paid to workers and managers. By definition, the pressure for wage increases and for the distribution of bonuses will exist as long as there is excess demand for labour. Utilisation of excess profit as a promotion indicator would provide an incentive for managers to employ labour rationally in the face of this pressure. In such a situation the complications of wage level and wage bill regulation can be replaced by careful determination of relative factor costs and 'uniform' profit-taxation rules.

We lack the space in this chapter to investigate this proposal any further, but it is worth mentioning several issues that have not been explored. Is it realistic to suggest that local Communist Party and labour-union organisations should reduce their power to resist reductions of staff? How are the centrally controlled retraining schools going to be established, given the present powers of branch ministries? Would the method of distributing investment funds influence this proposal? Would some form of ratchet effect exist, even though no explicit plan targets are calculated?

On the positive side, this proposal avoids macro-level unemployment and 'unacceptable' differentials among enterprises with respect to profit-sharing. It also takes into consideration the negative aspects of the second economy concerning wage regulation, suggests an alternative to the complicated wage-level and wage-bill form of regulation, and attempts to pin down the accountability of both managers and employees. Moreover, this proposal deviates from past practice by striving to stimulate labour productivity through the group pressure of those who do not want to be 'forcibly' transferred to new jobs. Thus, this proposal utilises the 'mow your lawn because this is a well-kept neighbourhood' view of life. Collective pressure to work efficiently may be as effective as community pressure to maintain a properly groomed lawn.

Acknowledgement and Notes: Chapter 4

I wish to thank István R. Gábor, Géza Kozma, Gábor Révész and the participants of the April 1979 colloquium on the Hungarian economy held at the University of Stirling for pointing out weaknesses in an earlier version of this chapter.

1   A multicoloured market mechanism encompasses legal, semi-legal and illegal markets. This concept follows the spirit of red, pink, white, grey, brown and black markets described by Katsenelinboigen and Levine (1977).

2   Members of the private sector claim that they have no choice, since complete compliance with these business laws would drive them out of business. For example, a private skilled construction contractor is only 'allowed' to hire additional labour at wages that approximate socialist sector wages. In reality, the contractor can find such labour at a minimum of 2½ to 3 times the legal rate yet cannot report the additional wage payments as costs. Hence, the contractor 'is forced' by the wage regulation to conceal a certain amount of his revenue to counteract the unreported wage costs.

3   Collective productivity refers to the productivity of a collective (e.g. an enterprise, factory or profit centre). Each individual in the collective shares the fruit of his own effort with everyone else in the collective.

4   Information for the 1950–6 period partly follows Meitner (1959, pp. 20–3).

5   Information for the 1957–67 period partly follows Székffy (1979).

6   Information for the 1968–70 period partly follows Sulyok (1969) and *A Népgazdaság Irányítási Rendszere* (1970, pp. 74–106).

7   This section is partly based on Ferge and Antal (1972) and Lökkös (1978).

8   This occurred even though the major problem may well have been that enterprises were still not interested in profits.

9   Changes that occurred in 1975 and 1976 follow Gadó (1976, pp. 39–67).

10 The discussion concerning the four forms of wage regulation reflects Gadó (1976, pp. 54–67).

11 Székffy (1979, p. 874).

12 Lökkös (1978, p. 178).

13 Comments concerning Balázsy's proposal follow from an interview with Sándor Balázsy as well as from the cited article.

14 A separate research effort on the second economy should be undertaken to design such a progressive enforceable tax system.

15 The levelling of potential profit due to oligopolistic power should be carried out through economic-specific lump-sum taxation; otherwise, the tax system should be uniform.

References: Chapter 4

Ipari Adattár (Budapest: Központi Statisztikai Hivatal, various issues).

Statisztikai Évkönyv (Budapest: Központi Statisztikai Hivatal, various issues).

Balázsy, S. (1978), 'A keresteszabályozás "megoldhatatlan" dilemmaja' (The 'unsolvable' dilemma of regulating earnings), *Közgazdasági Szemle*, vol. 25 (2), pp. 154–73.

Ferge, S. and Antal, L. (1972), 'Enterprise income regulation', in Gadó, O. (ed.), *Reform of the Economic Mechanism in Hungary: Development 1968–1971* (Budapest: Akadémiai Kiadó).

Friss, I. (ed.) (1969), *Reform of the Economic Mechanism in Hungary* (Budapest: Akadémiai Kiadó).

Gábor, I. R. (1979), 'A második gazdaság' (The second economy), *Valóság*, vol. 22 (1), pp. 22–36.

Gadó, O. (1976), *The Economic Mechanism in Hungary: How It Works in 1976* (Budapest: Akadémiai Kiadó).

Katsenelinboigen, A. and Levine, H. S. (1977), 'The Soviet case', *American Economic Review: Papers and Proceedings*, vol. 67 (1), pp. 61–6.

Lökkös, J. (1978), 'A keresetszabályozás néhány problémája és a továbbfejlesztés lehetőségei' (Some problems of regulating earnings and the possibilities for further improvement), *Közgazdasági Szemle*, vol. 25 (2), pp. 174–87.

Meitner, T. (1959), *Bérformák és Kereseti Arányok* (Wage Forms and Income Proportions) (Budapest: Tancsics Könyvkiadó Vállalat).

A Népgazdaság Irányítási Rendszere (1970) (The Regulating System for the National Economy) (Budapest: Közgazdasági és Jogi Könyvkiadó).

Révész, G. (1978), 'Keresetszabályozásunkról' (On the regulation of earnings), *Közgazdasági Szemle*, vol. 25 (7–8), pp. 917–34.

Sulyok, B. (1969), 'Major financial regulators in the new system of economic control and management', in Friss (1969).

Székffy, K. (1979), 'A bérek és a termelékenység kapcsolata az iparban, 1950–1974 között' (The relationship between wages and productivity in industry between 1950 and 1974), *Közgazdasági Szemle*, vol. 25 (7–8), pp. 831–47.

Part Three

Investment

Chapter 5

The Investment System in Hungary

1 Introduction

In all economies governments seek to exercise some control over the investment process, either by means of their influence over particular sectors of the economy (e.g. the nationalised industries in the UK) or by means of detailed regulation of most aspects of the process, as in the USSR and other centrally-planned economies. Hungary lies somewhere between these extremes, with some degree of central intervention in all sectors, although, as we shall see, it is closer to the USSR's end of the spectrum as far as investment is concerned. Whatever the institutional set-up, it is quite illuminating to think of the investment process in any given country (Hungary in the present chapter) in terms of three stages of determination, which are as follows:

(1) volume of investment;
(2) sectoral allocation; and
(3) project selection.

Now, in theory one could 'simply' establish a suitable investment criterion and accept in a particular planning period all those projects which, on the basis of information available at the time, appeared to satisfy that criterion. Thus, by starting with stage (3) and systematically examining all project proposals, one would simultaneously find solutions to stages (1) and (2) by aggregating over the accepted projects. Unfortunately, such a procedure could never function satisfactorily, either from the purely economic point of view or from the viewpoint of society's various interest groups, for available criteria, as we shall note later, are typically far too crude to bear all the burden of investment decision-making; at best they can be helpful in rejecting some particularly poor projects. Consequently, some additional guidance is needed to determine the allocation of investible resources. This is why stages (1) and (2) are important elements of the investment process, since they establish the framework of constraints within which project criteria may sensibly be employed. Although decisions on all three stages are subject to significant political intervention in Hungary, economic analysis retains an important role too, as is shown in the fuller discussion in section 2 below.

This conceptual formulation of investment stages does not correspond directly to the organisational and financial categories that have become conventional in discussions of Hungarian investment since the introduction of the 1968 reforms.[1] However, there is a closer connection than is apparent at first sight. Investment in Hungary is classified as either enterprise investment or state investment, the latter being further subdivided into three types: individual large projects, so-called aim-grouped investments and other state investments. The basic distinction between enterprise and state investment refers to the decision authority for the projects in each category. Thus, enterprise investment includes all projects for which the decision to invest is within the competence of some enterprise (or co-operative). Table 5.1 shows the breakdown of socialist sector investment into these categories in a few recent years.

Table 5.1   *Structure of socialist sector, investment by decision authority, 1971−5 and 1977 (%).*

Decision authority	All investment		Investment in industry	
	1971−5	1977	1971−5	1977
Enterprise investment	56·1	56·1	66·8	65·3
State investment:				
Individual large projects	14·2	14·0	30·8	28·6
Aim-grouped	19·7	20·9	1·6	5·9
Other state	10·0	9·0	0·7	0·2
Total state	43·9	43·9	33·1	34·7
Total (all sources)	100·0	100·0	100·0	100·0

Sources: *Magyar Statisztikai Zsebkönyv* (1978); *Beruházási-Epitö Ipari Adatok* (1977), p. 20.

Aim-grouped investments refer to areas of state investment in which the planners fix an overall financial target but leave individual projects within each 'aim' to be decided by lower levels. For example, the building of rural clinics and minor road developments both come into this category of investment, which is mainly concerned with infrastructure. The other categories of state investment are fairly self-explanatory.

Although Hungary possesses no capital markets for effecting transfers of investible funds between different sectors and institutions in the economy, the finance of investment is still fairly complicated. In particular, there is no attempt to restrict state finance to the support of state investments or enterprise finance to enterprise investment. Instead, all sources of finance can be used for either type of investment, although in different proportions, as shown in Table 5.2. Development funds

Table 5.2   *Financial sources for investment in industry by type of
finance provided, 1976 (%).*

Type of finance	State investment	Enterprise investment	Total investment in industry
Development funds only	2	10	12
Development funds and credit	4	11	15
Development funds, subsidy and credit	26	34	60
Development funds and subsidy	7	6	13
Total (all finance)	39	61	100

Source: Deák (1978), p. 29.

represent the resources provided by enterprises themselves. They
originate from the retained part of depreciation provisions and from
part of after-tax profits. (The remainder of after-tax profits forms a
small reserve fund and the sharing fund, the latter being the source of
finance for bonuses and wage increases.) Notice that virtually all
projects, whether initiated by enterprise or state authority, involve the
use of development funds. Also, it is clear that only a small proportion
of enterprise projects are funded solely by enterprise resources, thereby
escaping control by the planners and central agencies. But about 85 per
cent of enterprise investment involves some state funds, implying that,
at least in principle, centrally established criteria can be imposed. The
reality is more complex than that, as shown below.

In any discussion of the investment process in Hungary, it is
important to emphasise the distinction between investment outlays and
investment completions in any year; the distribution gives rise to the
associated indicator, namely, the stock of uncompleted investment.
Variations in these indicators from year to year show how balances or
imbalances in investment markets are developing and play an important role in determining the planners' responses, as elaborated more
fully in section 3. In the same context various inputs into investment
activity will need to be examined, especially the state of the domestic
construction and construction materials industries and the connection
between balance-of-payments problems and imports of machinery.

After considering these issues in section 3, we proceed in section 4 to
discuss the efficiency of the investment process in Hungary, both in
relation to generally stated goals and in relation to official investment
criteria and commonly used performance indicators. The final section
of the chapter attempts to extract a few general conclusions from the
preceding analysis. Any data presented in the chapter will refer either

to the socialist sector as a whole or to socialist industry; almost nothing will be said on the admittedly important and often neglected areas of services, agriculture, infrastructure, and so on.

2   The planning process

Although Hungarian enterprises no longer receive instructions telling them what to produce or what inputs they may use, planning activity within the central agencies (ministries, central planning board, price and material office, and so on) goes on very much as it did before 1968. As always a new five-year plan is based on an assessment of the preceding period's economic outcome and eventuates in a number of summary indicators, which are widely published and concern expected growth rates of production, trade flows, consumption, investment, and real wages among other things. Each year's annual plan then seeks to move in the direction of fulfilling the five-year plan, while taking account of any unexpectedly favourable or unfavourable changes in the economic situation. Typically, there is some attempt to assess the five-year plan itself towards the end of its third year, possibly introducing some modification at that time, as happened at the end of 1978 for the fifth five-year plan (1976–80).

An annual plan then comprises the following elements:

(1)   a list of general economic indicators to be achieved during the year;
(2)   specific targets relating to initiation and progress of state investment projects; and
(3)   economic regulators.

Categories (1) and (2) are self-explanatory and will be referred to again below, where appropriate. Category (3) consists of price, tax and subsidy policy, credit policy, wage guidelines and foreign trade controls. These are all intended to ensure that enterprise behaviour should be compatible with the plan objectives, in the sense of generating an allocation of resources acceptable to the central planners. In the sphere of investment, however, it appears that this regulation has been distinctly less than perfect, as Table 5.3 makes clear.

In formulating both annual and five-year plans the volume of investment is determined in order to ensure the satisfaction of a number of objectives and constraints. To put it simply, the plans should aim for the highest growth rates compatible with acceptable growth of consumption, full employment and a reasonable degree of equilibrium in trading activity, investment being seen as the main engine of growth. All this is not to suggest that outcomes are always as satisfactory as the

Table 5.3   *Investment in the socialist sector, 1971−80 (billion forints).*

Period	Enterprise investment		State investment		Total investment	
	Planned	*Actual*	*Planned*	*Actual*	*Planned*	*Actual*
1971−5	245−60	331·3	225−40	259·5	270−500	590·8
1976	72[a]	82·6	73[a]	69·5	145	152·1
1977	79	101·9	95	79·6	162−4	181·5
1978	94	112	96	84	180−2	196·0
1976−80	420−40	n.a.	420−40	n.a.	860−80[b]	n.a.
					940−60[c]	n.a.

[a] Indirect calculation.
[b] Fifth five-year plan target announced in 1975.
[c] Revised target for the fifth five-year plan announced in June 1978.

Sources: Beruházási-Epitöipari Adatok (1977); *Figyelö* (various issues); *Statisztikai Havi Közlémenyek* (1) (1979), p. 40; Tar (1976); Stark (1973), pp. 232 and 257; and Gadó (1972), p. 116.

initial plans, since circumstances are continually changing. Some of the constraints and trade-offs involved in this key decision about the volume of investment have been studied by Dániel *et al.* (1971) in their model of plan-sounding. This is a growth model constructed at a very high level of aggregation in order to facilitate the examination of general features of alternative growth paths. It is based on data for 1968 and projects the economy forwards to 1985. Over the period it has turned out that variations in the overall accumulation ratio would have made almost no difference to the expected growth rate of consumption, although over a longer period there would be some effect. Much more important than the volume of investment have been its structure and efficiency; these latter factors can have substantial effects on economic performance even over a fairly short period. Thus, changes in the investment ratio alone cannot be expected to achieve significant benefits − a conclusion evidently accepted by the Hungarian authorities, since in recent years they have planned no, or at most extremely small, changes in the ratio.

Over the 1970s, however, the ratio of net accumulation to net material product actually rose somewhat, from 23·5 per cent in 1970 to 27 per cent in 1977. This ratio includes both net fixed-capital formation and investment in stocks, the latter exhibiting considerable fluctuation. Later on, when discussing investment fluctuations, it seems most appropriate to use data referring to gross fixed-capital formation as the basis for the analysis, since it is the instability of fixed investment that has most concerned the planners.

In contrast to the stability of the overall investment ratio, there have been some attempts to plan changes in the branch structure of output and investment, although in practice the existing structure possesses considerable inertia, particularly within industry (see Table 5.4). A mixture of traditional and mathematical techniques has been employed in planning the output and investment structures, with the emphasis still probably on the former despite a vast outpouring of mathematical models and studies. The standard Hungarian procedure, reflected also in most of the models, has been to construct a set of economic balances (material balances, synthetic balances, and so on) corresponding to the final year of a five-year plan period, based on projected growth rates for the main economic aggregates and estimates of the pattern of demand. As far as possible, the balances should generate full employment and balance-of-payments equilibrium; if not, the initially assumed growth rates need modification, rather along the lines once proposed by Kalecki (in Kalecki *et al.*, 1963).

Table 5.4 *Planned and actual growth rates within industry, 1966−75 (%).*[a]

Branch	1966−70 Actual	Planned 1971−5	Actual
Engineering	7·7	5·9	9·0
Construction materials	6·3	9·2	5·8
Chemicals	11·6	8·9	12·8
Light industry	4·4	6·0	6·3
Food industry	4·7	4·1	5·0
Socialist industry total	6·3	5·7	7·4

[a] All figures refer to annual rates of growth of real output.

Sources: Stark (1973), p. 258; *Statistical Yearbook* (English edition) (1973), p. 134; *Statisztikai Évkönyv* (1976), pp. 120−1.

Given a set of balances for the final year, the planners can work out what new capacity has to be created over the plan period. (Apart from examination of this and its immediate implications, the intermediate years of the plan period receive remarkably little detailed attention.) Of course, the long gestation periods of investment in Hungary, which are referred to again in sections 3 and 4, mean that much of the required capacity should already be under construction by the end of the preceding five-year plan period. Thus, in the new plan ongoing projects will be completed, new projects will be introduced to meet the five-year plan targets, and further projects will be initiated in anticipation of requirements beyond the coming five-year plan period. All this investment has to be compatible with the economy's resources, not as they will be at the end of the five years, but year by year. In addition, much investment requires imported machinery, and this too must be consistent with available resources, in this case of foreign exchange, particularly dollars.[2] With the noted asymmetry between the treatment of the final and intermediate years of the planned five-year period, it is not surprising that inconsistencies do arise in the course of plan implementation and that the structure of investment is more resistant to change than the planners suppose.

Where models are employed to guide choices about economic structure by exhibiting the implications of alternatives, they have been built on an input–output framework. Hungary has developed input–output tables at varying levels of aggregation: 17–20 sector tables for most years since the late 1950s, and tables with up to 200 product groups every three or four years since the early 1960s. The available models reflect these differences. The more aggregated tables are incorporated into models that have been used to examine broad structural alternatives at the early stages of five-year plan formulation, while the more detailed tables have given rise to models that determine a fuller allocation of investment resources.[3] In most cases these models have taken a plan based on traditional methods of formulation as an initial constraint, seeking merely to improve on it or to estimate the consequences of relatively small variations in that plan. As a result the models have been assigned a fairly limited role in the process of plan formulation and investment allocation. Although the literature on optimising models contains suggestions that models could assume a much more important role, this has nowhere proved possible, partly because political systems (including that in Hungary) typically fail to generate well-defined objective functions, and partly for reasons to do with mathematical properties of the large-scale models currently amenable to solution.[4]

However, whatever their limitations the models and traditional methods in conjunction do give rise to a proposed allocation of investment resources, specifying:

(1) total amount to be spent over the five-year plan, broken down by branch (or in some cases, by product group within a branch), year and type of resource (construction, domestically produced machinery, imported machinery, other);
(2) resources to be devoted to the individual large investments, broken down by project, year and type of resource and including both ongoing and new projects; and
(3) capacities to be created over the five-year plan period.

With this framework established the next questions concern the choice of individual projects and of the procedures to be adopted to ensure that the national plan will be implemented, while attempting to secure the selection of an efficient set of projects. To a large extent choosing the individual large investments precedes this stage of analysis, since these projects completely transform and dominate the branches in which they occur. They should therefore be seen as strategic in character and often reflect prevailing views on major realignments of economic structure. For example, recent projects have been developing domestic energy production on the one hand and promoting expansion in areas thought to have a strong Western market on the other hand. Naturally, one would like such projects also to satisfy efficiency criteria, and it is required that the so-called D-index, discussed more fully in section 4, be computed for them. Frequently, however, this requirement seems not to be taken very seriously.

The more usual situation is that the plan establishes a level of investment in some area, for shares of which numerous projects compete. What tools are available to the planners to regulate the allocation? If some enterprise has a project that requires no external finance and involves no special import demands, the planners have no control at all. As we have seen earlier, however, this category represents only a small proportion of total investment. But for the remainder there are the following possibilities:

(1)   The enterprise requires credit. When the reforms were introduced in 1968, it was envisaged that credits would be allocated competitively on the basis of the rates of return offered by the submitted project proposals. Very soon, however, much of the available credit came to be pre-allocated to branches of production favoured in the plan. As a result the banks first check that the proposed project falls within one of the preferred categories of investment set out in the plan. If it does, the project can go ahead if the appropriate branch ministry approves, the particular credit category is not exhausted and the project itself promises a satisfactory payback period.

(2)   The enterprise requires special imports for the project. Again, the foreign trade ministry consults the appropriate branch ministry.

(3)   The enterprise seeks an investment subsidy. This is often given directly, but at least officially is now increasingly granted in the form of a so-called 'price favour', which increases the enterprise's creditworthiness. In such a case the National Materials and Price Office has to give approval, in consultation with the Ministry of Finance and the appropriate branch ministry. The enterprise then receives the subsidy as a price supplement for some or all of its products (although customers, of course, continue to pay the normal price), which generates more enterprise funds and raises the apparent profitability. More recently, the 'price favour' does not come into effect until the project itself begins to produce some output.

(4)   The project promises an expansion of exports to the West. Under the fifth five-year plan (1976–80) 45 billion forints have been set

aside as a special allocation of credit, to be distributed by the banks and not pre-allocated to branch ministries, for projects whose aim is to increase exports to the West. The usual payback period criteria still have to be satisfied; indeed, competition for these credits has been so strong that the banks have been able to insist on repayment of the credit within three to four years in most cases. It is probably too early to judge how effective this form of credit has been, although the very disappointing trade performance by Hungary in 1978 is not a good sign.

Apart from establishing various targets and constraints, the planners also regulate investment via their control over enterprise incomes. This is achieved by means of a combination of price and tax policy. Until the end of 1979, the tax system abstracted from enterprises a 35 per cent wage tax (reduced to 17 per cent in 1980) and a 5 per cent capital charge (eliminated in 1980). The remaining net income is subject to general profits tax at a rate of 36 per cent, plus various local taxes, leaving a residual to form the three enterprise funds: sharing fund, development fund and reserve fund. Thus, the size of these funds can be controlled either by varying tax rates appropriately or by adjusting producer prices to modify their net income content. Both methods have been used, but experience suggests that comprehensive price revisions are unreliable regulators of enterprise income. (This is not their only role, of course.) For instance, in the 1968 price reform and the revisions of 1975, 1976 and 1977, enterprise income was persistently underestimated, presumably because such adjustments provide enterprises with an opportunity to overstate their costs. This situation allowed enterprises to initiate a greater number of investment projects than the plan had anticipated.

It appears from the above that apart from (4) all other types of support for enterprise investment require consultation with, and approval of, the responsible branch ministries. In a similar way, although there are also several sources of finance for state investment, the appropriate ministerial consultations may be expected to ensure that the planned pattern of development is actually achieved, particularly as a considerable volume of enterprise development funds is assigned to state projects. Yet there is no doubt that investment plans are not realised in general; more specifically, the Hungarian economy seems to possess a built-in tendency towards the periodic creation of excessive demand for investment in relation to available resources. The task of the next section is to consider possible mechanisms to explain this phenomena, which go beyond the frequent references in the Hungarian literature to 'lack of financial discipline', 'too many investment starts', 'extended gestation periods', and so on.[5] These are merely symptoms and by themselves explain very little.

Table 5.5   *Fluctuations in socialist sector investment in Hungary, 1965–77 (%).*[a]

Year	Gross fixed investment	Year	Gross fixed investment
1965	100·4	1972	98·3
1966	110·2	1973	103·6
1967	121·8	1974	109·5
1968	84·6	1975	114·4
1969	131·7	1976	99·7
1970	116·5	1977	114·4
1971	109·7		

[a] The figure for each year represents investment in that year as a percentage of investment in the previous year.

Sources: Magyar Statisztikai Zsebkönyv (1978), p. 64; and *Statistical Yearbook*, English edition (1973), p. 870.

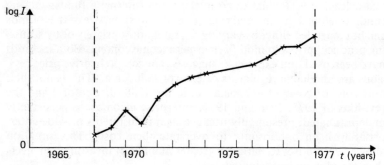

Note: Investment, I, is calculated as a quantity index, with $I(1964) = 100$.

Figure 5.1   *Investment fluctuations in Hungary, 1965–77.*

Sources: As Table 5.5.

3   Investment cycles

Table 5.5 and the accompanying graph (Figure 5.1) show the cyclical character of investment in Hungary by plotting the logarithm of investment against time. On such a graph steadily growing investment would be represented as a rising straight line. Evidently, growth has been far from steady. Yet, for many years, while it was taken as axiomatic that capitalist economies were subject to alternating periods of boom and slump, it was denied that socialist economies could experience similar phenomena. Starting with some work on Yugoslavia by Horvat (1970), this view became increasingly hard to sustain, until now it is widely accepted that the cycles occur, and the debate has moved on to consider their causes and consequences. In the Hungarian case the most interesting work has been carried out by Bauer (1975), Soós (1975), Portes (1978), Gács and Lackó (1973) and Marrese (1978a, b). There is no space to discuss all these approaches fully, but in this section I shall attempt to indicate their salient features, with particular emphasis on implications for the investment process in Hungary.

Bauer, Soós and Marrese studied the investment process and the resulting cycles directly, whereas Portes, and Gács and Lackó were more concerned to understand planners' behaviour as a rational response to perceived constraints and various characteristics of the economy. It turns out that such an approach, although not directly concerned with investment, is nevertheless very helpful in illuminating some aspects of that activity. It is certainly more useful than alternative approaches that regard the planners merely as exogenous agents seeking to impose their will on a recalcitrant economy.

In the previous two sections I have explained how the central agencies prepare investment plans and set economic regulators to control the investment process. It is now necessary to show how the economy generates periodic excessive investment, despite all the controls, and how the planners respond. There are a number of possible causes of overinvestment, which it is convenient to list with brief comments. These are:

(1) Overoptimistic plans, which result in the initially formulated plan's being too ambitious given available resources. This can happen if either productivity gains or construction capacity is overestimated.

(2) Costless investment for enterprises. Despite capital charges and appeals for financial discipline, it is clear that enterprises in difficulty will be subsidised and protected from world market forces. Requests to use world prices in investment evaluation are fruitless when it is politically impossible to permit a major enterprise to fail (and most enterprises in Hungary are major). Moreover, since 1976 personal incomes, including those of the managers, are only weakly related to enterprise performance.

(3) Lack of alternative outlets for enterprise development funds, combined with fears that the use of these funds may be restricted in the future (as happened in 1978). This induces the mental attitude 'Invest now and worry (and pay) later'.

(4) Persistent underestimation of enterprise financial resources (because the incentive system induces systematic overestimation of costs by the central agencies), combined with an insistence by the state in carrying out its planned part of investment.

(5) Underestimation of investment costs, particularly for individual

large investments but also for the other categories of state investment and for enterprise investment requiring state supports. This
particular problem is most plausible in the context of an economy
that is partially decentralised and contains a plethora of imper-
fectly co-ordinated and at times mutually antagonistic central
agencies. According to Marrese (1978a, b), this would be a fair
characterisation of Hungary.

If all these factors operate simultaneously, then, whatever intentions
the planners have, it is fairly sure that the demand for investment will
substantially exceed the plans. The only constraints on demand result
not from price and cost signals, which, I have already suggested,
function least effectively in the investment sphere, but from physical
capacity constraints and direct intervention by the planners. The
former gives rise to all the familiar features of overinvestment: exended
gestation periods as available construction capacity is spread over too
many projects, shortages of construction materials, balance-of-
payments deficits (due to diversion of some goods to the domestic
market and to large imports of machinery), labour shortages, and so
on.

One may wonder why the planners do not intervene to prevent the
emergence of these symptoms of strain. But how could they? As Bauer
(1975) pointed out, it is not until the symptoms are clear to everyone
that the planners can recognise the existence of a problem, for at any
earlier stage any small deviations from the planned path of development can be attributed to many possible causes and will be hard to
blame on the investment process. Moreover, as in all economies, information about production is usually produced with a lag of a few
months, and this too means that, by the time overinvestment has
revealed itself in the official statistics, the cumulative process is already
far advanced. Summarising, then, the planners cannot respond to
overinvestment until they recognise its existence, and the latter is
delayed at least until the relevant statistics become available. Otherwise, the planners would be reduced to making wild guesses about the
state of the economy and probably introducing completely inappropriate policy changes.

Subject to overall resource constraints, when deviations from plan
become too great, the planners can impose adjustments, either by
various forms of quantitative restrictions or by tightening the financial
constraints operating on some group of economic agents (e.g. enterprises). The systematic coherent response of the planners to disequilibria has been emphasised by Portes and Winter (1977) in their study of
consumer goods supply and by Portes (1978) in his more general
examination of equilibrium and disequilibrium in planned economies.
Although the latter paper treats both investment and consumer goods

markets, it omits any examination of foreign trade. This defect has been rectified by an earlier, although less systematic, study by Gács and Lackó (1973), which found, for example, that investment plans are inversely correlated with the state of the balance of payments, with a suitable lag. Such a result is exactly what would be expected in the light of our earlier remarks. Another paper by Gács (1976a) covers much of the same ground but adds a more detailed treatment of the relations between demand for investment and developments in the building materials industry. Again, the adaptive character of planners' responses to disequilibria is quite evident.

When clearly faced with a situation of severe overinvestment, it is very unusual for Hungarian planners to abandon projects altogether. This is quite surprising, since it is quite a common phenomenon in Western countries and can sometimes be the only rational response to an unexpected change in market conditions. The usual procedure in Hungary involves a temporary freeze on new project starts, allowing the backlog of uncompleted projects to be worked off to some extent and thereby reducing tensions in markets for investment goods to acceptable levels. Marrese's (1978a, b) concept of cyclical centralism sees this response as the only one politically acceptable in a context where several central agencies (ministries) are each engaged in a struggle for resources with a relatively weak central planning office and council of ministers. Thus, any degree of rationing short of a complete freeze would be seen as 'unfair' or 'unjustified' by one or other ministry. The fact that it is almost certainly a highly inefficient response to disequilibrium is quite beside the point, for it is politically feasible and does achieve its immediate objective.

Table 5.6 *Hungarian economic structure.*

Level I	Central Committee, Council of Ministers	} Centralised sphere
Level II	Branch and functional ministries, economywide agencies	
Level III	Managers of producing organisations, trade union-leaders and members of local councils	} Decentralised sphere
Level IV	Individual workers and consumers	

Source: Marrese (1978a), pp. 8 and 11.

This is not the place for a full discussion of 'cyclical centralism', but a few remarks are in order. First, Marrese (1978a) viewed the economy in terms of four hierarchic levels, as indicated in Table 5.6. Secondly, agencies within the centralised sphere set the constraints and parameters that regulate the decentralised sphere, but this happens in a framework of unclear or imperfect information and priorities and by means of a complex bargaining process. While not unreasonable as a description of what happens, this approach runs into difficulties when it postulates cyclical variations in the relative power positions within the directing group as part of the explanation for investment cycles. It is surely wrong to claim that power is greater in periods when it is exercised most visibly, as in times of strain, when investment priorities do obviously influence the allocation of resources, for at other times the more powerful agencies receive the resources that they need without a struggle. Moreover, Marrese's approach leaves unanswered many questions about the origins and significance of the postulated power relations in the Hungarian economy.

It is worth adding here a few remarks on Marrese's econometric findings relating to investment behaviour, as summarised in Marrese (1978b). His major conclusions indicate that: 'Level I decision-makers respond to indicators of well-being, targets, bottlenecks and foreign trade constraints, while Level II decision-makers argue in terms of branch priority, relative supply of the branch labour input, and success in maintaining branch GNP growth.' In addition, it turned out that annual planning does indeed have some impact on actual investment behaviour.

What is most striking about the econometric specifications, however, is that price and income variables play no role in them. This is rather surprising given the planners' belief that they can regulate enterprise investment to some extent by adjusting enterprise incomes, through either price or tax manipulations. Since Marrese's equations have substantial explanatory power, one has to conclude that the planners may be wrong to expect such manipulations to be effective. His formulations treat investment (both its total volume and its branch structure) as the result of interactions between (1) central objectives and priorities and (2) various forms of resource constraint. It is assumed throughout that there will be no lack of demand for investment from lower level units, but the behaviour of these units is not explicitly modelled. This is an important limitation of Marrese's analysis, although it does not detract from the interest of the conclusions that he reached, noted above.

What remains for me to mention here is the important work of Bauer and Soós, and this does provide a more satisfactory account of Hungarian investment cycles. Soós (1975) carefully documented the Hungarian experience, noting a shift in the 1960s from a centrally generated cycle, resulting from ambitious planners' aiming for excessive growth rates, to one resulting from pressure from below. Decentralisation combined with inadequate concern with efficiency generates unduly high demand for investment, which is not resolved or controlled by the relatively weakened and disunited central agencies. As already suggested, it is only when disequilibria become sufficiently widespread and visible, hence politically important or threatening, that the centre achieves sufficient unity to act decisively. Indeed it is only then that it is clear what needs to be done to restore equilibrium, hence the cycles. It seems that central controls, especially in the sphere of investment, are still more pervasive than the early supporters of the Hungarian reforms hoped. This is undoubtedly one reason why investors have not yet been prevailed upon to take full responsibility for their investment decisions. It also explains why both Bauer (1975) and Soós (1975) wished to see the Hungarian economic mechanism move further in the direction originally envisaged in the initial reform guidelines.

In this discussion of cycles, questions of investment efficiency have arisen from time to time. Since these questions and related issues are absolutely central to an understanding of the Hungarian investment process, the next section is devoted to a full analysis of them.

4 Efficiency of investment

The main social function of investment in most economies is usually taken to be the replacement of economically obsolete capital equipment, and the addition of new capital, with the aim of promoting growth in output. It would be incorrect to argue from this that more investment means faster growth, since Jánossy (1971) presented substantial evidence to the effect that the main determinants of growth over the longer term reside in the nature of the prevailing sociopolitical system and have little to do with fluctuations in the volume of investment. Western theorists have also argued that in the very long run the rates of growth of labour force and technical level are more important influences than the rate of investment.[6] Given Hungary's almost constant labour force, it follows that growth is only possible to the extent that output per worker (i.e. productivity) can be maintained on a rising trend; in recent years this has been around 5–6 per cent per year.

Now, some increases in productivity can be achieved through improved work practices and the elimination of so-called 'unemployment inside the factory gates', but for the most part it will be the opportunity to work with improved capital equipment that raises productivity. Consequently, although the volume of investment may have little long-run effect on growth rates, the economic efficiency of the projects that make up the total volume can have a decisive impact. In this section efficiency is discussed under the following items:

(1) formal criteria;
(2) prices;
(3) credits and the financial environment;
(4) individual large investments and concentration, and investment scatter; and
(5) other issues (scrapping, project preparation, and so on).

It should be emphasised from the outset that many of the points raised below can apply to the investment process in several other countries and that, taken individually, they will not necessarily be considered as major problems. Similarly, although Hungarian investment efficiency may be criticised, this is always with reference to planners' intentions and the real possibilities. The absolute level of performance and its rate of improvement are by no means bad in international terms.

The main formal criterion used in investment appraisal in Hungary is the so-called D-index:[7]

$$D = \frac{\sum_{1}^{15}(Y_i - I_i)R^i}{\sum_{1}^{n} K_i R^i - VR^{15}} \tag{1}$$

where Y_i = net income (i.e. value added) generated by the project in year i

I_i = additional capital costs in year i (to maintain or replace worn-out capital)

R = discount factor, $1/(1 + r)$, the discount rate, r, being usually 12 per cent

n = construction period of project (years)

K_i = capital outlays in year i.

V = residual value of the capital equipment after 15 years.

Superficially, this formulation is not the one most familiar to Western readers, but only the most trivial manipulation of equation 1 is required to express it in the usual net present value (NPV) form. It then follows that

$$D > 1 \text{ if and only if NPV} > 0 \tag{2}$$

Thus, ranking projects by means of the D-index is exactly equivalent to net-present-value analysis, the only novelty being the prescribed fifteen-year evaluation period. Given the inherent uncertainties of forecasting economic variables even this far ahead, that cannot be regarded as an important feature.

In principle, the D-index has to be used for all large investment, although it seems that its application is frequently an afterthought. For other projects this or at times simpler indices (e.g. payback periods) can be required by agencies like banks that provide credit, but again it is hard to escape the impression that their use is frequently a formality. This is for two related reasons.

First, investors know that, despite the reforms, the planners are still primarily interested in output and new capacity. Hence, most investment projects that run into difficulties will be bailed out somehow or other. At most, therefore, use of formal criteria may facilitate the rejection of a few hopeless projects, while in many other cases the criteria can be 'doctored' to reveal high profits in the knowledge that penalties for failure are minimal.

Secondly, the profits that affect incomes and the social esteem of the enterprise are those measured in domestic producer prices. Yet, in most cases investment criteria have to be evaluated in world prices, according to the official regulations. It was intended that by now there would be much greater concordance between the two sets of prices than has actually come about. To a rather limited extent world prices were used as the basis for some of the 1968 price-reform calculations, and the same principle has been asserted more strongly in the revisions since 1975.[8] Nevertheless, various taxes, subsidies and price adjustments have been imposed to ensure that, in terms of domestic prices, most domestic production should appear profitable. At times these profits have been so significant that socially unprofitable activities, rather than contracting, have been allowed to expand, as noted by Deák (1978) and Friss (1978) among others. All this implies that criteria measured in world prices are of little interest to domestic producing units.

These distortions in the pricing system are now widely recognised. Unfortunately, while the planners are aware that profitability calculations in present circumstances throw little light on the relative desirability of expansion in various branches, it is not clear what alternative criteria could be effective. In practice, this difficulty has meant that arguments about 'needs' or 'requirements' for certain capacities have been accepted quite readily, with inadequate attention to careful analysis. Such tendencies have been criticised recently by Nyilás (1976) and Tömpe and Vértés (1977).

Another aspect of the present price system, which is seen to be a source of imbalances on investment goods and labour markets, is the relative price between these two categories (i.e. the ratio, π, between a price index of investment goods and an index of unit labour costs). Until the end of 1979, producer prices incorporated a high tax on wage costs and sought a high rate of return on capital employed. The result was a high value of π, apparently resulting in the choice of relatively labour-intensive investment variants.[9] Given Hungary's labour shortage, such an outcome is not very helpful, and it seems that one objective of the 1980 price reform is to achieve substantial reduction in π. Presumably, this means that plans for the 1980s will anticipate investment programmes containing relatively fewer but more capital-intensive projects.

Turning now to credits and the financial environment, some potentially important changes were introduced at the start of the fifth five-year plan in 1976. A combination of price revisions and tax changes reduced enterprise incomes, but at the same time it relaxed earlier restrictions on the division of after-tax profits into development and sharing funds. Credit regulations were tightened in an effort to strengthen financial discipline. Penalty interest rates were to be charged for delayed repayments. In the case of state investments receiving state loans from the State Development Bank, repayment was to be made out of pre-tax profits, implying in effect that a lower rate of return was now acceptable on such projects.

In addition there was some hope, not yet realised, that investment subsidies could be reduced. Over the fourth five-year plan period (1971–5) these were initially to be available to support thirty-four types of investment, but the list of approved objects almost doubled during the five years. It appears that the projects (and indeed enterprises) receiving finance from several different sources (e.g. own funds, credit, state loan, subsidy) are generally the least profitable. Deák (1976, 1978) proposed that, in order to remedy this, a multiplicity of financial sources should be avoided, credits should be used more widely and subsidies should be based on general norms published in advance, not requiring special decisions or negotiation. Naturally, success would entail attendant changes in other regulators, particularly the price system, to eliminate excessive differentiation (by agent and product) and to achieve closer links between domestic and external prices.

During the fifth five-year plan period (1976–80) it was envisaged that enterprise investments would be financed in the following ways:[10]

Own resources (development funds)	220 billion forints
Bank credits	105 billion forints
State subsidies	95 billion forints

These figures are only approximate, of course, but they do give some indication of the immense scale of subsidies in relation to other forms of investment finance. They also explain why there may be pressure in the Hungarian economy to reform the price system and eliminate the need for many of the subsidies.

The last few years have seen a major effort to reduce the number of individual large investments under construction at any time, as part of a general campaign to concentrate investment resources. Thus, over the period 1971–5, as Pukli (1976) reported, there were thirty-seven major projects started and eighty completions, thereby reducing the number of ongoing projects from eighty-nine to forty-six. Outlays on these projects typically fall in the range 300–6,000 million forints. According to an interesting study by Szász (1977), projects of this size accounted for a little more than 3 per cent of the number of projects under way in 1973, although their completion would account for 60 per cent of the total investment outlays to complete all the projects under way then. Since only about 14–15 per cent of annual investment outlays are devoted to the individual large projects (Lang, 1978), it is not surprising that in an earlier study Szász (1974) found that the largest projects often take over nine years to build. Subsequently, referring not only to these projects, Turánsky (1978) argued that substantial gains in efficiency ensue from a serious attempt to plan for shorter construction periods and more concentrated investment activity. The benefits can be especially large for the major projects, however, since these frequently achieve rates of return much lower than initially expected and lower than the returns achieved by other types of project.

The importance of concentrating investment resources has also been illustrated by a recent study of Galla (1978), who found that the rate of spending on various projects examined in heavy industry rises much more slowly than the total cost of the projects. Consequently, expected project-gestation periods increase to very high levels for the largest projects, tying up huge amounts of resources for many years, with little or no return. It appears that the planning agencies concerned have little appreciation of the value of finishing some projects quickly. Presented with a set of projects to complete over a five-year period, the typical and extremely inefficient response would be to make a start on every project, spend resources at a slow rate on all of them and then finish them all more or less together.

As a related point, let us note that inadequate preparation of projects is mentioned by almost everyone who discusses investments in Hungary, although the real importance of, and costs imposed by, such shortcomings are very hard to assess. One indicator of poor preparation, admittedly an imperfect one, is provided by the disparities between the actual and planned investment costs of many projects. For example, in the case of some major state investments put into operation in 1976, actual outlays were expected on average to be around 110 per cent of those initially planned, with a range extending from 99·5 per cent up to 152·6 per cent (*Statisztikai Evkönyv*, 1976, p. 79). Presumably, such underestimation of costs leads the planners to believe that they can undertake more projects than actually turn out to be readily manageable at any one time.

Finally, Deák (1975) strongly criticised the tendency of enterprises not to replace obsolete capital rapidly enough. In the early 1970s only about 1·4 per cent of capital assets were scrapped each year, giving a replacement cycle of almost thirty years (based on an assumed growth rate of capital stock of about 6−6·5 per cent per year). To remedy this there should be much greater emphasis on major capital reconstructions involving large replacements of obsolete assets. Perhaps this would require disturbances to current production on a larger scale than the central agencies have so far been willing to accept.

5 Conclusions

Overall, it seems that the Hungarian investment process is reasonably effective in the sense that it sustains a not unreasonable growth rate of national income. But as the last two sections have shown, the institutional structure and incentive system, which jointly regulate economic development, generate a cyclical pattern of growth of total investment, while there are many aspects of the regulation of individual projects that apparently function much less efficiently than central agencies believe possible.

In particular, the boundless enthusiasm expressed for investment by most enterprises suggests that in some sense its price is regarded as being close to zero, despite which the planners believe that unduly labour-intensive project variants are often selected. The problem here seems to be a combination of imperfect macroeconomic management (i.e. a failure to restrain aggregate demand adequately) and incorrect relative factor prices. A further source of inefficiency, as we have seen, is the chaotic producer-price system, which is increasingly remote from both world prices and domestic costs of production and is increasingly recognised as inappropriate as a guide to important investment decisions.

It is therefore not surprising to find that most of the proposals to improve efficiency involve such changes as:

(1)   improvements in pricing by moving closer to world prices and eliminating special taxes and subsidies; and
(2)   enforcement of 'financial discipline' by enterprises.

It is easy to see technical and economic arguments for (1) and (2), many of which have been mentioned earlier, but it is hard to believe that they would really be implemented to the extent of granting enterprises the real autonomy that they entail, for this would involve a much deeper and more fundamental reform of the Hungarian economy than seems at all likely in present conditions.

When the New Economic Mechanism was first introduced, many of its observers believed for a while that enterprises had actually been granted an important degree of autonomy. But it soon became clear that it was autonomy 'within limits'. Central agencies, notably the branch ministries, retained the power to order enterprises not to cease production. Such a power, at first sight rather negative, nevertheless is sufficient to undermine any serious moves towards implementing (2), while (2) itself is the *sine qua non* for (1) to be effective. Consequently, although various features of the regulator system, including the prices, are being changed in 1980, I do not expect that to give rise to any dramatic improvements in Hungary's economic performance; minor benefits are not to be excluded, of course. This conclusion results from my belief that the basic institutional structure and power relationships that jointly regulate the development of the Hungarian economy are not likely to be reformed in the near future.

Notes: Chapter 5

1 For general accounts of the Hungarian reforms, see other chapters in the present volume, as well as Gadó (1972, 1976), Friss (1969), Portes (1977) and Hare (1976). For discussion of more recent developments, see Hare (1977) and Radice (1979).

2 This aspect of the investment problem is referred to again in Chapter 9 below.

3 For details of these models, see Kornai (1975), Ganczer (1973) and Dániel (1971).

4 For details, see Hare (1973).

5 Among the many possible references, see the discussions in Neményi (1975), Deák (1976, 1978) and Mandel and Huszár (1975).

6 See the excellent introductory survey of Western growth theory in Sen (1970).

7 See, for example, Faluvégi (1977, p. 231). The notation has been changed to bring it closer to Western conventions.

8 See Gadó (1972), Hare (1976) and Friss (1978), also *Figyelő*, vol. 22 (51) Összeállitás a termelöi árrendezés irányáiról (Collection of guidelines on the producer price revision) 1978, pp. 5–9, for discussions of pricing principles. Barta (1978) also discussed efficiency calculations.

9 This feature of the price system has generated considerable debate. See, for example, Megyeri (1976), Szakolczai (1975), Barta (1977) and Huszár and Surány (1977).

10 See 'Jotékonykodás helyett követelmény' (Requirements instead of charity), *Figyelő*, vol. 20 (29) (1976), p. 4.

References: Chapter 5

Barta, I. (1977), 'A termelöberuházások intenziv jellegének megitélése' (Judging the intensive character of productive investments), *Közgazdasági Szemle*, vol. 24 (12), pp. 1387–402.

Barta, I. (1978), 'A világpiaci árak szerepe a beruházás-gazdaságossági számitásokban' (The role of world market prices in investment efficiency calculations), *Külgazdaság*, vol. 22 (6), pp. 53–60.

Bauer, T. (1975), 'A vállalatok ellentmondásos helyzete a magyar gazdasági mechanizmusban' (The contradictory position of the enterprise in the Hungarian economic mechanism), *Közgazdasági Szemle*, vol. 22 (6), pp. 725–35.

Dániel, Zs. (1971), 'Planning and exploration: a dynamic multi-sectoral model of Hungary', *Economics of Planning*, vol. 11 (3), pp. 120–46.

Dániel, Zs, Jonás, A., Kornai, J. and Martos, B. (1971), 'Plan sounding', *Economics of Planning*, vol. 2 (1–2), pp. 31–58.

Deák, A. (1975), 'A vállalatok beruházási döntési lehetőségeiről' (On the possibilities for enterprise investment decisions), *Közgazdasági Szemle*, vol. 22 (1), pp. 97–103.

Deák, A. (1976), 'A vállalati beruházások állami támogatása' (State subsidies for enterprise investments), *Pénzügyi Szemle*, vol. 20 (4), pp. 243–9.

Deák, A. (1978), 'Vállalati beruházási döntések és a gazdaságosság' (Enterprise investment decisions and efficiency), *Gazdaság*, vol. 12 (1), pp. 17–36.

Faluvégi, L. (1977), *Állami Pénzügyek és Gazdaság-Irányítás* (State Finances and Economic Management) (Budapest: Közgazdasági és Jogi Könyvkiadó).

Friss, I. (ed.) (1969), *Reform of the Economic Mechanism in Hungary* (Budapest: Akadémiai Kiadó).

Friss, I. (1978), 'Tiz év gazdasági reform' (Ten years of economic reform), *Valóság*, vol. 21 (7), pp. 1–14.

Gács, J. (1976a), 'Adaptive planning and the cyclical character of economic activity', Institute for Economic and Market Research, Discussion Paper (December, mimeo.).

Gács, J. (1976b), 'Hiány és támogatott fejlesztés' (Shortage and subsidised development), *Közgazdasági Szemle*, vol. 23 (9), pp. 1043–60.

Gács, J., and Lackó, M. (1973), 'A study of planning behaviour on the national-economic level', *Economics of Planning*, vol. 13 (1–2), pp. 91–119.

Gadó, O. (ed.) (1972), *Reform of the Economic Mechanism in Hungary: Development, 1968–1971* (Budapest: Akadémiai Kiadó).

Gadó, O. (1976), *The Economic Mechanism in Hungary: How it Works in 1976* (Budapest: Akadémiai Kiadó).

Galla, L. (1978), 'Az időnyerés érdekében' (In the interests of saving time), *Figyelő*, vol. 22 (7), p. 6.

Ganczer, S. (ed.) (1973), *Népgazdasági Tervezés és Prográmozás* (National Economic Planning and Programming) (Budapest: Közgazdasági és Jogi Könyvkiadó).

Hare, P. G. (1973), 'Hungarian planning models based on input–output', D.Phil. thesis, Oxford University, Oxford.

Hare, P. G. (1976), 'Industrial prices in Hungary', *Soviet Studies*, vol. 28 (2 and 3), pp. 189–206 and 362–90.

Hare, P. G. (1977), 'Economic reform in Hungary: problems and prospects', *Cambridge Journal of Economics*, vol. 1 (3), pp. 317–33.

Horvat, B. (1970), *Business Cycles in Yugoslavia* (White Plains, New York: International Arts and Sciences Press).

Huszár, Mrs I. and Surány, B. (1977), 'A beruházások létszámigényének elszámolása a ráforditási költségekben' (Accounting for the labour intensity of investments in measuring costs), *Közgazdasági Szemle*, vol. 24 (11), pp. 1259–70.

Jánossy, F. (1971), *The End of the Economic Miracle* (White Plains, New York: International Arts and Sciences Press).

Kalecki, M. *et al.* (1963), *Essays on Planning and Economic Development*, Center of Research on Underdeveloped Economics, Research Papers, Vol. 1 (Warsaw: Polish Scientific Publishers).

Kornai, J. (1975), *Mathematical Planning of Structural Decisions*, 2nd edn (Amsterdam: North-Holland).

Lang, Mrs Gy. (1978), 'Helyzetkép a nagyberuházásról' (Situation report on large investments), *Figyelő*, vol. 22 (41), p. 5.

Mandel, M., and Huszár, Mrs J. (1975), 'A beruházási rendszer muködésének néhány tapasztalata' (Some experiences with the operation of the investment system), *Közgazdasági Szemle*, vol. 22 (12), pp. 1387–95.

Marrese, M. (1978a), 'Cyclical centralism: Hungary's gift to the understanding of bureaucracies', University of British Colombia, Discussion Paper 78–51 (mimeo.).

Marrese, M. (1978b), 'Cyclical centralism's explanation of Hungarian investment fluctuations', University of British Colombia, Discussion Paper 78–52 (mimeo.).

Megyeri, E. (1976), *Eröforrás-Értékelés és Jövedelem-Szabályozás* (Resource Evaluation and Income Regulation) (Budapest: Közgazdasági és Jogi Könyvkiadó).

Neményi, I. (1975), *A Magyar Beruházási Politika 30 Éve* (Thirty Years of Hungarian Investment Policy) (Budapest: Közgazdasági és Jogi Könyvkiadó).

Nyilás, A. (1976), 'Gazdaságossági követelmények a beruházások elosztásában és az exportban' (Efficiency requirements in the distribution of investments and in exports), *Gazdaság*, vol. 10 (3), pp. 103–14.

Portes, R. (1977), 'Hungary: economic performance, policy and prospects', in Joint Economic Committee, *East European Economies Post-Helsinki* (Washington, DC: US Government Printing Office).

Portes, R. (1978), 'Macroeconomic equilibrium and disequilibrium in centrally planned economies', Harvard Institute of Economic Research, Discussion Paper 638.

Portes, E., and Winter, D. (1977), 'The supply of consumption goods in centrally planned economies', *Journal of Comparative Economics*, vol. 1 (4), pp. 351–65.

Pukli, P. (1976), 'Az ipari beruházások alakulása a negyedik ötéves tervidőszakban' (The development of industrial investment in the period of the fourth five-year plan), *Ipargazdaság*, vol. 28 (11), pp. 40–3.

Radice, H. K. (1979), 'The Hungarian economic reforms: an assessment', Leeds University School of Economic Studies, Discussion Paper 72 (mimeo.).

Sen, A. K. (ed.) (1970), *Growth Economics* (Harmondsworth: Penguin).

Soós, A. (1975), 'A beruházások ingadozásának okai a magyar gazdaságban' (The causes of investment fluctuations in the Hungarian economy), *Közgazdasági Szemle*, vol. 22 (1), pp. 104–10.

106   *Hungary: A Decade of Economic Reform*

Stark, A. (1973), *Terv és Valóság* (Plan and Reality) (Budapest: Kossuth Könyvkiadó).

Szalolczai, Gy. (1975), 'A termelési tényezők és az árak' (Factors of production and prices), *Figyelő*, vol. 19 (53), p. 3.

Szakolczai, Gy., and Bárány, B. (1975), 'A termelés reális költségei és az árszintproblémák' (Real costs of production and price level problems), *Közgazdasági Szemle*, vol. 22 (11 and 12), pp. 1291–1311 and 1406–25.

Szász, T. (1974), 'Összefüggések a beruházáshatékonyság és a koncentrációs rendszer között' (Connections between investment efficiency and the system of concentrating investments), *Ipargazdaság*, vol. 26 (10), pp. 10–15.

Szász, T. (1977), 'A beruházások koncentrációja és a beruházások kivitelezési ideje' (The concentration of investments and their recoupment periods), *Pénzügyi Szemle*, vol. 21 (3), pp. 181–7.

Tar, J. (1976), 'Az V. ötéves tervidőszak beruházásai a gazdasági növekedés szolgálatában' (Investments over the period of the fifth five-year plan in the service of economic growth), *Gazdaság*, vol. 10 (3), pp. 47–61.

Tömpe, I. (1978), 'Beruházási lázgörbe' (Investment's temperature curve), *Figyelő*, vol. 22 (31), p. 3.

Tömpe, I. and Vértés, A. (1977), 'A beruházások néhány alapvető kérdése és a kivitelezési idő' (Some basic questions about investment and the recoupment period), *Pénzügyi Szemle*, vol. 21 (1), pp. 33–42.

Turánszky, M. (1978), 'Koncentrálható-e a beruházási tevékenység' (Should investment activity be concentrated?), *Figyelő*, vol. 22 (1), pp. 1 and 6.

Part Four

Transfer of Technology

Chapter 6

Industrial Co-operation between Hungary and the West

1 Introduction

The aim of this chapter is to assess the role of East – West industrial co-operation (hereafter EWIC) in the Hungarian economy since the late 1960s. For reasons that will become clear, it is not easy to assess the success of Hungarian policy in this field directly, let alone quantitatively. My approach therefore is to examine it in the context of trends in the economy and economic policy in general. In doing so I shall be drawing on the attitudes and behaviour of Hungarian enterprises involved in EWIC, as well as the relevant policies of the economic authorities.

Section 2 outlines briefly the forms of EWIC, available data on them and their interpretation. Section 3 gives an initial summary of the development of policy specifically directed towards EWIC. Section 4 assesses these developments by looking at the effects *on* EWIC of three aspects of the Hungarian economy: the relations between state and enterprise; industrial organisation and innovation; and patterns of foreign trade with both the Council for Mutual Economic Assistance (CMEA) and the West.

2 Patterns of EWIC in Hungary

McMillan (1977, p. 1178) defined EWIC 'as constituting arrangements whereby individual producers, based in East and West, agree to pool some assets and jointly to coordinate their use in the mutual pursuit of complementary objectives'. He went on to stress the bewildering variety of forms of EWIC, both as regards the method of 'pooling' (e.g. *ad hoc*, contractual, equity) and the elements to be pooled. While heeding McMillan's caveats about the use of oversimplified classificatory schemes, the most straightforward approach remains to list briefly the main forms of co-operation 'package' observed in practice in Hungary. These are:

(1)   contract manufacture;

(2)   receipt of technology, equipment or other inputs, with reverse flow of products;
(3)   co-production or product specialisation;
(4)   joint research and development; and
(5)   joint tendering.

In the main I am concerned with contractual EWIC, since equity joint ventures remain insignificant in Hungary. The contracts usually run for 5–10 years, and the Hungarian signatory may be any enterprise with foreign trade rights.

Facts and figures on EWIC are hard to obtain, although easier in Hungary than elsewhere. Different definitions of the various forms may be used. No regular statistics on even the number of agreements, let alone their value, are published; reports in the business press are patently incomplete; official statistics on foreign trade and licence payments do not separate out those undertaken within EWIC agreements.

Tables 6.1–6.10 (see appendix to this chapter) present the available data, drawing on both Hungarian and Western sources. A rough total for the *number* of extant agreements is 500 (Table 6.2), out of a total for the whole of the CMEA of about 1,200. Table 6.1 suggests that these agreements amount to 3·5–4 per cent of total Hungarian exports to the West. However, given the importance of engineering in co-operation (Table 6.2) and the relatively small role of engineering goods in exports to the *developed* capitalist countries, we can estimate that in this sector co-operation may account for as much as 25–30 per cent of trade with the latter.

As for the *time trend*, Table 6.2 and Table 6.5 on licence trade turnover, which is often related to EWIC, together with much impressionistic evidence, suggest that there was a quite rapid growth in EWIC agreements up to 1974, interrupted as a result of Western recession and inflation and resumed at a much slower rate in 1976–7.

Tables 6.2–6.4 break down the total number of agreements by sector, Western partner and type respectively. On *type*, the boundaries between the categories are very blurred (Radice, 1978), so that the figures do not mean much. The dominant *sector* is engineering, including within this machine-building, instruments, electrical, electronic and telecommunications equipment, and vehicles. The predominant *partner country* is the FGR. Thus, a typical case, if there could be one, would be between a Hungarian and a West German machinery firm and involve the supply of a licence and some parts, equipment and know-how by the latter, with a return flow of partially resultant products of roughly equal value over a contract life of seven years. On the other hand, short-term contract manufacturing as a form is common in the textiles industry.

Tables 6.6–6.10 provide further information covering the sector of 'metallurgy and machine-building' (i.e. all enterprises under the authority of the Ministry of Metallurgy and Machine-Building). A study of the agreements classified in Table 6.6 (Radice, 1978) suggests that in some sense co-operation activities can be ranged along a spectrum, with evolution anticipated from simpler forms (which may amount, for example, to little more than a licence purchase or a supply contract) towards more complex forms involving permanent co-operation in research and development, design, production and marketing over long periods. Tables 6.7–6.10 give the distribution of co-operation activity by subsector and country, and the time trends up to 1974. Unfortunately, the publication of these statistics has not been repeated. They cover industrial co-operation with socialist as well as capitalist countries, but the two are not distinguished in the analysis by subsector. Table 6.10 indicates that the proportions between East and West, and the shares of different countries, are broadly in tune with those for foreign trade turnover in general.

Tables 6.9 and 6.7, taken together, show that on average each active enterprise doubled the number of its co-operation agreements over the period 1969–74, while Table 6.7 shows that by 1974 the proportion of enterprises engaging in co-operation had still only reached 15 per cent. This concentration of EWIC within the sector is supported by other evidence. *Business Eastern Europe* (22 July 1977, p. 226) cites one firm with fourteen agreements, one with six and two with five. Collating these figures with my own (Table 6.6), we find that some 15–20 enterprises (i.e. 5–6 per cent of the total number) account for over half the EWIC agreements. This raises the question of why so many enterprises have *not* engaged in EWIC.

Apart from the general shortage of statistics, there are two particular pitfalls that must be noted. First, the great publicity given to EWIC, especially in the period around the signing of the Helsinki agreement, encouraged a large number of 'phoney' agreements in which *either or both* parties had little interest in moving towards 'real' or 'complex' co-operation. However, as I discuss below, this does *not* mean that these agreements were not mutually beneficial from the national or the enterprise viewpoint.

Secondly, the numbers of agreements reported are themselves misleading. Some partners sign a 'frame agreement' first and later one or more operating agreements, leading to double-counting. Many agreements become dormant without being formally cancelled. A 1977 Hungarian study found that only 340 out of 480 agreements were active (*Business Eastern Europe*, 22 July 1977, p. 226).

3 Hungarian policy on EWIC

Hungarian officials and economists have clearly and repeatedly stated why Hungary became a leading exponent of EWIC. Long-term contractual relations between Hungarian and Western enterprises are seen as offering definite advantages over traditional forms of trade in goods and technology in two key policy areas: 'upgrading' the structure of hard currency exports by increasing the share of industrial goods, and modernising industrial and agricultural production through imports of Western technology. In export development EWIC helps the Hungarian enterprise to enter Western markets by using its partner's outlets, goodwill and often trademarks; introduces it to Western standards in quality, delivery dates, servicing and maintenance; and by creating a mutual dependence weakens the impact of cyclical fluctuations and structural shifts in Western markets. In the 'transfer of technology' the Western partner has a much greater interest than in a normal licence sale in ensuring that the technology is effectively absorbed by the receiving enterprise, and the closer long-term relation gives the latter access to a broad technical culture, not merely a specific licence.

In promoting EWIC the Hungarian authorities have adopted a flexible approach, in keeping with the New Economic Mechanism. While they have passed legislation (1972–7) on equity joint ventures, contractual EWIC has not been given any legal framework. Any enterprise with foreign trade rights is free to conclude a contract, subject to the normal regulations governing foreign economic relations. Two specialised co-operation agencies exist, but there is no obligation to use them. Almost every conceivably relevant state body has a 'co-operation department', but again there is no obligation to consult them.

Nevertheless, most EWIC agreements require forint and hard currency outlays by the Hungarian partner and import licences, and in order to obtain these there is a complex system of regulation. Leaving aside equity joint ventures, which have a similar but separate structure, the typical Hungarian enterprise negotiating an EWIC deal has to submit proposals to the Hungarian National Bank (MNB), the Foreign Trade Bank (KKB) and its own sectoral ministry, culminating in the registration (or not) of its agreement with the Interdeparmental Co-operation Committee (Kooperációs Tárcaközi Bizottság, KTB). The KTB is located in the Ministry of Foreign Trade but includes representatives of the Ministry of Finance, Tax Office, National Planning Office and State Committee for Technical Development, as well as the bodies already mentioned. The KTB Secretariat and the agencies reporting to it assess the proposal in terms of industrial development policy, existing trade and co-operation patterns (including CMEA co-operation and specialisation agreements in whose negotiation it also has a say), the general competence of the enterprise, and the financial and technical viability of the specific proposal. Approval by the KTB leads to the granting of all necessary import licences for the contract period and to a variety of preferences. Fulfilment of the hard-currency payments aspects of the agreement is then monitored by the Foreign Trade Bank, which can have the import licences revoked if performance is not good enough, leading to a reappraisal back through the same machinery.

Since about 1975 the most important element in this has concerned the allocation of export promotion credits by the National Bank. Under the fifth five-year plan (1976–80) the share of these in the total credit has risen from about 10 per cent in the fourth plan (1971–5) to about 35 per cent. A key feature is that these credits are not pre-allocated to particular sectors, at least officially. They have preferential repayment periods and rates for forint investments, and they require the allocation of necessary hard currency to be repaid (in a much shorter period) out of export earnings. However, it is very important to note that these credits are available generally, not just to firms undertaking EWIC agreements.

The experiences of 1974–5 undoubtedly led to a certain disillusionment with EWIC among Hungarian enterprises and officials, although they put a brave face on it. The bankruptcy of two of the most well-known Western partners, Bowcan and Anker, was the most obvious evidence that conditions had changed, but many other agreements lapsed or had to be renegotiated. Many Hungarian firms using imported raw materials were caught out by contractually fixed prices for their material-intensive deliveries. Western firms that had been primarily interested in cheaper labour lost interest when they could not sell their products anyway and when trade unions at home made ominous noises about the export of jobs. In the most 'advanced' area of equity joint ventures, the 1972 law had produced only three joint ventures. Hungarian economists also began to voice complaints – not only the familiar ones about the obstacles posed by Western commercial policies, but also just-as-urgent problems on the Hungarian side. Why were so many enterprises not interested in EWIC? Were the incentives for exports to the West high enough? Did the excessive CMEA orientation of some of them block off EWIC as a sensible method of technical and market development? Were there dangers in encouraging dependence on big Western multinational firms, and could this ever be balanced by their dependence on Hungary alone?

The following section draws on the debates concerning these and other questions, necessarily without providing explicit answers to each of them. At this point I want only to stress the extent to which this questioning was a necessary reaction to the euphoria of earlier years; expectations had been unduly high. Today, the official position is much the same as before, only more cautious. In the field of equity joint ventures, the 1977 law allows joint ventures to engage directly in production activities, excludes these from the constraints of plan conformity, and in the ensuing directives reinforces their preferential tax treatment; it also allows Western firms to take majority stakes in non-production joint ventures. At the same time Hungarian joint-venture activities in the West, mainly in marketing, have expanded greatly. On contractual EWIC the guidelines and procedures are being tidied up and tightened up, both in the provision of information and advice and in the regulation and monitoring of EWIC.

4 The context of EWIC in Hungary

(a) *State–enterprise relations and the regulation of EWIC*
The Hungarian conception of EWIC was from the mid 1960s strongly influenced by the economic reforms, in particular by the much greater autonomy of enterprises embodied in the New Economic Mechanism. The advantages of EWIC, namely, technical development and Western exports, were logically seen as conforming to enterprise interests (through the profit motive) as well as to those of the economic and political leadership. The enterprises, subject to given economic, financial, technical and legal constraints, would pursue EWIC, conduct negotiations and implement contracts chiefly on their own initiative. The role of state bodies would be confined to influencing enterprise decisions by setting out a clear-cut structure of non-discriminatory preferences through the relevant economic regulators (tax rates, credit conditions, foreign exchange multipliers, wage and price controls, and so on). However, this would not exclude the initiation of EWIC by central bodies also.

(1) The first problem concerns the principles and practice of the application of the economic regulators to enterprises (e.g. see Bauer, 1976; and Tardos, 1976). 'Non-discriminatory preferences' may be understood as the differentiation of regulators with regard to *broad categories of products*, publicly announced in advance, based on clear and well-understood criteria, and applied uniformly to all enterprises producing (or trading) within a given product category. Clearly, the term 'broad category of product' is ambiguous, but the important implication is that bargaining over preferential treatment between the centre and the *individual enterprise as such* would be ruled out, including bargaining over trade-offs between different categories of regulator or between the applications of a given regulator to different products of the same enterprise. In practice, the operation of the regulators has not conformed to such principles. It has become, if anything, increasingly differentiated by product group on an *ad hoc* basis in response to changing practical requirements; and because of

the frequency of enterprise monopoly, this differentiation has been heavily influenced by bargaining with individual enterprises. This applies to credit conditions, import and export subsidies and taxes, price controls, wage regulation and production tax (*termelési adó*).

None of these regulators is specifically aimed at the regulation of EWIC activities. But co-operation work breaks down into particular components, notably: the import and export of equipment, licences, intermediates and finished goods, domestic investments and ancillary domestic sourcing of inputs; and sales of outputs. Any or all of these will be *directly* affected by the economic regulators, thereby influencing the interests of a given enterprise in a particular co-operation agreement. Given the lack of any clear demarcation between EWIC and other activities within the enterprise, *indirect* effects will be present too, through the impact of the regulators on the structure of output and employment, the financial condition of the enterprise, and so on. In short, the response of the enterprise to the opportunities created for EWIC by changing world and domestic market conditions will be profoundly influenced. There is no point in regarding these influences as 'distortions', since there is no *a priori* ideal situation with which to compare the 'distortions', but enterprise response becomes unpredictable, particularly as a result of enterprise-specific preferences and vertical bargaining with the authorities. The shortening of the time horizons of enterprise-planners, in response to frequent *ad hoc* changes, is also damaging in view of the long-term and uncertain nature of the benefits from EWIC.

(2) The second and related issue under this heading concerns the evaluation of both prospective and realised performance of enterprises in EWIC. In the registration process, particularly in applications for hard currency and export promotion credits, enterprises must submit detailed proposals and undergo investigation by superior bodies (see above, pages 112–13). Here, all the usual problems of information and misinformation apply. One view expressed to me was that 'Firms can cheat as much as they want in preparing figures', although this was strenuously denied by an official involved in vetting contracts. It is, however, inevitable that there will be conflicts of interest between different agencies involved in the vetting process. The relevant departments of the National Bank, for example, would be the Foreign Trade Department for the hard currency aspects, but the forint credit side would be handled by the relevant sector department, where the ongoing credit relationship with each enterprise is under the supervision of a given official. Although the Foreign Trade Department is free from such pressures, the sector departments tend, like the sectoral ministries, to promote the interests of 'their' enterprises. This conflict of interests has emerged over the question of allowing import

substitution projects to qualify for export promotion credits, with the Foreign Trade Department arguing that only an external market can provide an adequate check on price and quality.

A further aspect concerns how far it is possible to evaluate credit requests for co-operation deals (or generally an export promotion project) in isolation from the recent and expected performance of the enterprise as a whole. The existence of strong indirect or secondary benefits to the enterprise (or beyond), which are stressed by enterprise managers, argues for an evaluation of the total impact of the proposal on an enterprise, and indeed beyond it. This would be more complicated, but at the later stage of attempting objectively to assess results it might make matters easier. On the other hand, bank officials are well aware that indirect or supplementary *costs* may only surface after a project has been launched, so that further credits may have to be advanced, perhaps to supplier enterprises, without an independent evaluation, in order to safeguard the credits already provided.

(3) The evaluation and regulation process is not, and cannot be, immune from 'state preferences' for particular projects. This is not a question of whether the project fits in with the five-year plan (a formality), but a question of whether there is significant pressure for a project from sector ministries, other high state bodies and the Party. We know that many of the investments in the Central Development Programmes (e.g. bus production) have been financed by credits, which are effectively thus pre-allocated (Balassa, 1975). It is reasonable to assume that other large export-promotion projects, involving the bigger state enterprises (e.g. Tungsram, Raba, Aluminium Tröszt) and costing 1–4 billion forints each, undergo a qualitatively different evaluation process from small projects costing, say, 1 million forints. It is interesting to note that there were no new large-scale investment projects in 1979, and what remained in the export promotion kitty was oriented more to smaller projects, but this seems to have more to do with capacity bottlenecks in the construction industry than with any real shift in preferences towards smaller projects. Now, if 'real' EWIC is found more among small and medium-sized enterprises and projects, in the long run it may be in danger of being swamped by large-scale projects that do not take that form. Perhaps, however, the correct response is to question whether 'real' EWIC is really so valuable anyway.

Any system of state regulation relating to EWIC (directly or indirectly) would be liable to the problems outlined in this section. Other aspects of Hungarian economic policy and practice will shed light on the specific circumstances surrounding these problems in Hungary in recent years.

(b) *Industrial organisation and innovation*

If we abstract from the problems discussed above, the market conditions and market relations confronting the industrial enterprise within Hungary will also affect its willingness and ability to respond to the potential benefits of EWIC. Among the factors at work here are the competitive pressures on the enterprise in its markets for inputs and outputs and the responsiveness of suppliers and customers to new demands and new products respectively.

(1) The level of concentration of Hungarian industry at both plant and enterprise level is striking. A recent study (Economic Research Institute, 1974) provides comparative data on the share in total industrial employment of enterprises with more than 1,000 employees. Selected figures in descending order are:

	%
Czechoslovakia	90
Romania	80
Hungary	73
Poland	60
GDR	43
The Netherlands	41
FGR	39
Italy	17

Although the largest Hungarian enterprise would have ranked only 494th in the top 500 European firms by turnover in 1971 (Economic Research Institute, 1974), in the confines of the Hungarian economy it is not surprising that markets in individual industrial products are also highly concentrated. For consumer goods, if there exist a number of competing enterprises, effective competition may still require not only a degree of excess supply or market saturation but also import competition and the development of multiple competing wholesale and retail channels. Even given enough of these factors, if the good in question does not account for a significant share in the total sales of the enterprise, competitive behaviour may not occur (Laki, 1975). For producer goods the evidence suggests that on all these counts competitive pressures are weaker still. There is no obligatory central direction of supplies under the New Economic Mechanism, but in a seller's market there will be informal rationing by supplier enterprises, which is likely to distribute the supply according to the preferences of higher authorities. These preferences will in turn be subject to pressures from large consumer enterprises, via political and administrative channels, and to conflicts of interest among different authorities.

Competitive behaviour by enterprises is thus in many cases

unnecessary and/or constrained, particularly in producer goods sectors and among larger enterprises. This helps to explain why such enterprises are more likely to undertake EWIC in the context of centrally initiated projects and programmes, rather than as a response to market signals.

(2) A second significant feature of Hungarian industrial organisation concerns the horizontal and vertical diversity of the production profiles of enterprises and the powerful tendencies towards autonomy in parts and intermediate goods. Horizontal diversity makes it difficult for management to focus on the development or renewal of particular product lines and diffuses managerial energies. It means that, despite their size, enterprises do not enjoy economies of scale in production and elsewhere. ('They are conglomerates of small plants'; Schweitzer, 1978.) At the same time they prefer to make parts and subassemblies themselves rather than to buy them in (Róth, 1978; Sternthál, 1977). This tendency, as is well known, originates in the risks of dependence on other enterprises under conditions of scarcity in the traditional directive planning system, but it persists today. When 'do it yourself' is not possible, large enterprises prefer to buy in from other large ones, because small ones may be less open to the political–bureaucratic pressures with which the purchasing enterprise hopes to reduce the risks of dependence. But at the same time otherwise healthy enterprises are unwilling to put resources into new lines of intermediate goods for fear of dependence on the purchaser and because of the diversion of resources from their own development goals. The paradoxical result is that it is often inefficient firms in trouble that end up with such contract work, because they are in dire need of new product lines, or else (which is often better by far) agricultural co-operatives, for which the marginal cost of labour is low or zero.

The net result of this is the inadequate, or at any rate painfully slow, development of a 'background' industry, particularly in engineering, and the lack of production integration between enterprises. This has several effects on EWIC. First, it may mean that complementary inputs for a new product or process introduced under EWIC, using certain Western inputs, cannot be procured in Hungary – or at any rate, that the cost in terms of management effort, if not money, is very high. Further inputs from the West must therefore be incorporated into the agreement, reducing the hard currency balance. On the other side of production, the weakness of interenterprise production integration means that the domestic market for new processes and new intermediate products is fragmented, uncertain and hard to build up. Although in both cases the Western partner can help (in the latter particularly by licensing trademarks), often the only way in which the problems can be overcome is by enlisting the support of powerful authorities, notably in the supervising ministry, to develop a framework for mobilising financial support, advice and pressure on the reluctant suppliers and customers. Certainly, 'networks' of co-operation agreements involving vertically related technologies develop only under conditions of strong central initiative or involvement (e.g. buses, machine tools) or where market demand for the final product is particularly urgent (e.g. agricultural machinery).

(3) This last point is especially pertinent to the innovation aspect of EWIC (on which see Abonyi, Chapter 7 of this volume), but a number of further points can be made on this. In general, the role of the state in innovation is considerable, notably in major innovations and reconstructions of larger enterprises in producer goods sectors (Laki, 1977). In addition, it has been government policy to encourage the purchase of Western licences and know-how, but the growth in this area has been slow (Gerencsér, 1978). On the other hand, given an interest it appears that, at any rate under EWIC, technology assessment and the choice of partner are not seen as major problems, especially for enterprises with some experience in this area. Buy-back or counter trade requirements do not in principle restrict the choice of partner. This is helped by the fact that Hungarian enterprises get their hard currency credits from the National Bank, so that Western suppliers are not expected to compete in supplying credit.

Next, as already mentioned, there is the question of secondary or indirect effects (page 115). Several enterprises said that the state authorities were not willing to make allowance for these, concentrating instead on the supposedly more certain direct effects on production costs, exports, and so on.

Finally, many enterprises seem to prefer simple licence purchase to 'real' EWIC, especially if they have little interest in developing exports to the West. In such cases there may be 'fake' co-operation, in which the return flow is of unrelated products, even perhaps from another producer enterprise through the same foreign trade enterprise. In my view this is not necessarily a bad thing. Exporting the *resultant* product may provide an important guarantee of successful implementation of the technology and ongoing technological co-operation from the licensor; but if the enterprise has an adequate technological base of its own and does not aim 'too high', such a guarantee may not be necessary. Indeed, in the *long run* the success of the enterprise in absorbing Western (or any other) technology will be judged *not* by its ability to satisfy a Western market under the protective cloak of a Western partner but precisely by its ability to do so independently on its own terms and in its own name.

(c) *Foreign trade patterns*
Existing patterns and methods of foreign trade, discussed in detail by

Marer (Chapter 8 of this volume), inevitably influence the interests of Hungarian enterprises in EWIC by their effect on both costs and benefits. They also, of course, determine to a great extent the elaboration of state policy in this field. Given this policy, we can also look to changes in foreign trade patterns for indications of success or failure.

(1) As far as the volume and structure of Hungarian exports to the West are concerned, the figures in Tables 6.11 and 6.12 in the appendix to this chapter indicate virtually no improvement, but, of course, we cannot know what they would have been in the absence of EWIC. The export-promotion credit scheme as a whole is judged to have been a success; a sample of recipient enterprises had by 1977 achieved on average 22 per cent higher export earnings than they had agreed on. There are, however, doubts about the real economic efficiency of these investments (Sándor, 1978; Kun, 1978). As I have already indicated, it is hard to see how a national optimal investment efficiency could be calculated, but the extreme differentiation of subsidies and taxation certainly impedes such calculations. At a more intuitive level it appears that the easiest areas for expanding the *volume* of export earnings are in agriculture and the food and textiles industries, but in the long term this conflicts with the aim of building up exports of machinery and parts. A number of large enterprises, most notably Raba and Tungsram, have achieved notable successes in such 'higher level' sectors, but there is disquiet at the concentration of effort on large-scale export projects (Kun, 1978).

On the supposed advantages of 'real' EWIC, I have already noted the setbacks originating in the Western recession from 1974. In general, as long as a given agreement remains relatively unimportant to the Western partner, it has little reason for maintaining the agreement or extending it if market conditions change for the worse, even though the cost of doing so might be relatively slight. Hungarian enterprises must therefore learn to anticipate and allow for Western economic fluctuations of a conjunctural character.

A more interesting question is whether 'real' EWIC *ought* to attain a more significant level in Hungary's exports to the West. Most Hungarian economists accept the view that export-oriented economic policies are essential (e.g. Mándel and Müller, 1974). There is, however, disagreement about the extent to which the growth and structure of exports should flow from the decisions of profit-oriented enterprises or from deliberate and selective state policies. But whatever the mixture of these two in any particular case, the objectives of a Hungarian partner enterprise are less likely to be secured in establishing and in implementing an EWIC agreement if it is a less than equal partner in terms of bargaining strength. Thus, the terms of an agreement may prevent the Hungarian partner from adapting to changed market conditions, and dependence on the Western partner's sales outlets, service organisation, trademarks and goodwill postpones the necessary step of achieving 'world market status' in the enterprise's own right and on the basis of its own development strategy. For these reasons one foreign-trade-manager suggested to me that in machine tools the proportion of production developed on the basis of EWIC should not rise above an upper limit of 20–30 per cent, which has in fact been more or less reached. In essence, this amounts to arguing that an export-oriented policy must not be allowed to lead to the sort of dependent position that is common among less developed countries, in which the shifting patterns of demand, transmitted through Western (often multinational) firms, exercise a determining influence on the structure of industrial development. Nevertheless, the Hungarians understand very well that, for a small country that is poor in raw materials, an autarchic industrial strategy is not a serious alternative.

(2) There has been a long-standing debate about the relation between EWIC (and more complex economic relations with the West generally) and Hungary's participation in intra-CMEA trade, specialisation and co-operation. Initially, this concerned the possibility of a dynamic inter-relation between the two. EWIC would provide Hungarian industry with the technological base for winning a better position in CMEA trade by creating comparative advantages for Hungary; while on the other hand, CMEA specialisation agreements, by increasing the scale of production in the selected products and sectors, would make Hungarian enterprises more attractive to Western firms as co-operation partners, thereby reducing the effective cost of importing technology and other inputs (Ausch, 1972; Kozma, 1972).

In a later debate (Pécsi, 1975; Péter, 1975) the oversimplified nature of this argument became apparent, in the context of disappointment both with the achieved scale of EWIC and with the slow growth in CMEA specialisation and co-operation. First of all, such a dynamic would require a much more planned and selective strategy on the part of the Hungarian authorities, and the piecemeal nature of Hungarian EWIC attested to the absence of this (Pécsi, 1975).

Secondly, some degree of co-ordination of EWIC strategies among the CMEA countries would be needed. Although such a planned approach would fit in with the overall tendency for CMEA economic interaction to develop through planning rather than through market relations, it would come up against all the problems that Hungarian reform economists identify in present CMEA practice (e.g. politicisation of economic decision-making, bilateralism, inconvertible currencies, separation of end users from each other and from the decision-making process). Otherwise, there is the danger of competition among CMEA members for either specialisation 'rights' or Western technology or both, in order to secure the 'dynamic' in favourite sectors (e.g. semiconductors, advanced machine tools).

Thirdly, there is the question of enterprise interests. Péter (1975) argued that, as a result of both the position of the Soviet Union as dominant buyer and the nature of the intra-CMEA trade system (e.g. long-term contracts), many Hungarian enterprises are completely oriented to that market and are basically uninterested in exporting to the West. Although this is often due in part to relative prices on the two markets, it depends more importantly on the structural differences between them, reflected in perceived cost levels. The CMEA markets take very long series of identical products, allowing the producer to reap sizeable static and dynamic economies of scale, while Western markets, more often than not, are fragmented (especially in producer goods sectors) and have different design and technical standards, requiring frequent changes in production organisation and greater expenses on quality control, market research, and so on.

A good example of this is the bus industry. Regarded as one of the success stories of Hungarian industry, the Ikarus bus enterprise (under the public vehicles Central Development Programme) is one of the largest bus-producers in the world, with an output approaching 15,000 units per year. Of this, over two-thirds are exported to CMEA markets, with the Soviet Union taking the lion's share. Very few types are produced, and modern assembly-line technology has been developed in conjunction with West German equipment firms, so that great economies of scale are realised. Western technology is incorporated in the engine (produced by Raba under licence from MAN of the FGR) and in many other component areas, although parts (front axles) from the Soviet Union are also used. Buses are the leading item by value in Hungary's exports to the Soviet Union as a result. However, Ikarus lacks the material, technical and economic base for a successful penetration of Western markets. The narrow range of types is inadequate even for variations in domestic transport conditions, let alone the fragmented and highly differentiated Western requirements. As a result Ikarus's very minor production for Western markets involves the use of a very high proportion of imported parts (in some cases the whole chassis and engine to start with, then safety glass, and so on), and the assembly work takes place as a rule off the main production lines in traditional workshop conditions.

Related to this is a growing awareness that the more dynamic Western markets are not in narrowly defined products but in package form, as it were. This applies not only to such obvious areas as process plant but also to others, such as computers (hardware and software), educational products and health products (the latter linking pharmaceuticals, instruments and electronics as well as such 'simple' products as sanitary textiles and glass ampoules). Success in these fields, it is argued, requires a high degree of co-ordination among different enterprises, often under different supervising ministries. If the discussion above on industrial organisation indicates the difficulty of achieving this in a domestic context, it is clear that in the Western export-market context further complications are added (e.g. the role of foreign trade enterprises), while in the CMEA market context the existing system of foreign trade decision-making poses still greater problems. Nevertheless, these problems are under active discussion among economists, and in a number of areas (e.g. foreign trade rights) changes have been made in regulations to allow greater flexibility (Varga, 1978; Kozma, 1978; Marer, Chapter 8 of this volume).

I do not want to suggest that the expected dynamic between EWIC and CMEA specialisation has not materialised at all. But where it has, it seems to have operated in one direction or the other, rather than lead to a mutual reinforcement of developments, at least until now. Hungarian opinion seems to have shifted over the years: in the early 1970s great optimism on this 'dynamic'; after the Western oil-price rise and recession, a greater emphasis on CMEA specialisation; in the light of Soviet oil-price rises and the irredeemably 'traditional' nature of CMEA co-operation, renewed emphasis on the West.

5   Conclusion

Not surprisingly, no clear verdict can be given on the success or failure of Hungary's strategy in EWIC. It is clear that a number of firms have achieved considerable success, but this is by no means restricted to those engaged in 'real' co-operation. In recent years more attention has been paid by both enterprises and the responsible authorities to the *actual content* of relations with Western enterprises than to the sort of package that these relations are wrapped in. This seems to me to be absolutely justified, given the great diversity of motives and of elements that coexist, often uneasily, under the heading of co-operation. While the Hungarian authorities still have hopes of an increase in the number of equity joint ventures, and of the realisation of genuine production and technological co-operation with Western firms under contractual EWIC, the main policy emphasis is likely to be on the several components of the co-operative process: export promotion credits; purchase of Western licences; reform of the institutional structure of foreign trade; and, above all, reforms in the 'enterprise-orienting' spheres of prices and state–enterprise financial relations. EWIC may recede in importance *per se*, but it stands to benefit from these trends *if* they do in fact materialise in the 1980s.

Appendix: Tables

Table 6.1   *Turnover in Hungarian – Western co-operation agreements, 1975 – 6.*

Year	Co-operation imports ($m) (1)	Co-operation exports ($m) (2)	Total exports to developed capitalist countries ($m.) (3)	Co-operation exports as % of total (4)
1975	31	50	1,325	3·8
1976	39	52	1,553	3·3

Sources: Columns 1 and 2. Izikné (1979), p. 185.
  Column 3. Calculated from *Külkereskedelmi Statisztikai Évkönyv* (1977).

Table 6.2   *EWIC agreements by sector, 1972, 1974 and 1976.*

Sector	Mid 1972		End 1974		1976	
	No.	%	No.	%	No.	%
Engineering	122	73·5	245	66·4	366	76·3
Chemicals	13	7·8	33	8·9	19	4·0
Light industry	10	6·0	41	11·1	67	14·0
Agriculture and food industry	21	12·7	46	12·5	14	2·9
Construction			4	1·1	14	2·9
Total	166	100·0	369	100·0	480	100·0

Sources: Mid 1972. UNECE (1973).
  End 1974. Marketing in Hungary, no. 2 (1975).
  1976. Derived from *Business Eastern Europe* (22 July 1977), p. 226.

Table 6.3   *EWIC agreements by partner country, 1977.*

Partner's country of origin	% of total number of contracts	% of value of deliveries	
		Hungarian imports	Hungarian exports
FGR	50	45	41
Austria	9	7	10
Sweden	6	13	10
Italy	6	5	18
France	5	5	3
Switzerland	5	4	2
UK	5	2	2
Yugoslavia	5	17	12
Netherlands	3	0	1
USA	3	1	1
Other	4	2	1
Total	100	100	100

Source: Business Eastern Europe (5 August 1977).

Table 6.4 *Type of agreement: Hungary in comparison with other European CMEA countries, 1976 (%).*

Type of agreement	Hungary	Poland	USSR	Rest of European CMEA
Licensing (with at least some buy-back)	33	27	8	25
Deliveries of plant and equipment against counterdeliveries of product	14	25	63	29
Co-production or product specialisation	47	33	20	30
Subcontracting	6	3	3	5
Joint ventures	—	—	—	2
Joint projects in third countries	0	12	6	9
Total	100	100	100	100

Notes: Based on a sample of 300 out of 1,200 agreements extant in 1976.
(—) = none in sample.
Source: *UN Economic Bulletin for Europe*, vol. 29 (1) 1977.

Table 6.5 *Licence trade turnover, 1970—7 ($ million at current prices).*

Currency	1970	1971	1972	1973	1974	1976	1977
Imports							
Rouble	0·01	0·52	0·22	0·32	0·63	0·41	0·70
$ etc.	1·48	6·20	5·02	3·29	10·43	9·75	13·93
Total	1·49	6·72	5·25	3·61	11·06	10·16	14·64
Exports							
Rouble	0·004	0·12	0·18	0·11	0·09	0·09	0·18
$ etc.	0·43	0·62	0·75	2·87	1·21	3·32	2·37
Total	0·44	0·73	0·94	2·98	1·31	3·41	2·55

Source: *Külkereskedelmi Statisztikai Évkönyv* (1974, 1977).

Table 6.6   *Classification of co-operation agreements for twelve Hungarian engineering enterprises, 1975.*

	Type of agreement	No.	%
1	Contract manufacture	8	16
	– of which, evolving towards type 3:	1	
2	Supply of inputs with buy-back	16	32
	– of which, evolving towards type 3:	5	
3	Co-production	17	34
	– of which, evolving towards type (3 + 4)	8	
4	Joint development	2	4
5	Joint tendering	5	10
6	Turnkey supply outside Hungary	2	4
	Total	50	100

Notes: Type 2 includes agreements that involve the sale of a licence or know-how by one firm to another and those involving the sale of machinery or materials for processing. This category is not restricted to those cases in which buy-back is exclusively of 'resultant' products; this is in accordance with actual Hungarian practice.

In type 3 agreements each partner produces complementary subassemblies, parts or elements in a series. Either partner or both may complete the production and sale of the final product.

Type 4 includes joint research, development and design, up to but not including actual production.

Type 6 is included here because, although no contract partner is involved (as in type 5), such activity invariably involves close collaboration with the customer, other contractors, suppliers, and so on, and it indicates a high degree of competence in international business.

Source: Radice (1978), p. 286.

Table 6.7 *Participation in international production co-operation by subsector in the machine-building and metallurgy sector, 1969–74.*

							No. of enterprises in subsector
	No. of enterprises participating						
Subsector	1969	1970	1971	1972	1973	1974	1977
A Machines and machinery equipment	7	11	11	13	15	17	109
B Transport vehicles	2	4	5	5	5	5	44
C Heavy electrical equipment	3	3	4	4	4	4	34
D Telecommunications and vacuum technical	1	3	3	3	4	5	23
E Instruments	3	5	6	7	7	9	44
F Mass metal goods	—	3	7	8	9	8	67
Total for sector	16	29	36	40	44	48	321

Note: Tables 7–9 are based on data that include co-operation with CMEA enterprises as well as Western firms.

Sources: 1969–74. *Ipari Adatok*, no. 2 (1975), p. 94.
1977. *Statisztikai Évkönyv* (1978).

Table 6.8 *Production under international co-operation by subsector in the machine-building and metallurgy sector: final output as a percentage of total output in the sector, 1969–74.*

Subsector (as Table 6.7)	1969	1970	1971	1972	1973	1974
A	1·6	0·7	1·1	2·5	2·8	4·1
B	0·2	1·2	1·1	0·9	1·0	1·0
C	0·3	0·3	1·3	0·6	0·7	2·0
D	0·0	0·2	0·6	0·7	0·8	1·9
E	1·0	4·4	5·9	3·5	3·1	8·0
F	—	0·4	2·2	4·3	4·5	4·5
Total for sector	0·5	0·9	1·5	1·8	1·9	2·9

Note and sources: As Table 6.7.

Table 6.9 *Production under international co-operation in the machine-building and metallurgy sector: number of products produced, 1969–74.*

	1969	1970	1971	1972	1973	1974
Total for sector	21	44	68	94	108	138

Note and sources: As Table 6.7.

Table 6.10   *Participation in international production co-operation by country in the machine-building and metallurgy sector, 1973–4.*

Country	No. of international production co-operations		Country share in the value of output under co-operations (%)	
	1973	1974	1973	1974
Socialist countries				
USSR	10	15	38·9	28·2
Yugoslavia	14	10	13·4	5·2
GDR	10	11	12·8	8·2
Poland	5	9	4·2	4·8
Czechoslovakia	7	9	1·4	5·1
Bulgaria	2	1	0·0	0·5
Romania	—	1	—	0·6
Subtotal	48	56	70·7	52·6
Capitalist countries				
FGR	37	56	15·9	23·8
Sweden	3	5	5·1	5·9
Italy	6	10	4·5	5·0
Austria	4	6	2·5	1·3
Turkey	1	1	0·4	3·8
UAR	1	—	0·4	—
UK	4	3	0·3	1·2
Switzerland	2	7	0·1	2·0
France	2	1	0·1	4·3
Belgium	—	1	—	0·1
USA	—	1	—	0·0
India	—	1	—	0·0
Netherlands	—	2	—	0·0
Subtotal	60	82	29·3	47·4
Total	108	138	100·0	100·0

Source: As Table 6.7, p. 95.

Industrial co-operation 129

Table 6.11 *Structure of Hungarian foreign trade with non-socialist countries by sector, 1960–77.*

Sector	1960	1965	1970	1974	1977
Imports (% of annual total)					
FE	0·1	0·3	0·8	3·2	2·8
RS	74·1	60·7	60·0	62·8	57·7
MC	11·0	11·8	12·0	11·9	16·1
IC	2·5	2·6	6·1	4·2	4·7
AF	12·3	24·7	21·3	17·9	18·8
Total	100·0	100·0	100·0	100·0	100·0
Exports (% of annual total)					
FE	2·5	1·7	1·9	1·3	5·4
RS	30·0	32·8	41·6	40·4	34·7
MC	8·0	6·4	7·4	8·4	11·4
IC	19·8	19·9	15·9	19·3	20·8
AF	39·8	39·1	33·2	30·6	27·7
Total	100·0	100·0	100·0	100·0	100·0

FE = fuels and electrical energy.
RS = raw materials, semi-finished products and spare parts.
MC = machinery, transport equipment and other capital goods.
IC = industrial consumer goods.
AF = agricultural and food industry products.

Sources: 1960–74. Ipari Adatok, no. 2 (1975), p. 94.
   1977. Statisztikai Évkönyv (1978).
         Calculated from:
1960–74: Külkereskedelmi Statisztikai Évkönyv, 1974, table 12, pp. 30–33
1977   : KSÉ, table 18 (p. 41) and 19 (p. 47)

Table 6.12   *Share of developed capitalist countries in non-socialist trade by sector, 1974 and 1977 (%).*

Sector	Imports 1974	1977	Exports 1974	1977
FE	14·2	5·5	99·9	99·7
RS	87·9	91·9	83·8	83·4
MC	99·9	99·8	36·0	31·4
IC	82·8	77·4	78·8	78·2
AF	62·6	32·7	89·5	83·7
All sectors	82·2	79·0	80·8	77·4

FE = fuels and electrical energy.
RS = raw materials, semi-finished products and spare parts.
MC = machinery, transport equipment and other capital goods.
IC = industrial consumer goods.
AF = agricultural and food industry products.

Sources: As Table 6.11.
Calculated from:
1974: KSÉ 1974, tables 17 (pp. 42–3) and 19 (46–7)
1977: KSÉ 1977, tables 22 (pp. 54–5) and 24 (58–9)

Acknowledgement: Chapter 6

This chapter is based on research carried out under a Leverhulme Research Fellowship that I held at the Centre for Contemporary European Studies, University of Sussex, from 1974 to 1976, and under a grant from the Social Science Research Council (UK) to the Department of Economics, University of Stirling, for research on the Hungarian economy, in 1978–9. I am also grateful to the Karl Marx University of Economics, Budapest, and the Institute for World Economy, Budapest, for their help and hospitality during my research visits. Finally, I would like to thank Paul Marer for his perceptive comments on an earlier version of this chapter.

References: Chapter 6

Ausch, S. (1972), *Theory and Practice of CMEA Cooperation* (Budapest: Akadémiai Kiadó).
Balassa, A. (1975), 'Central Development Programs in Hungary', *Acta Oeconomica*, vol. 14 (1), pp. 91–108.
Bauer, T. (1975), 'A vállalatok ellentmondásos helyzete a magyar gazdasági mechanizmusban' (The contradictory position of the enterprise in the Hungarian economic mechanism), *Közgazdasági Szemle*, vol. 22 (6), pp. 725–35.
Business Eastern Europe (various issues).
Economic Research Institute (1974), 'On industrial big enterprises', *Acta Oeconomica*, vol. 12 (1), pp. 97–117.

Gerencsér, F. (1978), 'Venni vagy újra feltalálni?' (To buy or to discover anew?), *Figyelő*, vol. 22 (16), pp. 1–2.

Izikné, H. G. (1979), *Magyarország a Keleti-Nyugati Gazdasági Kapcsolatokban* (Hungary in East–West Economic Relations) (Budapest: Kossuth Könyvkiadó).

Kozma, F. (1978), 'Túlzott sietség nélkül' (Without excessive haste), *Figyelő*, vol. 22 (16), p. 5.

Kun, J. (1978), 'Az exportfejlesztési pályazat eredményei' (The results of the export development policy), *Figyelő*, vol. 22 (35), p. 9.

Laki, M. (1975), 'Competitive situation and product pattern of Hungarian enterprises on the market of consumer goods', *Acta Oeconomica*, vol. 14 (2–3), pp. 251–67.

Laki, M. (1977), 'The function of the state in the introduction of new products and new technologies', Institute for Economic and Market Research, Budapest (mimeo.).

Mándel, M., and Müller, J. (1974), 'Aims of an export-oriented economic policy', *Acta Oeconomica*, vol. 13 (1), pp. 35–47.

McMillan, C. H. (1977), 'East–West industrial cooperation', in Joint Economic Committee, *East European Economies Post-Helsinki* (Washington, DC: US Government Printing Office).

Pécsi, K. (1975), 'Még egyszer a Komplex Programrol és a keleti–nyugati kooperációról' (Once more on the Complex Program and on East–West co-operation), *Világgazdaság*, vol. 7 (36), supplement (21 February).

Péter, P. (1975), 'Hozzászólás a "Komplex Program és a keleti–nyugati kooperáció" cimü cikkhez' (Contribution to the article entitled 'Complex Program and East–West co-operation'), *Világgazdaság*, vol. 7 (16), supplement (24 January).

Radice, H. K. (1978), 'Hungarian engineering enterprises in East–West industrial cooperation', in F. Levcik (ed.), *International Economics: Comparisons and Dependences* (Vienna and New York: Springer-Verlag).

Róth, A. (1978), 'A "csináld magád" sokba kerül' (Do-it-yourself is costly), *Figyelő*, vol. 22 (19), p. 7.

Sándor, I. (1978), 'Az exportnövelő beruházások sorsa' (Export-increasing investments), *Figyelő*, vol. 22 (33), p. 7.

Schweitzer, I. (1978), 'Választék és vállalatnagyság' (Choice and enterprise size), *Figyelő*, vol. 22 (12), p. 3.

Starr, R. I. and Radice, H. K. (1976), *Hungary*, Chase World Information Series on East–West Industrial Cooperation and Joint Ventures (Chase World Information Corporation, New York).

Sternthál, J. (1977), 'Koncentráció és specializáció a szerszám-gépiparban' (Concentration and specialisation in the computer industry), *Ipargazdasági Szemle* (4), pp. 45–53.

Tardos, M. (1976), 'Enterprise independence and central control', *Eastern European Economics*, vol. 15 (1), pp. 24–44.

United Nations Economic Commission for Europe (UNECE) (1973), *Analytical Report on Industrial Cooperation among ECE Countries*.

Varga, Gy. (1978), 'Túlzott sietség–buktatokkal' (Excessive haste – with difficulties), *Figyelő*, vol. 22 (15), p. 3.

Chapter 7

Imported Technology, Hungarian Industrial Development and Factors Impeding the Emergence of Innovative Capability

1 Introduction

In the 1970s Eastern European states in general and Hungary in particular expanded their imports of Western industrial technology. The primary purpose of this strategy has been to attain intensive economic growth by increasing the efficiency of factors of production and achieving higher growth rates (Izikné, 1979, p. 70; Kozma, 1970, pp. 163–77; Szita, 1977, pp. 69–72). In order to realise such economic growth, the strategy also includes related policy objectives: changing product structures (eliminating outdated and uncompetitive products); increasing product specialisation; and altering trade structures through greater export-oriented production (Izikné, 1979, p. 70; Szita, 1977, pp. 69–72; Levcik and Stankovsky, 1979, p. 40). In Hungary this orientation towards greater division of labour is predicated on two important assumptions. First, it is presumed that enterprises using Western technology (licences, know-how and machinery) can escape from their past experience of industrial development and learn to assimilate and further develop imported technology (Kozma, 1976, p. 256). Secondly, it is accepted that Hungarian governmental agencies can regulate the impact of technology transfer and promote innovative capability in industry. The objective in this chapter is critically to evaluate these assumptions, arguing that the emergence of innovative capability and related attempts to stimulate the adaptation of imported technology collide with traditionally performed extensive-oriented production activities as well as with the historically generated structure of industrialisation.

Focusing on Hungarian industry, this study outlines the countervailing tendencies that undermine the emergence of innovative capability at the enterprise level and impede the effectiveness of the regulation process. First, it will briefly review some factors, emanating from the experience of past industrial development, that condition the absorption of imported technology in contemporary Hungarian industry. Secondly, by analysing some core attributes of industrial innovation and their impact on the adaptation of technology, it will assess the emergence of innovative capability within the present industrial structure, drawing on the experience of three sectors of the Hungarian metallurgy and engineering industry. Finally, the study will examine the role and effectiveness of Hungarian state agencies involved in regulating this adaptation process.

2 The pattern of industrialisation and factors shaping the contemporary domestic industrial environment

Before proceeding further it is necessary to clarify the term 'technology'. In the context of this study technology means systematic (scientific) knowledge about production activity, embodied in machines, designs, formulas and the like, and it also refers to general 'know-how', including, for example, organisational procedures used in co-ordinating production, procurement, marketing, and research and development (R and D) (Hewett, 1975, p. 377). This technology is transferred to Eastern Europe through a variety of channels, perhaps the most prevalent one involving the dissemination of information through foreign technical journals. Other types of transfers include: the purchase of foreign products for the purposes of reverse engineering; the purchase of products (i.e. machinery) for direct use in production; and the purchase of licences, know-how and training. This latter form of transfer introduces new production processes, possibly through turnkey plants or joint ventures, and so on, resulting in new products. It is an important type of transfer, because it involves complex institutional arrangements in the acquisition and payback phases. (For a review see McMillan, 1977.)

The capacity of enterprises to absorb foreign technology is conditioned by the prevailing domestic industrial environment (see Cooper, 1972; Patel, 1974; Sagasti, 1979). This environment has emerged from the historical experience of industrialisation and signifies the propensity to utilise and create endogenous technology. It is characterised by economic institutions based on the principle of either market or plan, which allocate scarce resources, including technology, between industrial sectors as well as firms. In Hungary the industrial environment has evolved from the country's historical role in the international division of labour as well as from the type of extensive autarchy-based industrialisation that has been pursued in the post-Second World War period.

(a)   *The PreWar background*[1]
Hungary's late industrialisation has shown the classic characteristics of industrial development in Eastern Europe in general. Before the First World War the country primarily supplied raw materials and agricultural products in exchange for machinery and other manufactured goods. This 'peripheral' form of industrialisation was reinforced by an archaic social structure dominated by a landowning aristocracy and by the subordinate position of Hungary in the Austro-Hungarian monarchy. Industrial development prior to 1919 was mostly linked to agriculture, often dependent on state subsidies and, once large-scale industry had begun to emerge in the 1900s, dominated by a small number of large banks with strong foreign connections. Pioneering work in certain industries (notably the electrical and pharmaceutical) could not compensate for the lack of a strong indigenous entrepreneurial class.

After 1919, with the country dismembered by the Treaty of Trianon and torn by civil war, economic recovery required huge foreign loans, which were used to promote a narrow and highly protected economic development in which an inefficient agriculture still took priority, thanks to its social and political power. Hungarian industry quickly fell behind that of Western Europe, and domestic invention and innovation became almost non-existent.

Through the 1930s Hungary became steadily more and more tied economically and politically to Germany, which was interested in the preservation of the agrarian character of the Hungarian economy. As industry became incorporated into the German war effort, its structure at last underwent significant changes, with an influx of German technology for production of aircraft, engines, and so on. Much of this new capacity was, however, destroyed in the closing years of the war.

(b)   *Technological development under the Soviet model of industrialisation*
In the aftermath of the Second World War, the Marxist–Leninist regime that came to power, with Soviet help, conformed to Hungarian tradition. It too relied on external forces to maintain domestic power. Inevitably, economic development was subordinated to the goals, values and norms diffused from the Soviet Union (Marer, 1976; Abonyi and Sylvain, 1977; Abonyi, 1978), and under such circumstances it is not surprising that the regime resorted to Soviet principles of economic organisation. It imposed a centrally planned model of economic management, with its own contradictions, on a weak industrial structure that had previously relied on external sources for technological development. Hungarian planners followed the Soviet model closely. They introduced an autarchy-based industrial strategy, isolating industry from its prior international connections, and redirected necessary trade to socialist countries, particularly the Soviet Union.

Compared to past levels, impressive gains were made in industrialisation, especially in such sectors as engineering, metallurgy and chemicals. Nevertheless, even within such sectors technological advancement was limited, and industrial innovative potential was impeded (Berend, 1969, pp. 84–5).

Organisational impediments. The character of centrally planned industrialisation and the peculiar trade relationship initiated with the Soviet Union have been major forces retarding Hungarian technological development. After the Second World War central planners were faced with the task of reconstructing industry as well as transforming an essentially backward economy. Consequently, they embarked upon a programme of forced industrialisation. Planning, especially in the 1950s, concentrated national resources in specific sectors to maximise industrial growth. This created an imbalance in the economy, leading to declining output in some sectors (e.g. agriculture) (Berend, 1969, p. 82). In their preoccupation with rapid economic growth, central planners resorted to extensive means, constantly increasing investment capital, labour and raw materials to achieve greater industrial output. Under such an industrial strategy the criterion for success had a quantitative orientation, not a qualitative one. The main objective was continually to increase output. As long as this could be achieved by adding extensive forces of production, little technological change was necessary.

From an organisational point of view, central planning did not sufficiently stimulate technological development during the 1950s and 1960s (Berend, 1969). First, it did not provide sufficient planning of R and D at the enterprise level, permitting systematic integration of technology with production. Instead, R and D were centralised to a great extent, funded primarily from state budgets and not necessarily intended to meet specific enterprise priorities. An artificial linkage emerged between technology and the production process – one subject to the direction and control of hierarchical decision-making. Planner preferences and ministry prerogatives prevailed, despite their being unresponsive to local enterprise conditions. Secondly, effective utilisation of technology was hampered by setting production targets from above. These goals produced incongruity among plans for sectors, industrial branches as well as enterprises. Thirdly, given the uncertainty created by such arbitrary decision-making, and in view of the supply bottlenecks caused by an unequal allocation of resources, enterprise-managers were less inclined to take the risks necessary to encourage innovation in the production process.

Finally, in general, under extensive growth the lack of incentives provided by institutional and organisational conditions of central planning poses major obstacles to the introduction of new technologies (see Woroniak, 1970, pp. 100–12). For example, a lack of parametric prices presents problems in calculating the efficiency of production methods and hence in determining the cost and utility of employing one technology as opposed to another (see Berend, 1969). The emphasis on planned quantitative production targets under central planning is at the expense of efficiency (Berend, 1969, pp. 82–3) – a phenomenon integrally related to the application of technology. Forsaking market and profit principles, moreover, also de-emphasises the need for technology, because there is no urgency to produce goods for discriminating buyers at lower cost and better quality.

The consequences of new trade relations. Its new trading relationship isolated Hungary from the capitalist world market, creating further obstacles to the development of technology. Throughout the 1950s and most of the 1960s, not only was Hungarian industry shielded from Western competitors – a fact that again decreased the need for efficiency and development of new technology – but also, and more importantly, its ties to advanced Western technology were severed. Western licences and know-how were not bought. So technological progress was attained primarily by usurping information from foreign technical journals or by 'reverse engineering' from imported Western machinery. In many cases enterprises were cut off from their traditional foreign sources of technology and had to rely on their own resources. This created problems, especially if the enterprise was a subsidiary of a foreign firm before nationalisation and its R and D capacities were centralised with the parent firm outside Hungary. In such cases enterprises had to take a fresh start at rediscovering technology.

The quasi-industrial development (see Jánossy, 1970) that occurred under extensive economic growth did not require much technological change. In view of organisational impediments and the absence of traditional ties to technology, enterprises, when left to their own resources, relied on the know-how that they had accumulated before 1950 (Tardos, 1979, p. 8). However, a higher technological level was not required. Hungary's predominant trade partner in the post-Second World War period, the Soviet Union, given its own level of industrial development and vast market, easily absorbed the lower quality and technologically less advanced production, until the early 1970s.

Pressures for economic reform. By the second half of the 1960s, there was a growing realisation that the sources of extensive growth were exhausted. With a labour shortage increased reliance on technology was required to maintain levels of output. More importantly, authorities recognised that the Soviet model of autarchic industrialisation is not applicable in a small country like Hungary, which not only lacks necessary manpower but also is resource-poor (Berend, 1969, p. 86). In addition, given the country's small internal market it was necessary to intensify foreign trade in order to raise the level of national income (Bognár, 1967, esp. p. 163). Debates on economic policy conducted under the auspices of the Central Committee concluded, in the mid 1960s, that increased production specialisation was necessary according to more discriminating 'selective' development policies, concentrating investment in those industries which would yield the most efficient results (Timár, 1975, pp. 138–47). Outdated low-quality production had to be eliminated (this was in line with the new Soviet trade demands in the early 1970s), and more export-oriented production had to be encouraged through greater international division of labour (see Bognár, 1967; Vajda, 1967; Szita, 1977, pp. 62–72). This emergent policy perspective required imports of Western technology to make factors of production more efficient as well as the introduction of a new form of economic management. Other Eastern European countries (i.e. Poland, Romania and, until 1968, Czechoslovakia), were contemplating similar import strategies, although not necessarily identical economic reforms. Moreover, given Soviet goals of normalising economic relations with the West under the rubric of *détente*, as well as of encouraging greater product specialisation in Council for Mutual Economic Assistance (CMEA) countries, the international environment made possible the pursuit of Hungarian policy objectives.

It is not the intention of this study to review the performance of the New Economic Mechanism introduced on 1 January 1968; that is done by others in this volume. The objective here is merely to point out that, as one of their objectives, the reforms intended to stimulate efficiency in the production process. This required greater technological change and a resort to imports of Western industrial technology to supplement domestic resources. One intended advantage of the reforms in this regard was the dismantling of direct planning procedures. Instead, indirect financial regulators (e.g. fiscal instruments, wage and price controls, credit policy, foreign exchange controls) were introduced to stimulate a market environment. The transfer of a substantial degree of decision-making authority to enterprise managers was another important aspect of the economic reforms. Less emphasis placed on instructions to enterprises was a move away from using plan indicators and quantitative output. Profitability became the measure of enterprise performance. Under a more decentralised investment scheme enterprises could retain funds from profits to generate new investments in many areas, one of which included technological development. In order to permit such enterprise autonomy, prices had to be made more flexible than before. They had to reflect actual production costs to a greater degree and also be responsive to market forces.

Although the New Economic Mechanism is a more complex

phenomenon than the above attempts to indicate, the brief reference to changes under this system shows that the reforms have led to a new environment for the utilisation of technology – one that is less associated with extensive-based industrial growth. Hungarian policy-makers recognise that 'it is not possible to ensure in all areas simultaneously the conditions for the introduction of the most up-to-date technology and for a further development which keeps up with the most advanced achievements of technological process' (Szita, 1977, p. 101). They stress, nevertheless, that imported Western technology can be channelled into traditionally advanced fields (Kozma, 1970, pp. 197–200). It is this position that section 3 attempts to evaluate by probing for the emergence of some core attributes of innovation in Hungarian industry.

3 Attributes of innovation and the role of imported technology in Hungarian industrial development

Due to limited R and D resources the objectives of Hungarian science and technology policy are oriented towards the adaptation of imported technology. Recent opinion has stressed that valuable R and D resources should not be wasted on rediscovering technologies available on world markets. Instead, research facilities should concentrate on adaptation (Kozma, 1970, pp. 198–200; Juhász, 1977, p. 225; Kardos, 1978, p. 11), fitting imported technology into domestic conditions and production activity. Moreover, dictated by policies of selective industrialisation and the need to remain competitive with rapidly changing international technology, it has been emphasised that imported technology will be further developed domestically (Kardos, 1978, p. 11). and lead to the introduction of new products (Juhász, 1977, p. 225). The ultimate goal of assimilation, then, is to lay ground for the development of innovative potential (Kozma, 1976, p. 256) – the ability to introduce new products through new production processes involving new types of technologies generated from the enterprise's own resources. There is an awareness that mere acquisition of foreign technology does not ensure maximisation of long-term industrial development and economic growth. Failing both to improve foreign technology and to develop the ability to reproduce it domestically in newer and more advanced forms, as Kozma (1970, p. 200) pointed out, will reduce affected sectors to technological dependence.

Ideally, the ability to adapt new technology in the production process is a precondition for the development of innovative potential. This has also been emphasised by Freeman (1974). Three important and mutually reinforcing attributes of innovation, which also have been the objective of regulation, include: a scientifically and technologically oriented industrial milieu (Freeman, 1974); a strong professional in-house R and D (Freeman, 1974, p. 170; Rekettye, 1978); and compatible technology with the rest of the plant as well as with suppliers (Rekettye, 1978, p. 139). If innovative potential is emerging, the three symptoms ought to be present in Hungarian industry.

By examining seven enterprises that I studied in 1978, in three sectors of industry under the auspices of the Metallurgy and Engineering Ministry, the remainder of this section will assess the presence of the above three attributes of innovation in Hungarian industry. For the purposes of reference, it is noted that enterprises A, B and C were part of the public vehicles sector, D and E belonged to the machine tools sector, and F and G formed part of the electrical generating-equipment sector. Each of the sectors had major acquisitions of Western technology in the early 1970s. Moreover, the ministry under which they function uses nearly 70 per cent of all imported licences and employs 38 per cent of R and D workers in Hungarian industry (Havás, 1975, p. 133). The information for the analysis was gathered through interviews with the enterprises and supplemented by extensive newspaper sources.

(a) Scientifically and technologically oriented industrial milieu (STOIM)

This orientation is revealed through a self-generated desire to develop and apply new (innovative) technology as well as through the disposition to renew in the production process. It is manifested in those institutions centrally concerned with reproduction of industrial culture, including education, infrastructure, marketing, and so on as well as production. Its existence can be determined by examining the following set of hypotheses. If STOIM is present in Hungarian industry, then:

(1) There is a tradition of applying (which also includes adapting) new technology successfully into the production process.
(2) There is a desire to renew technology.

The following subhypothesis also applies. If STOIM exists, then:

(3) There is a tendency to seek domestic rather than international solutions in the renewal of technology, at the enterprise or sectoral level.

With regard to the first hypothesis, Hungarian enterprises acknowledge that economic and technical resources are often insufficient, and in a majority of cases they lack a tradition in developing and applying new technology and see no immediate alternatives to importing it. The lacuna between basic and applied research reinforces this attitude. For instance, some enterprises, in conjunction with research institutes, have carried out basic research on some technologies that has proved quite productive. However, they have been unable to transfer the fruits of this research to the applied stage, and as a result they have later been forced to import these technologies from the West.

These general trends do not apply to all enterprises. One in particular, enterprise F, had a strong tradition of applying new technology successfully. This attribute was part of its historical development; the enterprise was already a technological leader in the second decade of this century. It had a rich heritage of technological achievements, which to a certain degree oriented its perspective towards the use and development of new technology. This was represented most prominently by its acquisition of a major technological system in the mid 1960s; the enterprise successfully adapted and further developed the system through its own resources and later marketed it in the West. Enterprises D and E, while not so rich in tradition, had also achieved relative success in the development and application of new technology through the utilisation of their own resources. Their success was in part due to intensive involvement in CMEA-co-ordinated R and D and primarily limited to particular single-product technologies not requiring the development and application of whole technological systems, usually involved in a new production process. Although both enterprises engaged in basic research on new technological systems in the early and mid 1960s, this activity did not advance to the applied stage, and the technologies were later imported from the West.

In the four remaining cases the enterprises (A, B, C and G) had generally been unable to develop new technologies of their own, despite the fact that they had previously imported licences. There were several reasons for this. First, as part of their historical conditioning some enterprises had received foreign technology and de-emphasised the development of their own technical capability. Secondly, others had been unable successfully to adapt previously imported licences and therefore had not progressed to a stage where they could generate their own technology. Thirdly, and perhaps the most important, there seemed to be insufficient economic and technical resources within these enterprises for development of new technology and, in some cases, for the successful adaptation of imported ones.

The second hypothesis, a desire to renew technology, is another indicator of an existing scientific–technological orientation. While there is a recognition that technology generally has to be renewed in order to remain competitive internationally, this perception is tempered by resource constraints and historical orientation. Large investments made in the acquisition of complete technological systems, as in the case of enterprises A, B and C, decrease the propensity for rapid renewal. There are less resources allocated for renewing the technology, and it has to be employed for longer periods of time (in comparison to the West or other single-product technologies employed in Hungary) in order to recoup high costs. In any event, given a lack of resources for the development of new technology and limited expertise, success in renewing imported technology has been achieved in smaller and less complex aspects of the system. The whole system can be renewed only if there is a strong professional R and D base, as discussed in section (b) below.

As previously suggested, the motivation to renew imported technology is present. However, in addition to resource constraints it is also moderated by a disposition to seek international solutions, and this leads to the examination of the subhypothesis. The tendency favouring international solutions is part of an historically conditioned technological syndrome that undermines the development of a domestic self-generating technological orientation in production activity. When technology is renewed, there is a strong desire to obtain it from foreign sources. Previous (pre-1945) trade connections had a significant impact on the sources of imported technologies in enterprises A, C, E, F and G. This is reinforced by the attitude in most cases that foreign, particularly Western, technology is better and of higher quality than domestically developed alternatives. It is also an easier solution when compared to the bottlenecks incurred in deploying developmental resources at home. This view is particularly underscored in enterprises participating in Central Development Programmes, which may require a rapid and extensive infusion of new technology on a sectoral level.

In assessing the existence of STOIM, the evidence refutes the first hypothesis, confirms the second and disproves the subhypothesis. Historical forces shaping industrialisation have produced a situation in which there is an underdevelopment of STOIM. This affects innovation potential. Without the emergence of STOIM around them, enterprise-managers, while they may understand the importance of the innovation cycle, are less inclined to take the necessary risks involved in introducing new products through new production processes. The present organisation of the economy also reinforces this attitude. Despite reforms managers still have to contend with hierarchically determined priorities (through bargaining), supply bottlenecks and uncertainties due to centralised investment. (For similar points see Deák, 1978; Laki, 1976; and Bauer, 1976.) Thus, the traditional weakness of central planning in applying new technology is maintained, because there is little stimulus in this environment systematically to integrate innovation with production. Furthermore, even in sectors or enterprises that can adapt imported technology more routinely, there is a tendency, conditioned to a great extent by experience of industrialisation, to seek international rather than domestic solutions. This creates a vicious circle; a lack of STOIM supports reliance on imports, which perpetuates a lack of STOIM.

The fact that technology has to be sought from external sources is not the impediment. Many other countries obtain foreign technology, and Hungary is certainly not a unique example. Industrialised countries, however, generally acquire foreign technology because: (1) they specialise in the development of certain types of technologies and import others; (2) although they have the economic and technical resources, it would be uneconomical for them to develop and market certain technologies; (3) they have a traditional R and D capability that can further develop imported technology; or (4) government commitments require the imports of certain technologies. In the Hungarian case, on the other hand, given a lack of STOIM the propensity to rely on imported technology can lead to a denigration of domestic alternatives, circumscribing full integration of innovation into production and consumption, so that innovation stimulates and supports a changing production and consumption structure and vice versa.

(b)   *Strong professional in-house R and D*
This characteristic derives from the experience that technical progress is a function of a highly organised R and D base in which there is a major emphasis on scientific content and professional specialisation in complex technology (Freeman, 1974). Moreover, scientists are engaged in a research function within the firm's overall division of labour, and their aim is to create new technology. To fulfil their objectives they interact on a regular basis with professional people (i.e. engineers and technicians) who are engaged in the production process. A professional in-house R and D capability therefore involves the coupling of two fundamental attributes, which are integral parts of innovative potential: first, the inventive idea that derives from the scientific end of research; and secondly, an adequate knowledge of the production process, into which development work is introduced. It is not being proposed here that in-house R and D are a substitute basis for all innovative activity. A liaison between other research institutes and enterprises can stimulate in-house activities. However, if innovation is to be efficiently integrated into the production process, an in-house R and D capability is essential.

Ideally, this coupling process in the R and D system should go through four stages (see Freeman, 1974, p. 23). The first includes basic research performed by scientists, who produce ideas, theories, formulas, and so on. The second stage involves inventive work and applied research. In addition to scientists, engineers and technicians are involved, and their combined efforts produce patents, working models, research papers, and so on. The third stage is characterised by experimental developmental work, in which the previous inventive output is augmented by the work of engineers and draftsmen. This level of activity usually yields blueprints, technical specifications, pilot plants, prototypes, and so on. The fourth and final stage of activity is represented by new-type plant construction to accommodate development output.

Although the above four stages are part of an 'offensive' innovation strategy – one designed to achieve technical and market leadership (Freeman, 1974, p. 259) – it is not unfair to apply them in an evaluation of the three sectors of Hungarian industry. Part of Hungarian import strategy seeks to convert the fruits of Western technology into a base for attaining leadership in certain products on the socialist (i.e. CMEA) market (Kozma, 1974). In view of this and the fact that the public vehicle and machine tool sectors manufacture specialised products containing Western technology for the CMEA, and given that enterprise F has co-production agreements with Soviet enterprises in the electrical generating-equipment sector, it seemed appropriate for me to analyse innovation as an 'offensive' strategy.

In contrast to the above requisites of R and D, the Hungarian enterprises surveyed conducted only a minimal amount of basic research. In fact, most – four out of seven, including enterprises A, B and C, which formed the nucleus of a whole product sector and used imported technology systems on a wide scale – contracted out their basic research to external institutions. The R and D network is by and large organised outside the enterprise unit, along sectoral and functional lines. This means that each ministry, including the Ministry of Metallurgy and Engineering, also has its own research institutes. These institutions, which perform most of the scientific work, receive a majority of their financing from central authorities – the state budget, ministries or the State Committee for Technical Development – and locate their research in an overall scientific and technical plan. This is part of a centralising tendency in scientific research (Rupp, 1977) that encourages vertical integration and isolation from the production process. Although these institutes also work on research contracts for enterprises, only enterprises D and F had developed close and fruitful interaction between basic research and the production process. On the whole the scientific research remains segregated from enterprise production activity.

While enterprises are endowed with a Technical Development Fund (TDF) that includes monies for research, the primary aim of TDF is not to stimulate basic in-house research but to promote product development (adjustments to product technical parameters) and the development of production (bringing new technology into the production process and constructing new facilities). Citing total enterprise expenditures for R and D in 1975, Havás (1975, p. 133) noted that the proportions allocated in TDF included 16·7 per cent for research, 33·6 per cent for product development, and 16·5 per cent for the development of production processes and facilities. The R and D performed by enterprises themselves through TDF were 66·8 per cent of their total expenditure on R and D. From the remaining 33·2 per cent, 22·98 per cent was contracted out, and 10·3 per cent was spent on miscellaneous R and D objectives.

The above distribution has been confirmed by the enterprises surveyed. All but two of the enterprises, namely, D and F, expended their R and D energies on technical adjustments to products and development of the production process. As one enterprise official remarked: 'The R and D division is now constantly preoccupied with resolving the daily problems that plague production. It should be involved in mid- and long-range development of production.' This statement characterises the dominant R and D activities carried out under TDF. It also draws attention to the minimal amount of research done under TDF, by implying that it is of short duration. This has been confirmed by Havás (p. 138), who indicated that most research in this category consists of continually monitoring information on international technology and research for short-term gains. Long-term research, more representative of professional in-house R and D activity, is not feasible at the enterprise level, because, as Havás suggested (pp. 135–8), financial resources are centralised.

From the preceding discussion it is clear that a strong in-house R and D capability is lacking among the enterprises surveyed, by virtue of the fact that a major part of basic research is divorced from the production process. This also undermines innovative potential. The research activity that does take place in-house concentrates on small and less complex technologies, which take less lead time to develop. More importantly, R and D within the enterprise emphasise adjusting and resolving technical problems. All these factors associated with in-house R and D capability have significant implications for imported technology. A weak enterprise R and D capability means that imported technology is not incorporated into a long-term research plan. As a result there is less likelihood of imported technology's being further developed or innovated. On the other hand, the preoccupation of R and D with adjusting technology indicates a potentially strong adaptive capacity that can successfully integrate imported technology into the enterprise's production process. However, this does not escape the issue that the combination of a weak innovative and strong adaptive capacity will further increase technological imports.

(c) *Compatible technology*
One important attribute of innovation is congruence of technological levels, so that new technologies can readily be diffused. By its very

nature innovation affects most of a firm's activity. Innovation does not occur in isolation; one of its most prominent features is the external benefits that it creates within and between firms. If innovation is to fulfil its potential in both intra- and interfirm manufacturing activity, the production processes that have to be linked together must be compatible in terms of their technological levels. There is a similar prerequisite for the diffusion of imported technology in Hungary, because it is intended to be a stimulus to industrial development, and like domestic innovation it is supposed to scatter technological spin-offs in both intra- and interenterprise production activity. Therefore, it is necessary to determine how compatible intra- and interenterprise technology levels are in transmitting these spin-off effects.

The importance of external effects in the innovation context is that they may stimulate innovation elsewhere. Horizontal spin-offs both within the firm and more broadly in the sector may include direct effects. In some cases they may reduce cost (e.g. 'free knowledge' passed on from one engineer trained under an East–West industrial co-operation deal to his colleague who has not been so trained; free use of certain specialised equipment), but more important is increased stimulation to imitate, which can also lead to cost reduction. This means employing a process or method once exposed to it, because it provides an easier solution to the production problem. Enterprises or individuals, on the other hand, not subjected to such a process may not readily resort to imitating it. Many of the external effects are intangible and have already been reviewed by Radice in this volume (Chapter 6). The vertical external effects are similar in nature but, in terms of STOIM, much more important. End users may not only get better value inputs but also be stimulated to undertake their own innovations, which in turn feed back down the chain to other suppliers. Suppliers impelled to improve quality or produce new products for a given innovation find that their own induced changes have wider benefits; some are horizontal at that stage, some again back up to their other users.

In assessing compatibility of technological levels, two general characteristics emerged among the Hungarian enterprises surveyed. First, all had difficulties attaining compatibility, except enterprise A, which was vertically integrated with large acquisitions of imported technology and in relative isolation from the rest of the economy. Secondly, in many cases imported technology (licences or machinery) had been made necessary because previous imports had been incompatible. Intraenterprise problems were generated most frequently by outdated machinery. In enterprise E, for instance, 32 per cent of all machinery was depreciated to zero. In a majority of the cases, machinery and production processes could not provide the quality necessary for effective utilisation of imported technology. As a result there was a slow accumulation of inappropriate technology functioning side by side with the new imports.

The more significant aspect of compatibility relates to interenterprise or, in some cases, sectorwide production activity. Again, all enterprises were affected by compatibility problems, which in some instances seriously hampered the performance of imported technology. The source of the irritant usually varied, depending on the enterprise's division of labour. Out of the seven enterprises, C and G had hardships in securing proper-quality rolled steel for their new technologies, and E could not get delivery of adequate castings for its production process.

Enterprise C acknowledged inappropriate technology among its suppliers at two levels. First, co-operatives that furnished small components were not adequately prepared to supply their products at the proper technical level demanded by the enterprise. As a result the enterprise was forced to provide these suppliers with the necessary know-how, technical assistance and proper materials for production. At another level the same enterprise had trouble securing major parts from no less than six large co-producers. In three of these cases, the parts were not forthcoming because the enterprises in question had difficulties employing newly imported Western technology.

Enterprise B was in a similar position to enterprise C. However, it pointed to some explanations for the bottlenecks. First, most of its co-producers were in monopoly positions and were not quick to respond to external interests. Moreover, such monopolies produced a large assortment of products and did not possess the resources necessary to import technologies for every product line. In some cases this meant that they did not readily acquire licences or other technological imports necessary to make co-producer technological requirements compatible. Enterprise F pointed to another interesting feature, namely, the effect of CMEA co-producers, which could not meet the technical parameters of imported technology. The Hungarian enterprise made technical adjustments to parts after receiving them from the CMEA partner, or it completely took charge of producing the part by vertically integrating it into its own production activity. Indeed, this latter solution is naturally fostered by the structure of Hungarian industry and has been frequently employed by enterprises involved with domestic suppliers.

The concentration of large enterprises in the economy (Inzelt, 1978; Economic Research Institute, 1974) has sometimes been artificially increased by their mutual production activities. These enterprises, some of which are export-oriented in an attempt to balance the cost of imports, are more preoccupied with creating a division of labour and establishing compatible technology within rather than between themselves. A secondary effect of such concentration leaves a technologically and organisationally inadequate background industry (Varga, 1977). Even where Central Development Programmes have established, with a large infusion of imported technology, the basis for intrasectoral compatibility between enterprise technologies, as demonstrated by enterprises A, B and C, their operation is regularly short-circuited by suppliers whose production performance is constantly affected by inappropriate technologies. So there is a built-in tendency vertically to integrate supply linkages within the enterprise, in order to permit effective utilisation of imported technology and create compatibility. While this exacerbates centralisation of production, it goes a long way towards resolving the incompatibility problem between enterprises. The only other solution is to rely on imports instead of domestic suppliers; but quite apart from the short-term balance-of-payments effects, this clearly reduces the overall impact of the imported technology on the domestic economy.

Although presented separately, the above three attributes of innovation do not function in isolation from one another; they are mutually reinforcing. For instance, compatible technologies are more likely to emerge: first, where R and D is determined to capitalise on spin-offs derived from technologies imported into other sectors; and secondly, when there is an orientation towards rapid self-generated renewal of technologies in the production process. If one of the attributes is absent, it is likely to impede the development of others. In the enterprises examined the resource and organisational constraints imposed on in-house R and D, for instance, had a rippling effect on the other two attributes of innovation. These constraints were part of a wider set of countervaling forces reinforced by the historical experience of industrialisation, undermining conditions for full development of the three attributes of innovation analysed above.

On the other hand, the regulation of technology transfer has been one of the most significant policy instruments at the disposal of Eastern European states, and Hungarian governmental agencies are actively engaged in deflecting the negative consequences of imported technology, while at the same time attempting to stimulate its absorption in industry. The following section offers a brief analysis of the role and effectiveness of state agencies involved in this process, with some specific references to their impact on the three attributes of innovation already discussed.

4 The regulation of imported technology

Regulation of imported technology in Hungary can be seen as a process of harmonisation – one that attempts to reconcile the distribution of international technology and capital with government objectives for domestic planned industrial development. Such harmonisation is a decided advantage for Eastern European states, because, as Lodgaard (1973) suggested, it will enable them to import technology into highly endowed R and D sectors, where it is more likely to be successfully absorbed. One aspect of this general harmonisation is the regulation of acquisition, which provides an institutional (technical and financial) umbrella, including a monopoly position for socialist enterprises during the transfer of technology. For instance, this form of regulation enhances enterprise (or foreign-trade enterprise) bargaining power and assures more favourable access to Western technology. Thus, the main purpose of such regulation is to maximise the benefits from importation of technology, relating it to the production of local technology while minimising its adverse effects (Sagasti, 1979, pp. 89–91).

A second aspect of regulation involves the policy instruments that are used to stimulate absorption of technology in the domestic economy. For example, various governmental programmes have been established, with administrative-oriented monitoring and incentive systems, the purpose of which is to assimilate imported technology into intraenterprise as well as into domestic production activities, translating it into innovative potential. Based on detailed interviews with the state organs listed below, it can be said that the function and performance of these systems largely depend on the institution that administers them and on the particular role that it plays: first, in the overall operation of the economy (e.g. financial, technical consultant, planning); and secondly, in the original decision to acquire technology. Some agencies (e.g. the National Planning Office, the ministries) are structurally inclined towards 'direct' planning solutions in the process of regulation, while others (e.g. the Ministry of Finance, the Hungarian National Bank) tend to prefer 'indirect' market forces.

(a)   *Ministry of Metallurgy and Engineering*
One of the most prominent institutions engaged in regulation is the branch ministry. For the purposes of this study, officials in the Ministry of Metallurgy and Engineering were interviewed. It became evident that the Ministry monitors directly the integration of technology from a control office, at least in the preliminary phase. This office and the ministry in general make on-site inspections six months after acquisition to assess how the technology is functioning. Probably the most extensively relied-on monitoring system is the 'registry' data sheet. It is completed by enterprises, detailing the cost, utilisation and perspective performance of each licence acquired. The 'registry' sheets are filed with the ministry every six months (see Nadudvári, 1973). It can check how actual productivity, and therefore employment of technology, correspond to estimates made during licence acquisition.

However, officials admitted that these sheets can be, and are sometimes, manipulated to mislead ministry officials. Unless periodic surprise inspections are made, such deceptive information can continue to mask deficiencies in utilising technology.

The ministry regulates adaptation through technical assistance by financing the acquisition of new technology, making earlier imported technologies more compatible within the enterprise or between enterprises within a sector. Perhaps the best example of this is its participation in the public vehicle sector. The ministry also finances extraordinary R and D (these funds are usually split between research institutes and enterprises), development of new production processes, and construction as well as reconstruction of plant facilities, in order to help to integrate technology. It participates in interministerial committees mapping out long-range industrial strategy and concomitant technological development, attempting to conform to long-range objectives through the above monitoring process. Moreover, if imports involve the expenditure of hard currency, the ministry, as the primary state organ responsible for enterprise performance, has to review and approve the technical merits of foreign technology to be acquired by enterprises under its jurisdiction. Only with the ministry's permission will the enterprise receive the necessary importing licences from the Foreign Trade Ministry, the required credit from the Hungarian National Bank and the essential foreign exchange from the Foreign Trade Bank. In this type of hierarchical situation, enterprises with stronger management and a more developed technological base are in a better position to bargain for the kind of technology that they desire to obtain. Weaker enterprises may find themselves dictated to by ministry officials, as the latter can redefine proposals for importing and utilising the desired technology.

While they indicate an awareness of the importance that innovation plays in industrial strategy, ministry officials remain encapsulated in the priority-oriented world that characterises central planning. This is best reflected by the reliance on hierarchical bargaining with enterprises to enforce ministry objectives, as well as the employment of administrative monitoring systems in regulating the absorption of imported technology. The ministry, it seems, lacks the creative energy required to stimulate enterprise orientation towards innovation. This is demonstrated by the fact that it has no immediate solutions for the problems that exist between basic and applied research. In addition, it is not very anxious to promote greater in-house R and D capability. This is understandable in view of the fact that the ministry would stand to lose resources from its own research institutes.

(b) *National Planning Office*
This office is also engaged in the regulation process. It is directly

involved in interministerial work committees designing and debating Central Development Programmes (e.g. modernising the public vehicle sector), which involve the assimilation of imported technology and usually affect more than one sector (see Balassa, 1975). The Planning Office attempts to build in adjustments between and within sectors, emphasising compatibility of technology. In some cases this may involve direct financial assistance to an enterprise for the procurement of foreign technology so as to create compatibility with previous imports within and between enterprises.

Although the Planning Office makes on-site enterprise inspections, it is less involved with the actual utilisation of technology and more concerned with setting industrial goals, based on technical consultations with ministries, financial organs and the State Committee for Technical Development. It attempts to co-ordinate sectors by integrating enterprise performance, including technological development, on which data are assembled on a regular basis.

(c)   *State Committee for Technical Development (SCTD)*
The routine function of this committee can be traced to co-ordinating, through various work committees, the design and debate of technical conceptions, which later serve as the basis for importing technology between enterprises and across sectors. It employs a staff of experts and hires many specialists on contract to study the feasibility of, and set criteria for, utilising technology, including that which is derived from foreign sources. The SCTD attempts to stimulate the use and integration of new technology through its own R and D, financed by a fund into which each enterprise is required to contribute. By performing on-site inspections the SCTD monitors technology and evaluates the employment and assimilation of imported technologies, particularly ones that have been obtained through its financial assistance.

The SCTD helps to finance the introduction of new technologies (numerical control technology in the machine tool sector is a good example) to develop technological harmony within the sector. As in the case of numerical control technology, it also finances the construction of new production facilities and the development of prototypes. It runs technical seminars where producers familiarise themselves with the imported technology and learn how best to integrate it into overall production. These seminars are also held for Hungarian end users which buy domestically manufactured products containing imported technology. They are also informed of the adjustments necessary for incorporating the new technology content into their own production activity.

In its attempt to promote greater awareness of, and reliance on, technology in Hungarian industry, the SCTD has enjoyed some success. Its performance in introducing numerical control technology in the machine tool industry is a case in point. In stimulating R and D, however, it has been less than effective. It has failed to link imports of technology to the development of in-house R and D capabilities. Creating viable in-house R and D capabilities, however, is probably against the long-term interests of the SCTD. Like the Ministry of Metallurgy and Engineering, the SCTD now receives important contributions for its own centralised R and D fund from the Technical Development Fund of each enterprise. If in-house R and D were to become a major source of activity in the innovation process, both the SCTD and the ministry would stand to lose valuable resources from their own R and D funds. Leaving bureaucratic considerations aside, there are other creative instruments to promote the innovation process. For instance, the SCTD could design a monitoring programme for enterprises, requiring further development of imported technology, thereby ensuring, albeit in a forced way, the eventual emergence of innovative capability. In all likelihood the reluctance to undertake such a programme, or to take strong initiatives in co-ordinating technological development, stems from the fact that the SCTD is only a consultative body and has little power to enforce enterprise conformity.

(d) *Foreign Trade Bank, Hungarian National Bank and Ministry of Finance*

Financial institutions are also involved in the regulation process. These three state financial organs provide credits during the acquisition phase. Both the Foreign Trade Bank (see Gáspár, 1978) and the Hungarian National Bank provide credit to enterprises to increase exports. The Foreign Trade Bank handles the foreign exchange component of the credit. In this relationship National Bank credits are a prerequisite for obtaining the foreign exchange component. Increasing exports usually necessitates increasing imports of Western technology (e.g. machinery, equipment, licences, know-how), which can foster, assuming that it is appropriate, compatibility and raise productivity of other imported technology already situated in the enterprise. Some of the credits from the Ministry of Finance and the National Bank also go towards new construction, intending to integrate imported technology into a more modern and productive environment.

The regulatory impact of these financial institutions emerges by default rather than through calculated effort. Their technical competence is limited. During the credit-granting stage they primarily depend on the Ministry of Metallurgy and Engineering, the SCTD and the Planning Office to assess projects from the technical and planning viewpoints. However, they do monitor the application of imported technology.

For instance, the Foreign Trade Bank monitors export and import performance. In this process it can detect enterprises that do not meet contractually required outputs. Such outputs are usually agreed upon when the enterprise receives hard currency financing to obtain imported technology The bank has the power to conduct on-site inspections to determine the cause of poor performance. This may reveal problems with the handling of imported technology (e.g. poor handling, lack of assimilation, not enough complementarity with other equipment). If flagrant abuse of the technology is detected, the bank is empowered to impose fines on the respective enterprise.

The National Bank also reserves the prerogative to inspect the financial records of enterprises when they are not repaying credits. While such examinations can discern inappropriate use of technology, they are not intended to be a check on the actual utilisation of the technology. Instead, the bank is interested in ascertaining why the enterprise is not attaining projected production goals, as this 'promised' performance was the original basis on which the bank issued the credits. If it desires, the bank can cut off further credits or raise interest rates to those enterprises not conforming to proposed production targets.

A more systematic monitoring mechanism is operated in the Ministry of Finance. Monthly data sheets are supplied by every enterprise to the ministry, where they are assessed and overall productivity is gauged. In case of unsatisfactory results, ministry officials can backtrack, albeit somewhat inefficiently, to a possible source of the problem, namely, the use of technology.

In sum, the weakness in regulating the adaptation of technology and in promoting innovative capability stems from: a conflict of interest on the part of regulatory agencies; an inadequate strategy for receiving and further developing imported technology; and an incoherence among the regulatory functions of agencies, which only exacerbates the problem of designing a forward-looking strategy to promote innovative capability. First of all, it has been shown that the Ministry of Metallurgy and Engineering and the SCTD have a fundamental conflict of interest in creating a sound in-house R and D base at the enterprise level. Secondly, the monitoring processes in place are ineffective for stimulating innovative capability. While these administrative measures can be useful in assessing how effectively imported technology is being used, they do not present enterprises with alternative industrial strategies for the purposes of systematically integrating new technology into production and thereby promoting, from enterprises' own resources, the development of new products through new production processes. A system of regulation so narrowly confined employs foreign technology to resolve past problems in production processes, without duly anticipating the prospective evolution of production in order to fuse these imports to domestic technological advancement.

Finally, and not surprisingly, the consequences of deficient regulation necessitate further imports, as industrial innovation is unable to propel domestic industry. International solutions not only aggravate the balance-of-payments problems but also generally contradict the intended goal of regulation, namely, to encourage the assimilation and regeneration of imported technology. This contradiction is rooted in the distribution of regulatory functions between state agencies, for the negative results of ineffective regulation (e.g. those reflected by more severe balance-of-payment problems) do not fall under the purview of either the Ministry of Metallurgy and Engineering, the SCTD or the Planning Office. Instead, responsibility for resolving balance-of-payments difficulties rests with the Ministry of Finance, the Foreign Trade Bank and the National Bank – institutions that have the least impact on regulating the adaptation and improvement of foreign technology.

5 Conclusions

An Hungarian strategy for greater international division of labour, predicated on the assumptions that industrial enterprises will absorb and further develop imported Western technology and that state agencies will promote this process, has to contend with powerful historical forces that shaped the country's industrial past, the consequences of which are still evident today. In the three sectors, public vehicles, machine tools, and electrical generating equipment examined in this study, this is reflected by factors undermining emergence of the three attributes of innovation and the ineffectiveness of regulation – a process that remains endowed with the bureaucratic contradictions of central planning.

The obstacles to innovation will be less dramatic if policy-makers decide to concentrate on removing current bottlenecks. Emphasis should be placed, first, on transferring more resources to enterprises for basic research, and its success must be tied to realisation in the production process. Secondly, new monitoring programmes have to be established at the enterprise level, linking in-house R and D to imported technology. In other words, new technology has to be accepted into a wider programme of R and D at this level. Such enterprise programmes can be monitored by an agency like the SCTD in order to ascertain the *advancement* made by enterprise R and D in further developing the technology in new forms and new products. Thirdly, managerial attitudes, at both enterprise level and Ministry of Metallurgy and Engineering level, have to place greater emphasis on the self-generated renewal of technology, preferably through new programmes, such as the ones suggested above as well as others. Fourthly, organisational changes have to decrease concentration in industry and increase the assortment of products being produced. This may permit more effective utilisation of imported technology. Finally, there has to be recognition of the necessity to diffuse imported technology throughout the industrial system. Instead of being isolated, as presented by the case of vertical integration, it has to travel through backward and forward linkages in order to establish compatibility and avert imbalanced growth and productivity.

Instituting these changes would not be an easy task, for it would involve revising old policy instruments and devising new ones in the process of economic management. The alternatives to change mean reliance on imported technology in order to fulfil production needs left unmet by domestic innovation. This might have unintended consequences. Although imported technology *per se* is not detrimental to industrial development, its improper utilisation is. If it fails to stimulate domestic technological development through innovation, eventually further imports will be required. The net result of this is a vicious circle, which many students of international political economy, including Kozma (1970, p. 200), have described as technological dependence.

Acknowledgement and Note: Chapter 7

The research for this study was carried out under a Canada Council Doctoral Fellowship, which I received in 1978–9. I am grateful to the council for its financial assistance as well as to the Institute for World Economics, Budapest, for its cordiality and help with my research. I am also indebted to Hugo Radice for his extensive and helpful comments on an earlier version of this chapter. I, however, take the responsibility for any remaining errors or shortcomings.

1 Lack of space prevents more than a bare summary of pre-1945 industrial development. See especially Berend and Ranki (1976), Jászi (1966) and Berend and Szuhay (1978).

References: Chapter 8

Abonyi, A. (1978), 'Internationally diffused innovation and conditions of change in Eastern Europe', in A. Gyorgy and T. Kuhlman (eds), *Innovation in Communist Systems* (Manhattan, Kansas: Westview Press).

Abonyi, A., and Sylvain, I. J. (1977), 'CMEA integration and policy options for Eastern Europe: a development strategy of dependent states', *Journal of Common Market Studies*, vol. 16, pp. 132–54.

Balassa, A. (1975), 'Central Development Programs in Hungary', *Acta Oeconomica*, vol. 14 (1), pp. 91–108.

Bauer, T. (1976), 'The contradictory position of the enterprise under the New

Hungarian Economic Mechanism', *Eastern European Economics*, vol. 15 (1), pp. 3–23.

Berend, T. I. (1969), 'The historical background of the recent economic reforms in East Europe', *East European Quarterly*, vol. 2, pp. 75–90.

Berend, T. I., and Ranki, Gy. (1976), *Közép-Kelet Európa Gazdasági Fejlődése a 19–20 Században* (Economic Development in Central Eastern Europe in the Nineteenth and Twentieth Centuries) (Budapest: Közgazdasági és Jogi Könyvkiadó).

Berend, T. I., and Szuhay, M. (1978), *A Tokés Gazdaság Története Magyarországon, 1848–1944* (History of Capitalism in Hungary, 1848–1944) (Budapest: Kossuth Könyvkiadó and Közgazdasági és Jogi Könyvkiadó).

Bognár, J. (1967), 'Principles of foreign trade in the New Economic Mechanism', *New Hungarian Quarterly*, vol. 8, pp. 156–71.

Cooper, C. (1972), 'Science, technology and production in the underdeveloped countries: an introduction', *Journal of Development Studies*, vol. 9, pp. 1–18.

Deák, A. (1978), 'Vállalati beruházási döntések és a gazdaságosság' (Enterprise investment decisions and efficiency), *Gazdaság*, vol. 12 (1), pp. 17–36.

Freeman, C. (1974), *The Economics of Industrial Innovation* (Harmondsworth: Penguin).

Gáspár, G. (1978), 'A Magyar Külkereskedelmi Bank Rt; a kelet–nyugati gazdasági kapcsolatok szolgálatában' (The Hungarian Foreign Trade Bank serving East–West economic relations), *Pénzügyi Szemle*, vol. 22 (11), pp. 803–9.

Economic Research Institute, 'On industrial big enterprises', *Acta Oeconomica*, vol. 12 (1), pp. 97–117.

Havás, G. (1975), 'A vállalati kutatás-fejlesztés finanszirozásáról' (On the financing of enterprise research and development), *Pénzügyi Szemle*, vol. 9 (2), pp. 128–38.

Hewett, E. A. (1975), 'The economics of East European technology imports from the West', *American Economic Review*, vol. 65 (3), pp. 377–82.

Inzelt, A. (1978), 'A vállalati centralizációról' (On enterprise centralisation), *Gazdaság*, vol. 12 (2), pp. 58–75.

Izikné, H. G. (1979), *Magyarország a Keleti–Nyugati gazdasági Kapcsolatokban* (Hungary in East–West Economic Relations) (Budapest: Kossuth Könyvkiadó).

Jánossy, F. (1970), 'The origin of contradictions in our economy and the path to their solution', *Eastern European Economics*, vol. 8 (4), pp. 357–90.

Jászi, O. (1966), *The Dissolution of the Habsburg Monarchy* (Chicago, Ill.: (University of Chicago Press).

Juhász, J. (1977), 'Elenjáró műszaki ismeretek átvételének általános kérdései Magyarországon', (General questions of technology transfer in Hungary) in B. Bojkó (ed.), *Technológia-Transfer a Keleti–Nyugati Kapcsolatokban* (Technology Transfer in East–West Relations) (Budapest: Institute of World Economy).

Kardos, P. (1978), 'Licencvásarlás vagy hazai fejlesztés?' (Buying licences or domestic development?), *Külgazdaság*, vol. 22 (7), pp. 9–17.

Kozma, F. (1970), *A Két Europa Gazdasági Kapcsolatai és a Szocialista*

Nemzetközi Együttmüködés (Economic Relations between the Two Europes and Socialist International Co-operation), Budapest: Kossuth Könyvkiadó and Közgazdasági és Jogi Könyvkiadó).

Kozma, F. (1974), 'International division of labour and the development strategy of the Hungarian national economy', *Acta Oeconomica*, vol. 13 (1), pp. 19–33.

Kozma, F. (1976), *Gazdasági Integráció és Gazdasági Stratégia* (Economic Integration and Economic Strategy) (Budapest: Közgazdasági és Jogi Könyvkiadó).

Laki, M. (1976), 'Téves üzleti döntések' (Mistaken factory decisions), *Közgazdasági Szemle*, vol. 23 (11), pp. 1296–313.

Lederer, E. (1952), *Az Ipari Kapitalizmus Kezdetei Magyarországon* (The Beginnings of Industrial Capitalism in Hungary) (Budapest: Közoktatásügyi Kiadóvállalat).

Levcik, F., and Stankovsky, J. (1979), *Industrial Cooperation between East and West* (White Plains, New York: M. E. Sharpe).

Lodgaard, S. (1973), 'Industrial cooperation, consumption patterns and division of labour in the East–West setting', *Journal of Peace Research*, vol. 10 (4), pp. 387–99.

Marer, P. (1974), 'The political economy of Soviet relations with Eastern Europe', in S. J. Rosen and J. R. Kurth (eds), *Testing Theories of Economic Imperialism* (Lexington, Mass.: D. C. Heath).

McMillan, C. H. (1977), 'East–West industrial cooperation', in Joint Economic Committee, *East European Economies Post-Helsinki* (Washington, DC: US Government Printing Office).

Naduvári, Z. (1973), 'Elemzési lehetöségek a gépipari vállalatok licencforgalmáról beszámoló jelentések adatai alapján' (Analysis based on data from reports on licence trade involving engineering industry enterprises), in *Ipari és Épitöipari Statisztikai Értesitö*, No. 3 (Budapest: Központi Statisztikai Hivatal).

Patel, S. J. (1974), 'The technological dependence of developing countries', *Journal of Modern African Studies*, vol. 12, pp. 1–18.

Rekettye, G. (1978), 'A környezeti változások hatása–innovatív reagálás' (The effect of environmental changes–innovative response), *Marketing és Piackutatás* (2), pp. 135–41.

Rupp, A. (1977), 'Tudományirányitás és kutatásfinanszirozás' (Science management and the financing of research), *Pénzügyi Szemle*, vol. 21 (5), pp. 344–52.

Sagasti, F. R. (1979), *Technology, Planning and Self-Reliant Development* (New York: Praeger).

Szita, J. (1977), *Perspectives for All-European Economic Cooperation* (Budapest: Akadémiai Kiadó).

Tardos, M. (1979), 'The diffusion of imported technology in Hungary', paper presented at University of Michigan Research Conference on East–West relations in the 1980s, Bellagio, Italy (June).

Timár, M. (1975), *Reflections on the Economic Development of Hungary, 1967–1973* (Akadémiai Kiadó).

Vajda, I. (1967), 'Foreign trade and economic reform in the new technical age', *Hungarian Survey*, vol. 2, pp. 19–35.

Varga, Gy. (1977), 'Vállalati nagyság és rugalmas alkalmazkodás' (Enterprise size and flexible adjustment), *Gazdaság*, vol. 11 (2), pp. 51–63.

Woroniak, A. (1970), 'Technological transfer in Eastern Europe: receiving countries', in S. Wasowski (ed.), *East – West Trade and the Technology Gap* (New York: Praeger).

Part Five

International Issues

Chapter 8

The Mechanism and Performance of Hungary's Foreign Trade, 1968–79

1 Introduction

This overview chapter on foreign trade focuses on the institutional features of Hungary's foreign trade system and on the country's foreign economic performance. Section 2 describes the foreign trade aspects of the New Economic Mechanism – its blueprint, implementation and evolution since 1968. Section 3 analyses the country's convertible-currency (CC) trade balance between 1968 and 1978. In a small resource-poor country like Hungary (with about 50 per cent of national income exported to pay for correspondingly large imports), developments in the domestic economy, in the Council for Mutual Economic Assistance (CMEA) and on the world market all have an impact on the CC trade balance, which can thus be viewed as a barometer of the country's foreign trade performance. Section 4 describes the new reforms and policies that Hungary has adopted during 1979–80 to improve its CC balance of payments and draws attention to some of the major obstacles to their implementation.

During the 1970s Hungary and the other Eastern European countries had substantial deficits in trade with the West, accumulating large CC debts. Indebtedness in and of itself is neither good nor bad; it depends on what has caused the deficits, how large the debt burden has become and what the country's future economic prospects are. These aspects are explored for Hungary in sections 3 and 4 below.

All Eastern European countries have large and growing CC debts, which they are finding increasingly difficult to contain, given the shortcomings in their economic system and the deteriorating external environment. Energy prices continue to skyrocket, the USSR is less willing to provide incremental supplies of energy and raw materials, and increased competition and protectionism are encountered on the world market. To keep the CC indebtedness within manageable limits has become Hungary's highest economic priority as it enters the 1980s.

The significance of what Hungary is trying to do to improve its CC trade balance extends beyond its borders. If successful, Hungary may well point the way for other planned economies. But if Hungarian-type policies turn out to be patently unsuccessful, the domestic and international repercussions of Eastern Europe's large and still rapidly rising indebtedness to the industrial West will become a critical problem during the 1980s.

2 Foreign trade system under the New Economic Mechanism

(a) *Changes in the planning system*

The New Economic Mechanism, introduced on 1 January 1968, abolished detailed plan instructions to enterprises. Since 1968 macroeconomic plans have been implemented through the use of economic regulators and consultations rather than through compulsory plan directives to enterprises. *Long-term plans* deal with the most important ten- to fifteen-year development targets and balances (e.g. national income, standard of living, the distribution of production by sectors and main branches, technical development programmes, and the sources and uses of labour). *Medium-term plans* project in more detail what the economy is expected to accomplish during a five-year period. These include projections of the volume and growth of foreign trade, estimates of trade balances by principal foreign markets and outlines of commodity composition. Of particular importance are plans for investments in the domestic economy and in the economies of the other CMEA countries under the so-called CMEA joint projects, to fulfil Hungary's obligations under CMEA agreements (see Marer and Montias, 1980). Major changes in economic regulators are usually introduced at the beginning of each five-year plan. *Annual plans* are the economic action programmes of the government; to implement them heavy reliance is placed on market-type instruments.

When the New Economic Mechanism was introduced in 1968, many 'brakes' still appeared to be necessary; that is, direct controls on prices, occasional intervention by the authorities in the activities of firms, and taxes and subsidies tailored to the needs of industrial enterprises or branches were still needed. These 'brakes' were to be gradually removed during an approximately ten-year transition period.

A substantial part of the remaining administrative authority over enterprises was redistributed, away from the National Planning Office and branch ministries to the banking system, to the National Materials and Price Office and to the functional Ministries of Foreign Trade, Finance and Labour. The branch ministries continue to appoint the managers of enterprises and to prepare sectoral development plans, but their direct intervention into enterprise decisions is supposed to have ceased.

In the banking system the Hungarian National Bank (MNB) is the institution most directly involved in international transactions. The National Bank administers the state's gold reserves and foreign exchange and carries out payment, credit and other international banking operations through its correspondent links with approximately 2,000 foreign banks. The bank quotes foreign exchange rates in terms of the forint and administers exchange controls. Credits to finance imports are generally satisfied by the bank. Foreign exchange credits can be obtained by any Hungarian entity directly from a foreign lender only with the approval of the bank. Approval is granted only in exceptional cases, because supplier credits directly to the Hungarian importer are considered too expensive (although the higher interest rate is often hidden in the price) and in order to preclude the possibility of enterprises' circumventing the intent of domestic credit policy with the help of foreign loans. Consequently, about 95 per cent of imports from the West are paid for on a cash basis (Hungarian National Bank, 1980, p. 31). Hungarian exporting enterprises may *grant* short-term credits on their own account and medium- or long-term credits with the authorisation of the Minister of Foreign Trade. These credits are usually refinanced by the National Bank or, in the case of intergovernmental agreements, by the budget. The only other commercial bank authorised to conduct business in foreign exchange and to specialise in financing trade is the Hungarian Foreign Trade Bank Ltd (Hungarian National Bank, 1979, p. 16). In recent years its main task has been to finance joint ventures at home and abroad.

The Planning Office prepares forecasts and plan alternatives for party and government leaders. Once the government has formally adopted an economic policy plan, the Planning Office breaks it down into co-ordinated suggestions to the ministries for implementation. The Planning Office also co-ordinates the elaboration of the system of economic regulators.

The Materials and Price Office recommends price policy to the government and develops the system and methods of official price regulations designed to implement the price policy adopted by the government. The office also controls the allocation of materials in those limited spheres where central allocation was retained after 1978.

The Ministry of Foreign Trade elaborates the foreign trade aspects of the national economic plan and works with the Ministry of Finance and other bodies on the system and methods of economic regulators designed to implement foreign trade policy. Together with the Ministry of Finance, it monitors foreign trade performance and alters the regulators as necessary. The Ministry of Foreign Trade is also responsible for concluding intergovernmental agreements of trade and represents Hungary in international economic organisations. The Ministry of Finance elaborates and helps to control the implementation of financial regulators affecting foreign trade and finance.

(b) *Enterprises involved in foreign commerce*

Production, distribution, transportation and other services are carried out for the most part by state or co-operative enterprises that are autonomous legal persons, independent of each other and of the state, with separate assets and with legal liability for their actions to the extent of their assets. Enterprises can associate to set up share or limited liability companies, or they can form partnerships for specific purposes. As in all CMEA countries, the state maintains a monopoly on foreign trade. In Hungary this means that foreign trade activities can be pursued only by enterprises authorised by the Minister of Foreign Trade. The bulk of foreign trade is performed by state-owned firms called foreign trade enterprises (FTEs), established for the sole purpose of pursuing such activity. In addition, a significant and increasing number of producing and commercial enterprises have been granted the right to engage directly and independently in foreign trade. In some cases two or more producing or commercial enterprises can join to form an FTE, which works under their control as a share company. Finally, an enterprise, institute or organisation that has no foreign-trade right may solicit and be granted, on a case-by-case basis, permission to transact business abroad if such direct dealings can be justified.

A large portion of total exports and imports are conducted by FTEs on behalf of producing enterprises, on a commission or agency contract basis, under which FTEs are compensated by a price mark-up; these mark-ups are regulated uniformly by products for each of the two main groups of partner countries (Gadó, 1976, p. 118). Less than 10 per cent of the total turnover is transacted by the FTEs for their own account. Because foreign trade prices skyrocketed after 1973, as did volume, many FTEs have done very well financially. For that reason, in 1974 import commission fees were frozen at their nominal 1973 levels, and a substantial and widely differentiated *commercial tax* was imposed on FTEs in 1975. Tension has been created in recent years between the authorities, the FTEs and the producing enterprises on how to formulate policies to reconcile, on the one hand, the need to stimulate FTEs to obtain as favourable a price as possible abroad and, on the other, the pressures to tax away 'excess profits'.

Foreign firms can be represented in Hungary by Hungarian agencies established for that purpose; the usual method of payment is a commission. The agencies are not specialised, so a foreign firm can choose from among them and can change agencies if it is not satisfied, or it can establish its own representative office in Hungary.

(c) *The licensing system*

All import and export transactions require a licence from the Ministry of Foreign Trade, which permits the conclusion of a transaction and the delivery or receipt of goods. An import licence authorises its holder to buy the necessary foreign exchange if it has the required amount of forints at its disposal. A licence can be *general* or *individual*. A general licence authorises conclusion of a deal, up to the value of the licence, in a defined range of goods appearing on a list issued periodically by the Minister of Foreign Trade. Individual licences authorise the conclusion of the transactions that they refer to. By law the time limit for deciding on a licence application is thirty days (which may be extended in justi-fied cases to sixty days). Most general licences are *global*, which means that goods up to the stated value can be imported from any country. In the late 1960s approximately 60 per cent of Hungary's imports from countries belonging to the General Agreement on Tariffs and Trade (GATT) were transacted on the basis of global licences. From 1 January 1969 a licence fee of 2 per cent of the import value of purchases from CC areas was levied.

The licensing system is the means to ensure that only enterprises authorised to trade actually do so, to control and influence the fulfil-ment of bilateral obligations, and to safeguard the balance of pay-ments. Understandably, Western exporters and importers want to know the criteria that govern the issuance of licences. It is not clear, for instance, how GATT membership is consistent with the use of licences to fulfil bilateral obligations and to safeguard the balance of payments. The Hungarians point out that quotas agreed upon in bilateral agree-ments with market economy countries entail an obligation to issue import licences up to the value of the quota, if such licence requests are made. Moreover, since for many goods the value of general licences issued is higher than the value of the sum of the quotas found in bilat-eral agreements with market economy countries, the system of general licences is more liberal than a purely bilateral system would be. Still, from a Western perspective the impression remains that the Hungarian licensing system provides a fail-safe device to control and influence CC imports.

(d) *Import quotas and deposit schemes*
The importation of certain goods is subject to quantitative restrictions. In 1968 quantitative restrictions covered electric energy, automobiles, foundry and furnace coke, fertilisers and consumer goods. In that year the quantitative restrictions on goods from CC areas only were as follows: foundry and furnace coke, 100,000 tonnes; fertilisers, $10·6 million; consumer goods, $28·7 million (GATT, 1969, p. 18). The global import quota for consumer goods from CC areas had success-ively been increased to $30 million in 1973, $60 million in 1976, $73 million in 1977 and $83 million in 1978. The intention is, conditions permitting, to abolish this quota in the near future.

An important change introduced with the reform was the abolition

of maximum foreign-exchange allocations to enterprises, except for
domestic trade in consumer goods, as noted above. The basic idea and
practice are that, if an Hungarian enterprise has the import licence and
the forints, the National Bank automatically grants it the necessary
foreign exchange. One aspect of this new system is that barter business
and leasing arrangements are no longer pushed by Hungarian enterprises just to get around foreign exchange 'limits'.

Some quotas serve to limit the importation of certain goods, mainly
from CC areas, other quotas are designed to make sure that enterprises
will import goods that the government is obligated to purchase under
bilateral agreements, mainly from the CMEA countries. The exchange
between GATT and the Hungarian government on whether the
existence of quotas and the bilateral agreements with the CMEA
countries are consistent with GATT principles is interesting:

Question by GATT:
　　Can the Hungarian government explain their system of centralized
　　purchasing procedures in their trading arrangements with certain
　　foreign countries and its implications for other suppliers to
　　Hungary?

Answer by Hungary:
　　Bilateral trade agreements do not provide for compulsory levels;
　　they establish quotas that are either directive (i.e., in trade with
　　CMEA countries), or merely contain obligations for the two sides
　　for issuing the necessary licences, or are merely indicative (i.e. in
　　trade with market economy countries). Interstate agreements are not
　　binding on Hungarian enterprises; they are binding only on the
　　Hungarian government.

Question by GATT:
　　. . . with CMEA countries, we understand Hungary enters into bilat-
　　eral obligations to export and import specific products and commo-
　　dities in specified quantities and values. Since lists of items imported
　　under the terms of these agreements amount to about two-thirds of
　　total Hungarian imports, it would appear that Hungary is in a posi-
　　tion to extend real MFN treatment to only about one-third of
　　Hungarian imports, i.e. imports not covered by these barter-type
　　agreements.

Answer by Hungary:
　　. . . bilateral trade agreements . . . represent in the first line an inter-
　　state fixing of the contracts concluded by enterprises on the basis of
　　market research. Consequently, in these cases there is no question of
　　giving orders by the authorities independent of the interest of enter-
　　prises. The actual situation is that everything agreed upon

previously in the form of contracts between enterprises becomes an intergovernmental obligation. (GATT, 1969, p. 9)

(e) *Foreign trade aspects of the price system*
The nature of the price system – how prices are determined, how flexible they are and how far they are permitted to influence resource allocation – is at the heart of Hungary's New Economic Mechanism. In an open economy like Hungary's, how the price system works is critically important for understanding the country's foreign trade system and for analysing its foreign trade performance. This section will discuss briefly: (1) theories of price formation in a planned economy, (2) the basic principles of the price system envisioned by the architects of the New Economic Mechanism, and (3) the nature and role of exchange rates in the post-1968 economic system, including (4) the question of convertibility. The relationship between external and internal prices is affected also by (5) tariffs, (6) the turnover tax system, and (7) special subsidies and taxes related to exports and imports.

Theories of price formation. In preparation for the New Economic Mechanism, Hungarian economists began to search for a more objective, but still Marxian, criterion for forming producer (i.e. wholesale) prices than the arbitrary 'administrative pricing' then prevalent in the USSR and elsewhere in Eastern Europe (see Bornstein, 1977; and Gadó, 1976). According to Marx the value of a commodity is composed of current labour (measured by employee compensation), labour embodied in materials and in machinery and equipment (the latter measured by depreciation) and surplus value (which goes to the employer under capitalism and to the state under socialism). The various price-formation models proposed for a planned economy, which does not permit prices to be determined by market forces, differ mainly in how they allocate surplus value:

(1)   in proportion to wages ('value prices');
(2)   in proportion to the sum of material costs and wages ('cost value prices');
(3)   in proportion to the amount of fixed and working capital ('production prices'); or
(4)   a combination of (1) and (3) ('two-channel prices').

Since all these models omit relative scarcities and demand as factors in price formation, the results cannot be optimum guides to resource allocation.

Principles of price formation under the New Economic Mechanism. In *fields not related to foreign trade*, the theoretical basis for Hungary's

1968 price reform for industrial commodities was (to oversimplify matters greatly) the 'production prices' formula. A 5 per cent charge was levied on assets, the rate of profit was expressed as a percentage of the value of assets, and profit taxation was related to the proportion between the value of assets and the size of the wage bill. In *fields closely related to foreign trade*, Hungary's open economy was to rely on prices determined by supply and demand on the international markets. One of the key reforms of the New Economic Mechanism was to try to set the relative prices of tradables (except in agriculture and the retail trade) according to world market prices, with Hungarian and foreign prices linked by proxy exchange rates. (This concept is discussed later.)

Initially, the implementation of this concept presented no major difficulties in *exports*, which were accounted for at actual foreign-trade prices received, converted to domestic prices at the prevailing proxy exchange rates. But difficulties arose in *imports*, where many goods were purchased simultaneously from socialist and non-socialist markets and prices differed. One possible solution to dual price imports is to use a weighted average price – a system heavily relied on up to 1980. Another is to set prices on the basis of where the additional imports will come from, which almost always will be the Western world market. This approach would have been the most efficient, but it seemed to create difficulties (e.g. measuring and interpreting comparative advantage deriving from Hungary's CMEA specialisation). There was an additional problem of how often changes in world market prices should be allowed to alter the domestic prices of imports. In principle, Hungarian economists wanted *permanent* price changes to be mirrored in domestic prices and *temporary* price fluctuations to be buffered. But the rules for distinguishing one from the other were not clear – a problem that came back to haunt them after the 1974 world-market price explosion.

Because in many areas demand exceeded supply at prevailing prices and because keeping inflation under wraps was considered critically important, six types of prices were introduced: *fixed, maximum, limited* (by which a starting level as well as permissible margins for fluctuations, generally in the 5–15 per cent range, were set), *free, minimum* (for certain agricultural commodities) and *orientation* (mainly for services provided by the private sector). But even the nominally free prices of many final products were largely determined by the fixed prices of most raw materials and semi-finished goods. Moreover, on important commodities a *preliminary notice of intent to change the price* had to be submitted to the Materials and Price Office, which used its considerable clout to 'persuade' enterprises to heed its recommendations. Between 1968 and 1979 more than 70 per cent of prices were 'administered' in one form or another.

It is not surprising that under such a mixed system the profit rates of enterprises varied not only from branch to branch but also often from firm to firm. One reason was that the price levels, and therefore the profitability, of industries or firms heavily involved in exports were determined on the basis of international prices; another was that supply–demand relations in the domestic consumer market dictated relatively higher prices, and therefore profits, in some industries.

The architects of the New Economic Mechanism envisioned a consumer price level 6–10 per cent higher than the producer price level (so that 1 forint spent on investments would have approximately the same purchasing power as 1 forint in consumption). This relationship was maintained for several years after the reforms were introduced. However, the rapidly increasing price of imports after 1973–4 (neither contained at the border by revaluing the proxy exchange rates nor allowed to affect retail prices, which had to be subsidised more and more heavily) caused the level of producer prices by the mid 1970s to become about 4 per cent *higher* than the consumer price level, unlike the situation in all other CMEA countries. In 1977 the subsidy paid on basic foodstuffs, as a percentage of retail price, amounted to 26 per cent (a 66 per cent subsidy was paid on milk, 26 per cent on cereals, 16 per cent on meat); on gasoline, 38 per cent; on home-heating, 168 per cent; and on mass transit, 117 per cent; whereas the sales tax on luxury goods represented 38 per cent of the retail price (e.g. 31 per cent on automobiles, 5 per cent on clothing) (Kramer, 1979).

Exchange rates. There are two exchange rates for the forint: *a commercial rate*, used for all enterprise foreign-trade transactions; and a *tourist rate* (also called the non-commercial rate), used for transactions by individuals (e.g. by tourists and for private remittances of gifts or earnings).

(1) The commercial exchange rates (called the foreign trade multiplier until 1 January 1976) introduced in 1968 were calculated separately for dollar and ruble trade as follows:

$$\frac{\text{Exchange}}{\text{rate}} = \frac{\text{Actual exports valued at Hungarian wholesale prices}}{\text{Foreign exchange received for the exports}}$$

Export revenues in dollars (i.e. sales to CC areas) were calculated at prices actually prevailing in Hungary's trade with the industrial West, and revenues in rubles (i.e. sales to CMEA countries) at contractual prices in CMEA trade, subtracting in each case the direct and indirect costs of foreign trade operations. In 1968 these calculations yielded roughly the exchange rates of 60 forints = $1·00 and 40 forints = 1 ruble. Within the Western currency area the forint value of the various other currencies is calculated according to their official parities against the dollar; within the CMEA area a commercial exchange rate is calculated only for the so-called transferable (clearing) ruble.

For a country that does not have full external convertibility of its currency for current account transactions – the definition of convertibility adopted by the International Monetary Fund (IMF) – but that still wants to establish approximately correct exchange rates to guide its economic decisions, the exchange rate can be based on the purchasing power of its currency relative to the currency(ies) of its major trading partner(s). Such calculations typically establish the weighted average ratio of a representative bundle of goods and services produced or consumed at home and in selected foreign countries (i.e. wholesale or retail prices or gross domestic product (GDP) – deflator items). This type of calculation yields meaningful exchange rates in the sense that goods that can be produced more cheaply at home than abroad become potential exports or import substitutes, while goods costing more to produce at home become potential imports.

The above procedure is not the Hungarian method of exchange rate calculation, as shown by the formula above. One difference between the Hungarian and more standard calculations is that the commodity coverage of the former is much more limited, based only on the actual (and possibly quite rigid and perhaps disadvantageous) structure of Hungarian exports. Another difference is that, since the calculations reflect not foreign prices but the prices that Hungary actually obtains, the exchange rate is affected by such factors as the commercial policies of Western importing countries towards Hungary and the negotiating skill of Hungarian exporters. These considerations tend to depress the exchange rate compared with the standard method. A third and less obvious difference arises from the artificially high level of Hungarian producers' prices, which include a significantly higher allocation of 'surplus value' (i.e. taxes of various kinds plus tariffs plus profits) than is typical in Western and in most or all other CMEA countries. The effect again is to depress the exchange rate.

These three considerations suggest that it would be misleading to call the quotient in the Hungarian formula simply an exchange rate without qualifying that term. Let us therefore coin the term 'proxy exchange rate' as our designation for the quotient in the Hungarian formula.

Before the introduction of the proxy exchange rates there was a long debate on whether the calculations should be based on average or marginal costs of earning a dollar and a ruble respectively. Advocates of the marginal concept wanted an exchange rate based on the domestic cost of earning a unit of foreign exchange in the least economical 10–20 per cent of exports that would still be necessary for balance-of-payments equilibrium, given a certain volume of imports. Opposition to the marginal rate centred on its potential inflationary effect (see Brown and Marer, 1973). It was noted too that the dollar price level of Hungary's exports was (and remains) considerably lower than the dollar price level of its imports, because Hungary is not able to export at fully competitive prices, due to inadequate marketing efforts and to Western discrimination. Thus, when the proxy exchange rate is determined on the basis of the average forint cost of exports, this already yields relatively high domestic prices for imports.

The most important consequence of using the current Hungarian formula for determining the proxy exchange rates is that large subsidies must be granted to enterprises to generate the volume of exports required to pay for imports. This conflicts with one of the main objectives of the New Economic Mechanism, namely, efficiency. Enterprises producing for exports become much more interested in bargaining with their superiors about subsidies than in reducing costs or increasing profits by improving the product or their marketing efforts. A further corollary of proxy exchange rates based on average costs (as noted by Kozma in Chapter 9 of this volume) is that the price elasticities of import demand and of export supply become much lower than would otherwise be the case.

Regarding elasticities, there is reason to believe that the *price elasticity of demand for imports* is low because the predominant share of imports consists of raw materials and intermediate goods essential to production or of capital goods essential for technical progress. Moreover, the export supply of such products from CMEA sources is price inelastic. Consumer goods imports are little affected by exchange rates because they are regulated by quotas and because there is a thick layer of insulation between world market prices and the retail prices for many products.

The true *price elasticity of supply for Hungary's manufactured exports* to CC areas is difficult to measure as long as the prevailing economic environment for enterprises makes it is so much more attractive for them to sell to the domestic or to the CMEA markets than to the West. For this reason the key to the *supply elasticity of exports to CC areas* is the level of domestic and CMEA demand. If these were reined in – domestic demand by tight monetary and fiscal policies and CMEA demand by export restrictions – then enterprises would be forced to seek Western buyers and would be able to increase exports.

The consensus of experts in Hungary and in the West (e.g. see Portes, 1978) is that, given the economic environment prevailing in Hungary, devaluation of the forint's dollar proxy exchange rate would not improve the CC balance of payments but would fan inflation. Computer simulations of devaluation have shown that a 1 per cent depreciation of the forint would increase producers' prices by 0·8 per cent.

What, then, is the role of the exchange rate under the New Economic Mechanism? The head of the Materials and Price Office, Béla Csikós-Nagy (1979, p. 6) argued that exchange rate policy must: (1) insure the relative stability of the value of the domestic currency (i.e. help to protect against imported inflation); (2) correctly orient enterprises involved in foreign commerce about the relative value of foreign currencies; and (3) influence exports and imports to insure a reasonable equilibrium in the balance of payments.

Regarding objective (3), it has just been noted that the elasticity conditions are unlikely to be satisfied for a devaluation to improve the balance of payments. Objective (2) is achieved automatically, because the proxy exchange rates of the forint *vis-à-vis* currencies in the dollar area are set on the basis of their official parities against the dollar. The achievement of objective (1) must therefore be the main focus of exchange rate policy under the New Economic Mechanism – a conclusion confirmed by János Fekete (1976, p. 58), Vice President of the National Bank and the country's leading spokesman in the international financial community.

To help to protect against imported inflation, the proxy exchange rate has to be modified whenever the world-market price *level* for the relevant basket of goods and services changes, but this should not mean stability in *relative* prices, since that would distort production and consumption decisions. A difficult theoretical problem is posed whenever the foreign price levels of exports and imports diverge significantly. For example, if the terms of trade deteriorate, as they did after 1974, should a revaluation then be based on the price changes of exports or on those of imports? (See Kozma's Chapter 9 below for an analysis of this problem.)

Table 8.1 presents changes since 1970 in the price levels of Hungary's dollar exports and imports and in the extent of the forint's appreciation. Although after 1971 the forint was revalued periodically to follow the devaluation of the dollar, the appreciation of the forint was much less than the rise in foreign trade prices in dollar terms. By the end of 1978, prices in dollar (i.e. CC) trade had more than doubled (rising by 152 per cent in imports and 103 per cent in exports), while the forint had been upvalued by only 24 per cent against a basket of CCs and by 35 per cent against the US dollar. Producers' prices increased slightly in 1973−4 and considerably during 1975−6, but the main impact was the explosive growth of subsidies from, and taxes to, the state budget.

(2) The tourist exchange rates are calculated to approximate the purchasing power of the forint at the retail level. From 1968 until February 1979, the ratio between the commercial and tourist exchange rates was about 2:1; that is, the tourist forint was approximately twice as valuable as the commercial forint. As a result of the February 1979 devaluation of the tourist forint, the ratio changed to about 1·75:1. In September 1979 the tourist rate was 20·33 forints = $1·0, and the commercial rate was 35·58 forints = $1·00; in February 1980 the

Table 8.1 *Price indices of Hungary's dollar imports and exports and the extent of the forint's appreciation, 1968–78.*

Year	Price indices in dollar trade[a] (1970 = 100)		Percentage revaluation of the forint (Ft) since 1968 (cumulative)		
	Imports	Exports	Against a basket of CCs[b]	Against the US dollar ($)	Against the transferable ruble (TR)
1968			n.a.		0
1969			n.a.		0
1970	100·0	100·0	n.a.		0
1971	102·2	101·4	n.a.		0
1972	113·4	114·0	n.a.	5·1[c]	0
1973	152·0	149·1	n.a.	15·6	0
1974	217·6	181·9	n.a.	19·8	0
1975	232·5	180·9	13·0	26·7	0
1976	217·6	180·6	21·2	30·7	12·5
1977	238·4	190·4	21·8	31·7	12·5
1978	252·5	203·5	23·8	35·2	16·3
Exchange rate, 1968			n.a.	60·0 Ft/$1	40·0 Ft/TR1
Exchange rate, mid 1978			n.a.	38·88 Ft/$1	33·50 Ft/TR1
Exchange rate, 15 February 1979			n.a.	35·58 Ft/$1	32·00 Ft/TR1
Exchange rate, 1 February 1980			n.a.	33·50 Ft/$1	28·00 Ft/TR1

Note: n.a. = not available.

[a] Price indices calculated in dollar terms reflect actual changes in the foreign-trade price level, while price indices computed in forint terms (not shown) combine changes in foreign trade prices and changes in the commercial exchange rate, thus partly offsetting the extent of external inflation by the official forint revaluation.

[b] The basket reflects the pattern of Hungarian exports.

[c] Cumulative changes in value up to the end of 1972, inclusive of a 3 per cent across-the-board subsidy on CC exports.

Sources: *1968–77.* Brown and Tardos (1980), table 3 and appendix table 3.

1978. Price indices from Hungaropress, *Economic Information*, no. 5–6 (1979), pp. 3–4.

1978–9. Exchange rates from Hungarian National Bank (1979), p. 30, and monthly updates.

tourist rate was 20·38 forints = $1·00, and the commercial rate 33·50 = $1·00, the ratio narrowing to 1·64:1.

The significantly greater purchasing power of the tourist forint in terms of consumer goods and services at the retail level can be traced to three factors. One is the continued large subsidisation of many consumer items – or more generally, the Hungarian system of internal taxation and subsidisation – which results in the consumer price level's being *lower* than the wholesale price level. This situation is unique among the CMEA countries and possibly among countries anywhere in the world. In Hungary, up to 1979 much of net social income (i.e. budget revenues) was built into wholesale prices, in contrast to the international practice of levying most taxes on personal income or consumption. Because the government has heavily subsidised those consumer items on which tourists tend to spend money (e.g. food, restaurant meals, entertainment, public transportation), the millions of foreign tourists visiting Hungary each year were in 1978 being subsidised (even at the present tourist exchange rate) to the tune of about 1·6 billion forints – more than 1 per cent of the national income. Another reason for the large difference between the two exchange rates is that Hungary exports to the West too many high-cost goods whose production and sales are not warranted by the country's comparative advantage. The third factor is poor marketing and Western discrimination against Hungarian goods, both of which depress the dollar prices obtained by Hungarian exporters. According to Hungarian economists, one precondition for achieving a convertible forint is the unification of the two exchange rates – a stated objective of Hungary's economic policy for the 1980s – which in turn requires the shifting of net social income from the sphere of production to the sphere of consumption.

Forint convertibility: current status, future prospects. Conceptualisation. What is the meaning of currency convertibility for any country? *Absolute convertibility* means that every physical or juridical person, resident or non-resident in the country, is free to obtain, convert and transfer to/from abroad balances in domestic or foreign currency, for any purpose. Absolute convertibility also requires the absence of major trade restrictions (e.g. licences, tariffs, quotas, non-tariff barriers, bilateralism). Absolute convertibility has not been achieved by any country in the postwar period; the world is comprised of countries with various *degrees of convertibility*.

The IMF's definition of convertibility is: no restrictions on the use of currency balances acquired by *non-residents* in connection with current account *transactions* in the balance of payments (i.e. trade in goods and services and short-term facilitating credits; payments due as interest or amortisation on loans or as depreciation and net income on equity investments; and modest personal remittances for family living expenses).

Given the above definitions and the different institutional frameworks for Hungary's commerce with the West and East, the forint's convertibility must be assessed separately for transactions:

(1) with Western versus CMEA and other planned-economy countries;
(2) for Hungarian residents (enterprises and the population) versus non-residents; and
(3) involving the current account versus the capital account in the balance of payments.

Convertibility for Hungarians with the West. With respect to current account transactions, any Hungarian *enterprise* that has secured the import licence and has the forints can obtain the necessary foreign exchange from the National Bank. Thus, the question of forint convertibility for enterprises revolves around the ease or difficulty of obtaining the import licence. Today, I understand, obtaining the licence is almost automatic in many cases. Convertibility for the Hungarian *population* would mean being able to obtain CC freely, with no distinction between official and black market rates, for foreign travel. By this definition the forint is not convertible, although it is important to note that a certain amount of CC is available to most citizens, once every few years, for travel. In 1979, 5·1 million Hungarians travelled abroad (number of border crossings), of whom more than 400,000 went to Western countries, the latter group obtaining from the National Bank the equivalent of $85 million in CC (Hungarian National Bank, 1980, p. 33). Although the number of tourists travelling to the West and the amount of CC available from official sources are smaller than the likely effective demand in the absence of rationing, the figures are impressive compared with data of a few years ago or in comparison with the number of tourists permitted to travel to the West from the other CMEA countries. With respect to capital account transactions, neither Hungarian enterprises nor individuals enjoy convertibility, fundamentally because such transactions are prohibited.

Convertibility for Western non-residents in Hungary. With respect to current account transactions, a Western exporter of goods or services or granter of CC loans to Hungary (or to any other CMEA country) enjoys *de facto financial convertibility* because payment is always in CC. But can CC be used to purchase freely goods produced in Hungary; that is, can an importer from the West compete freely with domestic and CMEA buyers? In principle, yes; in practice, there are limitations, which arise mainly from the centralised long-term quantitative export commitments of the state to its CMEA partners. But since Western exporters can spend freely on the world market, the CC that they earn in Hungary, this is not a serious limitation on convertibility. Western tourists can exchange CC for forints and purchase goods and services available in Hungary's retail sector, without significant restrictions. In 1979, 15·1 million foreign tourists crossed Hungary's borders, of whom 2·1 million came from Western countries, the latter group spending $157 million (Hungarian National Bank, 1980, p. 33). Sending personal remittances to families in Hungary is also easy.

Future prospects. Given the current status of the forint, what do Hungarian economists mean when they talk about achieving convertibility for the forint during the 1980s? With respect to CCs, the Vice President of the National Bank, János Fekete, elaborated what I understand is the official position on this matter:

> In the event of the introduction of external forint convertibility, we would pay with a convertible forint for those imported goods and services for which before convertibility we were willing to settle in freely CC. For those nonresidents who thus would have the right to ask for payment either in CC or in convertible forint, we would make the creation of convertible-forint deposits advantageous by guaranteeing unconditionally and at any time the conversion of such deposits into CC and by offering attractive interest rates relative to those available on the international financial markets. The introduction of the forint's external convertibility would not mean, however, either free access to CC for Hungarian citizens travelling abroad or free capital mobility . . .
>
> The introduction of a convertible forint would be a spectacular proof of the stability and continuous development of our economy and would improve Hungary's international position and creditworthiness. Convertibility of the forint would make it possible to attract foreign capital on advantageous terms. (Fekete, 1977, p. 71)

Perhaps I do not understand it fully, but, for a non-resident, taking this next step appears to be of psychological importance only. To be sure, the changes in price levels and ratios required in the domestic economy to support this move may well represent very important improvements in Hungary's New Economic Mechanism. But from the point of view of an outside observer, what is notable and different in Hungary compared with the other CMEA countries is the substantial degree of convertibility achieved *already* for Hungarian enterprises wanting to import from the West and for Hungarian citizens wishing to travel abroad.

Convertibility within the CMEA. Much more important than forint convertibility *vis-à-vis* Western currencies is the convertibility of intra-CMEA transactions on the current account. With respect to trade, little progress has been made up to now, except for that small share (about 5–20 per cent) which is priced at current world-market prices and settled in CC. Examining the financial integration in the CMEA, Brainard concluded that integration has been achieved only in so far as trade and credit transactions are conducted in CC (see his chapter in Marer and Montias, 1980). For the remaining transactions there is no convertibility, which forces commerce into bilateral channels. This means that the repayment of any trade surplus is tied to the future ability and willingness of the deficit country to export something to the surplus country. One adverse consequence of bilateralism is a forced reduction of each country's exports to some partners (because the potential importer can pay neither with goods nor with a currency desired by the exporter, and because the 2 per cent or so interest paid on any surplus is a further disincentive to export), which forces each country to restrict imports from third countries. An alternative method of avoiding becoming a creditor is to increase non-preferred imports, which reduces the gains from trade. Non-convertibility of currencies thus alters the volume and composition of exports and imports and generally worsens the quality of trade.

Prospects for achieving convertibility within the CMEA, as defined by the IMF, are not good as long as fundamental economic reforms of the Hungarian type are not introduced in several countries.

With respect to tourism, there are various degrees of convertibility among CMEA countries, in the sense that limited amounts of foreign currencies are available, to selected citizens, for the purpose of travel to other CMEA countries.

The tariff system. Imports are subject to customs duty levies, introduced on 1 January 1968. The customs duty is a factor in price calculations; that is, it is actually paid by the importer, and its effect is felt by the end user. The purpose of the tariff system is to serve as an instrument of trade policy; that is, it is used to grant reciprocal bilateral or multilateral customs concessions, including special preferences to less developed countries; to help to regulate the quantity and composition of imports; and to protect domestic production. The Commercial Customs Tariff has three columns. The rates in column I apply to developing countries enjoying preferential customs treatment, the rates in column II apply to goods originating in countries to which Hungary grants most favoured nation (MFN) status, and the rates in column III apply to all other countries.

The average level of tariff rates in Column II is about 30 per cent. (For raw materials it ranges between 0 and 5 per cent; for semi-manufactures, between 5 and 20 per cent; for manufactures and consumer goods, between 40 and 50 per cent.) The basis of the tariff calculation is the customs value of the goods (i.e. foreign price plus the aggregate cost of delivering it to the Hungarian border, including transportation, insurance, packing, commission, and so on). The customs value of the goods expressed in foreign exchange is converted into forints on the basis of the commercial exchange rate valid on the day of internal customs inspection.

The import turnover-tax system. The enterprise taxation system is composed of: (1) capital charge on the average amount of fixed and working capital employed by enterprises; (2) wage and social security taxes; (3) income tax on audited enterprise profits; (4) 'production tax', levied on excess profits originating from special advantageous conditions (the economic equivalent of rent); and (5) turnover taxes on consumer goods. This last tax is of special importance to foreign sellers of consumer goods attempting to penetrate the Hungarian market.

The turnover tax is imposed when goods or services are delivered to the retail trade or to consumers. The same tax rate is levied on imported and domestic products, but the rates differ from product to product. The turnover tax is paid by the organisation (producer, wholesaler or FTE) that sells the goods to the retailer; the basis for the calculation is the wholesale selling price.

Special subsidies and taxes. There are now more than 50 grounds on which an enterprise can receive a subsidy (Kramer, 1979). *Export subsidies* are set in an *ad hoc* fashion for individual enterprises or products, usually as a percentage of the export value. Subsidies do not create inflationary pressures, because domestic prices and wages are controlled, so that enterprise liquidity is not permitted to spill over into market demand.

As long as domestic prices of many commodities are administered by the government, it is necessary to subsidise a certain portion of imports. An *import price subsidy* is granted from the state budget when the price of a product manufactured from imported materials is administered and the increased cost of imports would otherwise cause a loss.

As long as enterprises trade the same or substitute products on three separate and partitioned markets – namely, domestic, CMEA and Western – it is necessary to 'harmonise' their price through various subsidy and tax schemes. A *special import-turnover tax* was introduced because the prices of many raw materials and of a lot of consumer goods purchased on the CMEA market used to be lower than the forint prices of goods produced domestically or imported from dollar areas. Price unification is achieved by elevating the prices of goods obtained from the least cost market to the average level via the special import turnover tax.

To mitigate the effect of temporary price fluctuations of goods imported from the world market, a *reserve fund for import price equalisation* has been created at those industrial enterprises (in some cases the wholesaler) which use imported materials in products with administrative prices (e.g. certain chemicals, textiles, clothing, iron and steel products, non-ferrous metals) as well as for consumer goods with fixed prices that are imported in large quantities (e.g. citrus). Savings attained compared with *reference* prices are deposited in the fund, from which losses can be covered. To encourage firms to import as cheaply as possible, only a portion of the price gain must be deposited and, similarly, only a portion of the loss may be claimed; the rest adds to or depletes the enterprises' own (development or sharing) funds. The fund's net losses or gains are periodically settled with the state budget. For further discussion of this topic, see Gadó (1976, ch. 10).

Foreign trade performance: focusing on the convertible-currency trade balance

(a) *Statistical indicators of performance*
Table 8.2 presents Hungary's total and CC trade during 1968–79 on the basis of official Hungarian sources, together with its estimated CC indebtedness to the industrial West on the basis of Western calculations up to 1978 and of officially reported CC debt, available for the first time for 1979. Hungary is the only CMEA country that reports not only trade with 'socialist' and 'non-socialist' countries but also 'ruble-denominated' and 'non-ruble denominated' trade. The two series differ, because a certain portion of trade with the socialist group is settled in CC, including all trade with Yugoslavia, the People's Republic of China and Cuba and a portion of trade with each of the European CMEA countries. In 1977, for example, 18·7 per cent of Hungary's exports to, and 12·2 per cent of its imports from, socialist countries were settled in CC. According to Brown and Tardos (1980), in intra-CMEA trade alone (excluding Yugoslavia and Cuba) Hungary was able in 1977 to earn a CC surplus covering 13 per cent of its balance-of-trade deficit with the West, or approximately $100 million. According to another Hungarian source, in 1978 the volume of CC transactions with the Soviet Union alone was $370 million. However, when this figure is broken down in the same source into exports and imports, there is an inconsistency, maybe because of a misprint. Hungary's 1978 dollar exports to the USSR are said to have been $117 million (comprising such items as pigs for slaughter and alumina), while its dollar imports from the USSR are said to have amounted to $185 million (including crude oil, timber products, cotton, chemicals, rolled metal products, leather and asbestos) (*Külgazdaság* report, 1979, pp. 4–6). As a rule goods shipped to CMEA partners over and above the quantities stipulated in the five-year and annual trade agreements are settled

Table 8.2 *Hungary's total and CC trade and estimated CC indebtedness, 1968–78 (millions of dollars at current prices).*

Year	Imports Total (1)	CC $ (2)	(%) (3)	Exports Total (4)	CC $ (5)	(%) (6)	Balance of trade Total (7)	CC $ (8)	(%) (9)	Estimated net CC indebtedness (10)
1968	1,803	561	(31·1)	1,789	513	(28·7)	−14	−48	(8·6)	500
1969	1,928	604	(31·3)	2,084	647	(31·0)	156	43	(7·1)	600
1970	2,505	856	(34·2)	2,317	776	(33·5)	−188	−80	(9·3)	600
1971	2,934	1,109	(37·8)	2,532	912	(36·0)	−402	−197	(17·8)	900
1972	3,329	1,159	(34·8)	3,596	1,157	(32·2)	267	−2	(0·2)	900
1973	3,845	1,598	(41·6)	4,459	1,774	(40·0)	614	176	(11·0)	900
1968–73	16,344	5,887	(36·0)	16,777	5,779	(34·4)	433	−108	(1·8)	
1974	5,337	2,701	(50·6)	5,041	2,227	(44·2)	−296	−474	(17·5)	1,500
1975	6,578	2,714	(41·3)	5,370	2,229	(40·1)	−848	−415	(15·3)	2,000
1976	7,118	2,916	(41·0)	6,401	2,491	(38·9)	−717	−425	(14·6)	2,800
1977	8,283	3,514	(42·4)	7,534	2,894	(38·4)	−749	−620	(17·6)	3,400
1978	7,715	4,221	(54·7)	6,172	3,072	(49·8)	−1,543	−1,149	(27·2)	4,600
1974–8	35,031	16,066	(45·9)	30,878	12,983	(42·0)	−4,153	−3,083	(19·2)	
1979	7,921	4,221	(53·3)	7,234	3,881	(53·6)	−687	−340	(49·5)	5,000

Note: Data in forints converted to dollars at 39 forints = $1 rate.

Sources: *Imports, exports and balance of trade.* Data for 1968–77 from *Külkereskedelmi Statisztikai Évkönyv* (various years); for 1978 from *Magyar Statisztikai Zsebkönyv* (1979); and for 1979 from *Statisztikai Havi Közlemények* (January 1980).

Estimated CC indebtedness. Data for 1968–72 from Snell (1974), table 4, p. 198; for 1973–5 from Zoeter (1977), table 2, p. 1352; for 1976–7 from Kolarik (1979), table 2, p. 198; for 1978 from my own estimate, by assuming that debt increased by the amount of the 1978 current account deficit, which is shown in Hungarian National Bank (1979), p. 29; and for 1979 from official figures published for the first time in Hungarian National Bank (1980), p. 31.

in CC if the goods could be sold readily on the Western world market. For a statistical estimate of Hungary's socialist trade settled in CC in 1975, see Marer (1977, pp. 565–6).

Total CC trade is shown in Table 8.2 because the key question for Hungary is its CC trade balance, not its balance with a group into which countries are classified on the basis of their political system.

Between 1974 and 1978 an average of 46 per cent of Hungary's imports and 42 per cent of its exports were settled in CC – a significantly higher share of the total than a decade ago. This is attributable to the rapidly increasing volume of trade with the industrial West and to the growing importance of CC settlements in intrasocialist trade. No great significance should be attached, however, to year-to-year fluctuations in the share, because this may simply reflect substantial price changes either in Western or in intrabloc trade. It should also be noted that there are alternative ways of calculating the share of trade denominated in CC; for example, the National Bank (1979) showed that in recent years 54–5 per cent of total imports and 50 per cent of exports were settled in CCs. The appendix to this chapter presents and reconciles the different official series on trade and explains alternative trade-share calculations.

Columns 7–9 present the balance of trade, total and in CC only, and the relative size of the annual CC deficit or surplus as a percentage of CC imports. The estimated CC indebtedness in the last column is a cumulative figure.

The 1968–78 period can be divided into two subperiods. During the first six years of the New Economic Mechanism, 1968–73, total trade and trade with the West were approximately in balance; the cumulative CC deficit represented less than 2 per cent of total CC imports during the period. By contrast, in each of the five years from 1974 to 1978 Hungary ran a large CC trade deficit, totalling more than $3 billion. On the average, approximately 20 per cent of CC imports were obtained on credit. (If intrasocialist trade settled in CC were excluded, the figure would rise to about 25 per cent.) During these same years Hungary also ran a deficit in ruble trade, except in 1974 (as shown by total deficits' being larger than deficits in CC trade only), which probably reflects in good part the drawing down of a loan that the USSR granted to Hungary (and to the other Eastern European countries except Romania) to help to mitigate the sharp deterioration in the terms of trade in the wake of intra-CMEA price increases beginning in 1975. Evidence that the Soviet Union extended credits is based on the Soviet announcement in 1975 that it was willing to provide ten-year loans to Eastern Europe and on the large trade deficits that these countries were running with the USSR during 1975–7. The amount of these deficits, however, is not necessarily a good proxy for credits actually drawn, because part of the deficit may reflect Eastern

European surplus on invisibles or debt repayment by the USSR on earlier credits. Moreover, during this same period there was a sizeable flow of Eastern European investment credits to the USSR to finance participation in joint CMEA projects, which would partly offset Soviet credits. (For a detailed discussion of these issues, see Kohn, 1979.)

In 1979 Hungary's foreign trade performance improved significantly. Exports to CC areas rose by 26 per cent, and imports stagnated (preliminary data), decreasing the CC trade deficit from $1,149 million to $340 million. This improved performance is attributable to the significant slowdown in the rate of growth of the economy, the entering into production of new export projects financed by the National Bank under its export development programme, and the curtailment of the activities of uncompetitive industries.

Before analysing the causes and implications of Hungary's growing CC trade deficit up to 1979, let us look at the aggregate performance of the Hungarian economy and at the role that foreign borrowing has played in shaping that performance.

Table 8.3 presents annual percentage changes in constant prices of national income produced and national income absorbed (i.e. distributed or consumed), both according to the Hungarian definition of the concepts. The table also shows the major categories of absorption: *consumption* (total only, including private and social consumption) and *net investment* (including its three principal components), as well as the weight of each category in total absorption.

In comparing the growth rates of national income produced and absorbed, it is striking that the latter has fluctuated much more than the former. In fact, rather extreme yearly changes appear to be the rule. Another striking fact is that, in the five years after the 1973–4 world economic crisis, distributed national income grew substantially faster than produced national income: 7·2 versus 5·4 per cent per year during 1974–8. It is interesting to compare these figures with those achieved during the 1966–70 five-year plan, when in many respects the best economic performance had been achieved in the postwar period. In these five years national income produced and distributed each grew at approximately 7 per cent, consumption by more than 6 per cent and net investment by 12 per cent per year. Compared with the 1966–70 period, while the rate of growth of produced national income slowed during 1974–8 by an average of about 1·5 per cent per year, the growth of distributed national income remained practically unchanged (7·4 per cent in 1966–70 versus 7·2 per cent in 1974–8), made possible by recourse to heavy foreign borrowing.

During 1974–8 the growth of distributed national income – and, by implication, some of the resources borrowed from abroad – was used to maintain a solid and uninterrupted real growth of consumption of about 4·5 per cent per year in spite of the major external economic

Table 8.3 Rate of growth of national income produced and absorbed, 1966–79 (annual percentage change at constant prices).

Year	National income produced	National income absorbed	Major categories of absorption				Components of total net investment					
			Total consumption		Total net investment		Net fixed-capital formation		Changes in unfinished investment		Changes in inventories	
			%	(Weight, %)	%	(Weight, %)	%	(Weight, %)	%	(Weight, %)	%	(Weight, %)
	(1)	(2)	(3)	(4)	(5)	(6)	(7)	(8)	(9)	(10)	(11)	(12)
1966–70	6·8	7·4	6·2	(n.a.)	11·6	(n.a.)	14·6	(n.a.)		(n.a.)	n.a.	(n.a.)
1971	5·9	11·3	5·4	(n.a.)	30·4	(n.a.)	1·6	(n.a.)	2·3	(n.a.)	n.a.	(n.a.)
1972	6·2	-3·7	3·1	(78)	-21·4	(22)	8·9	(20)	7·3	(2)	n.a.	(0)
1973	7·0	2·0	3·7	(79)	-3·8	(21)	5·7	(21)	6·9	(1)	n.a.	(-1)
1974	5·9	12·7	6·9	(74)	34·2	(26)	-5·6	(18)	-0·2	(5)	n.a.	(3)
1975	6·1	6·4	4·7	(74)	11·5	(26)	39·7	(23)	24·1	(1)	n.a.	(3)
1976	3·0	1·2	2·1	(74)	-1·4	(26)	-12·7	(20)	-5·1	(2)	n.a.	(3)
1977	8·0	6·2	4·6	(73)	11·0	(27)	-0·1	(18)	1·7	(6)	n.a.	(3)
1978	3·9	9·6	4·0	(n.a.)	24·8	(n.a.)	7·8	(n.a.)	n.a.	(n.a.)	n.a.	(n.a.)
1979	1·8											

Note: n.a. = not available.
Sources: 1966–78. Columns 1, 2, 3, 5 and 7 from *Magyar Statisztikai Zsebkönyv* (1979), pp. 53–4; columns 4, 6, 8, 9, 10, 11 and 12 from *Main Economic Indicators* (1977), as cited in Brown and Tardos (1980), appendix tables.
1979. Hungarian National Bank (1980), p. 22.

disturbances suffered by the Hungarian economy during this period. It was evidently the government's policy to isolate the Hungarian consumer, for a while at least, from the adverse impact of the external economic shocks suffered through the foreign trade sector.

During 1974−8 the growth of distributed national income was also used to finance a rapid expansion of total net investment, which grew at 16 per cent per year, exceeding the growth tempo even of the 1966−70 period (12 per cent). Extreme year-to-year fluctuations in the tempo of expansion of total net investment suggests that a good part of this growth may have been unplanned, with the government having to use foreign credits, *ex post facto* as it were, to finance the large stock of unforeseen investments. This was almost certainly the case in 1974 and again in 1978 − two years when total net investments grew by 34 and 25 per cent respectively, both years witnessing the largest CC deficits to that time (see Table 8.2). Some insight into the reasons for the growth of, and fluctuations in, total net investment may be gained by focusing on its components, all of which showed rather extreme yearly fluctuations during this period. (See Hare's discussion of investment fluctuations in Chapter 5 of the present volume.)

(b)   *External causes of the CC trade deficit*

Deteriorating terms of trade. Table 8.4 presents Hungary's terms of trade with dollar and ruble areas, showing that their worsening in trade with both areas contributed substantially to the large CC trade deficit during 1974−9. Had Hungary's terms of trade with the dollar area remained unchanged during 1974−8 compared with the 1970−2 period, the same volume of imports that Hungary actually purchased and paid for in dollars could have been obtained for $13 billion instead of $16 billion. The $3 billion difference is of the same order of magnitude as Hungary's cumulative dollar-trade deficit during the same period.

The deterioration in the terms of trade with the ruble area was more gradual, but by 1979 the extent of net price losses had become about the same as that with the dollar area. This, of course, reflects the fact that price changes in intra-CMEA trade follow price changes on the world market. Since 1975 prices in intra-CMEA trade have been based on an annually moving average of world market prices during the previous five years. Since the Soviet Union is the principal supplier of energy, raw materials and semi-finished products in Hungary's ruble trade, the rapid rise of prices of these commodities on the world market was the main cause of the sharp deterioration in Hungary's ruble terms of trade; price changes in trade with the USSR dominate the ruble terms-of-trade index.

The worsening of Hungary's terms of trade was particularly severe

Table 8.4 *Hungary's import and export price indices and terms-of-trade with dollar and ruble areas, 1970–8 (1970 = 100).*

Year	In trade with dollar areas			In trade with ruble areas		
	Imports	Exports	Terms of trade	Imports	Exports	Terms of trade
	(1)	(2)	(3)	(4)	(5)	(6)
1970	100·0	100·0	100·0	100·0	100·0	100·0
1971	102·2	101·4	99·2	101·8	99·6	97·8
1972	104·4	105·0	100·6	104·0	100·2	96·3
1973	121·6	119·3	98·1	104·2	100·7	96·6
1974	169·6	141·8	83·6	105·2	102·0	97·0
1975	170·2	132·5	77·8	132·2	117·0	88·5
1976	150·9	125·3	83·0	128·8	112·4	86·6
1977	162·5	129·8	79·9	138·1	116·0	84·0
1978			80·5			82·1
1979[a]			79·5			80·5

Note: Import and export price indices and terms of trade are calculated in forint terms, so that the import and export price indices show not only changes in import and export prices but also changes in the commercial exchange rate. This will, however, not affect the terms-of-trade index.

[a] Preliminary index.

Sources: *1970–9. Külkereskedelmi Statisztikai Évkönyv* (1978), p. 408.
1978–9. Hungarian National Bank (1979), p. 25.
1979. Hungarian National Bank (1980), p. 27.

with both dollar and ruble areas during 1974–5. The combined loss in those years was the equivalent of 7·5 per cent of the national income (Brown and Tardos, 1980, p. 10).

The worsening of the dollar terms of trade occurred not only because Hungary imports mainly raw materials and semi-finished products and exports principally manufactured and agricultural products, but also because the terms of trade deteriorated *within* each broad commodity group. For instance, in 1975 import prices for machinery rose by 39 per cent, while export prices increased only by 7 per cent; for raw materials and semi-finished products import prices rose by 64 per cent, export prices by only 14 per cent; for industrial consumer goods the price index of imports rose by 26 per cent, that of exports by only 23 per cent (Köves, 1978, p. 109). That Hungarian exporters could not react flexibly to the changing situation on the world market, to adjust the commodity composition of imports but especially that of exports, was clearly a factor. To be sure, events that were beyond Hungary's ability to control also contributed to the loss. An example is the way in which import and export prices changed in the agriculture and food sector. Between 1970 and 1977 export prices in this sector approximately doubled, but import prices increased more than threefold. The divergence was due mainly to the skyrocketing prices of animal feed and fertilisers, while the export price of meat and cattle for slaughter, exported principally to the European Economic Community (EEC) markets, did not increase much (that of cattle actually declined in some years). This was a major factor in the 34 per cent decline in Hungary's terms of trade in the agriculture and food category – a substantially greater decline than that in overall dollar trade (Brown and Tardos, 1980, p. 14).

Deterioration in the terms of trade may reflect not only price changes but also *changes in the commodity composition* of imports and exports. Because in recent years Hungary could buy only small additional quantities of energy, raw materials and semi-finished products from the ruble area (not nearly enough to meet its demand), it increasingly had to obtain these goods from the dollar area. Between 1970 and 1977 approximately two-thirds of the weighted rise in dollar import prices occurred in the energy and raw material sectors – an amount that would have been considerably smaller had Hungary been able to increase the import of these goods from the ruble area in proportion with the growth in their consumption. Thus, for these two reasons it is incorrect to attribute the deterioration in Hungary's dollar terms of trade *entirely* to causes originating in Western world markets – a point that will be elaborated below.

Insufficient growth of essential imports from CMEA countries. During the 1970–7 period the volume of Hungarian imports increased approximately at the same rate as that from the ruble and from the CC area. But considerable differences within the aggregates should be noted. Take, for instance, energy imports. Between 1970 and 1977 the volume index of imports from the ruble area increased by 50 per cent and that from the dollar area by 390 per cent (*Külkereskedelmi Statisztikai Évkönyv*, 1977, p. 30). In 1972 Hungary still had a slight surplus in fuel and energy trade with CC markets, but by 1977 its net energy imports for CC had become substantial, accounting for 14 per cent of the CC trade deficit in that year (Brown and Tardos, 1980, p. 12).

While energy imports are important, these purchases should be placed in perspective. Table 8.5 shows the commodity composition of Hungary's 1977–9 imports from dollar and ruble areas. (See the appendix to this chapter for a statistical note on trade share calculations.) During 1977–9 energy comprised a little over 20 per cent of Hungary's total imports of primary and semi-finished products and only about 13 per cent of total imports. Western experts on Eastern Europe tend to focus on energy imports, especially crude oil, pointing out that the bulk of foreign oil is supplied to Hungary (and to the other Eastern European countries except Romania) by the USSR. For Hungary, however, considerably more important than energy have been raw material imports, which in 1977 were obtained in approximately

Table 8.5 Commodity composition of Hungary's dollar and ruble imports, 1977–9.

Commodity category at current prices	Paid in dollars			Paid in rubles			Total imports		
	1977	1978	1979	1977	1978	1979	1977	1978	1979
Imports (billions of forints)									
Energy	9	13	15	21	25	31	30	38	46
Raw materials	22	24	27	22	23	21	44	47	47
Semi-finished products	46	52	52	18	18	18	64	70	70
Agricultural products and food	27	23	21	3	4	4	30	27	25
Total primary and semi-finished goods	104	112	114	64	70	74	168	182	188
Machinery and equipment (with spare parts)	32	43	40	45	51	55	78	94	95
Industrial goods	8	10	10	14	15	15	22	25	25
Total manufactures	40	53	50	59	66	70	99	119	120
Total imports	144	165	165	123	136	144	267	301	309
Percentage from dollar and ruble sources									
Energy	30	34	33	70	66	67	100	100	100
Raw materials	50	51	57	50	49	43	100	100	100
Semi-finished products	72	74	74	28	26	26	100	100	100
Agricultural products and food	90	85	84	10	15	16	100	100	100
Total primary and semi-finished goods	62	62	61	38	38	39	100	100	100
Machinery and equipment (with spare parts)	42	46	42	58	54	58	100	100	100
Industrial goods	36	40	40	64	60	60	100	100	100
Total manufactures	40	45	42	60	55	58	100	100	100
Total imports	54	55	53	46	45	47	100	100	100

Note: See the appendix to this chapter for an explanatory note in interpreting trade statistics.
Sources: Külkereskedelmi Statisztikai Évkönyv (1977), pp. 38–40, and (1978), pp. 39–41; Statisztikai Havi Közlemények (January 1980), p. 94.

equal shares from ruble and dollar sources and in 1979 more than half (in current value terms) from dollar sources. Most important and striking, however, have been the imports of the energy- and raw-material-intensive semi-finished products (mostly chemicals and ferrous and non-ferrous metal products), which in value terms account for nearly as large an expenditure as energy and raw material purchases combined. In this commodity category Hungary buys nearly three times as much, in value terms, for dollars than for rubles! And in the late 1970s 84–90 per cent of agricultural and food imports were obtained for hard currency.

As a consequence of these developments, about 70 per cent of Hungary's CC imports comprise primary products and semi-finished goods (including food), and only 30 per cent comprise finished manufactures. It is evident that Hungary has not been able to secure adequate imports – not only of energy but also (and more importantly) of raw materials and semi-finished products – from the CMEA. The problem is not only the growing shortage and increased reluctance of CMEA exporters of energy and raw materials to supply more of these products to their bloc partners, but also (and more importantly) the fact that the semi-finished goods sector has not been adequately built up *any-where* in the CMEA during the postwar period. Consequently, Hungary is unable to meet its demand for semi-finished goods in required quantities and quality either from the domestic or from the CMEA market; hence, it has to increase rapidly their import for CC.

It is in the light of these facts that the significance of Soviet credits granted to Hungary and to the other Eastern European countries after 1975 to help to finance their deteriorating terms of trade must be evaluated. Such credits, I understand, are agreed upon by political leaders at the highest levels, but they often cannot be utilised fully because the goods that Hungary and the other Eastern European countries need the most – namely, energy, raw materials and semi-finished products – are not available. What are offered (e.g. standard machinery, watches and cameras) are not the kinds of goods that are needed.

Growing dollar content of exports to the CMEA. A corollary of the deteriorating terms of trade and insufficient growth of imports from the CMEA is the rapidly growing dollar-import content of the products that Hungary exports to the USSR and to other ruble markets. According to Hungarian calculations, between 1972 and 1974 the dollar import-material content of a unit of ruble exports increased by 123 per cent:

> Mainly because of the import difficulties we faced, imported materials we could previously purchase from socialist markets, in 1974 could be secured predominantly from capitalist markets only or against payment not in rubles . . . This suggests that an expansion of

our ruble exports requires a much more rapid increase in our dollar imports. (Beke and Hunyadi, 1977, pp. 496–7 and 502).

Considering the continued relatively slow growth of the volume of energy, raw material and semi-finished goods imports from the CMEA since 1974, and the rising dollar price of these goods on the world market, the import content of a unit of ruble exports that Hungary must purchase for dollars has surely continued to increase since 1974. The relationship between Hungary's growing exports to the CMEA and its deficit in dollar trade has been analysed by an Hungarian economist:

> Worsening terms of trade with socialist countries are less difficult to counter-balance by the quantitative increase of exportable commodities [than deteriorating terms of trade with the West]. Therefore, exports to socialist countries constitute the most dynamic part of Hungarian foreign trade ... Growth of exports to socialist countries impairs, however, the balance of trade with capitalist countries, for two reasons: ... it requires Western imports to an increasing degree [and] ... it restricts the volume of commodity stocks potentially exportable to the West. (Köves, 1978, p. 119)

Shortcomings in the CMEA trading mechanism. The existing CMEA trading mechanism does not put strong enough pressure on enterprises to manufacture goods that will also be competitive on Western markets. Under the existing CMEA trading mechanism, quantities to be traded are agreed upon first, prices afterwards. Prices depend less on the quality and modernity of the products than on efforts to achieve balance in bilateral trade, because, in the absence of currency convertibility, a country with an unplanned surplus is obliged to buy something to avoid becoming a creditor. A quantitative increase in imports therefore tends to be viewed as more important than quality – a tendency reinforced by the absence of direct contact between producer and user enterprises in the CMEA countries. (For a detailed discussion see Marer and Montias, 1980.) A consequence of this CMEA mechanism is a lack of competition on the CMEA as well as on the domestic market, which weakens incentives to improve quality, to provide service and to innovate new products, leading to inability to compete successfully with manufactures on Western markets. (Competition in the CMEA takes mainly the form of competing for *hard good imports*.) Lack of competition contributes to the 'saleability illusion', in Holzman's phrase; that is, since planners and enterprise-managers find that most of their products are saleable either on the domestic or on the CMEA market, it is difficult for them to see the need to adapt to the requirements of Western markets (Holzman, 1979, p. 77).

Sluggish economic conditions and increased protectionism in the West.
Various studies have shown that the Eastern European countries often
tend to be 'residual' suppliers in Western markets. This means that
their exports to CC markets tend to increase more rapidly than world
trade during the expansion phase of the business cycle and that their
sales tend to fall off more rapidly than those of other suppliers during a
recession. This situation has been exacerbated by increased Western
protectionism since 1974, especially in Western Europe, which is the
main market for Hungary's manufactures and agricultural products.
Notably important in this regard are the policies of the EEC: first, its
highly restrictive Common Agricultural Policy, a manifestation of
which is noted below in concrete terms; secondly, its recent
enlargement, causing the exports of new members to displace some of
the exports of third-party suppliers; and thirdly, its granting of special
trade preferences to an increasing number of non-member Western
European as well as Third World countries. EEC preferences mean
that, practically speaking, Hungary and the other Eastern European
states remain the only countries in the region not having preferential
access to the Common Market; thus, they are being effectively discri-
minated against.

EEC protectionism is illustrated dramatically by what happened to
Hungary's food exports between 1973 and 1976. Live animals and food
products have traditionally been a chief source of Hungary's CC
earnings, with exports of cattle to Italy and the FGR accounting for
between one-quarter and one-half of those earnings. As a result of a
drought in Western Europe in 1974, a sudden rise of slaughtering in the
EEC led to an overproduction of meat. To protect domestic producers
the EEC imposed an import ban on cattle from non-members. The
impact is shown in the declining share of agricultural products and
foodstuffs in exports to non-socialist countries (Brown and Tardos,
1980, pp. 12–14):

	1972	1976
Agricultural products and foodstuffs	37·4%	25·1%
Including live animals	18·2%	6·2%
Including cattle for slaughter	11·8%	1·6%

Fortunately, Hungary was able to sell some of the displaced exports to
the USSR and to Arab countries for CC.

Focusing on manufactures, how badly Western protectionism
affects a country's exports depends in part on the share of exports
concentrated in import-sensitive products. We call 'import sensitive'
those products for which import restraint petitions have been initiated
recently in various Western countries by import-competing industries.
A recent US study found that *highly sensitive* products are textiles,
clothing, steel and footwear (at the two-digit level of the Standard

Industrial Trade Classification). *Moderately sensitive* products are: textile fibres; chemical elements, compounds and products; manufactured fertilisers; plastics; manufactures of metal other than steel; electrical equipment; electronic products; and transport equipment (Taylor and Lamb, 1979). The same study analysed the exports of the Eastern European countries and found that Hungary (along with Czechoslovakia, Bulgaria and Romania) was dependent on exports in highly sensitive sectors to a somewhat greater degree than the world average. Of Hungary's shipments to countries of the Organisation for Economic Co-operation and Development (OECD) during 1973–7, more than 20 per cent consisted of goods in the highly import-sensitive category, the most important item being clothing (Taylor and Lamb, 1979, table 1 and p. 152).

Increased competition on Western markets. Hungarian and other Eastern European exports to CC areas have also been buffeted in recent years by increased competition from Third World suppliers, other Eastern European countries and, generally, those nations which have promoted their exports in response to deficits in their balance of payments induced by the oil price rise. The situation has been depicted graphically by Brown and Tardos:

> World markets of the mid-1970s, especially in certain industrial manufactures, became a Darwinian survival-of-the-most-flexible environment. Suppliers who could not satisfy world market requirements in terms of range of assortment, quality requirements, and observance of terms of delivery were left behind. Those who were novices in this keen competition of buyer's markets were particularly handicapped . . . Hungarian enterprises were not under the type of vital pressures at home as their competitors either in the acquisition of markets or in price bargaining. (Brown and Tardos, 1980, p. 16)

(c) *Domestic causes of the growing CC trade deficit*

Poor investment performance. Table 8.3 has shown that in 1974 and 1975, the two years when Hungary suffered the greatest external shock from deteriorating terms of trade, the rate of growth of both investment and consumption accelerated. Investments, especially when growing rapidly, are dollar-import intensive, because a significant share of machinery and equipment and any increase in inventories must be purchased from the West. Moreover, when projects come on-stream, their efficient operation often requires continuous dollar imports. These may be required even when a project is planned to use inputs from CMEA sources. For example, when a modern, electronically controlled printing-machine assembly purchased in the West was put into operation, it was found that the quality of the paper available from CMEA sources was inadequate. It became more economical, therefore, to use paper imported from the West for CC than to put up with frequent machine breakdowns. Especially during 1974–5, but in subsequent years also, a large share of the increase in investment went into accumulating inventories and swelling unfinished investment projects; their combined sum during 1973–7 amounted to about 60 per cent of Hungary's aggregate foreign-trade deficit.

Investments were cut drastically in 1976 – even the absolute volume declined – and this helped to moderate the CC trade deficit in that year. But in 1977 total net investments increased by 11 per cent, and this in turn helped to increase the CC deficit by nearly 50 per cent. In 1978 total net investments grew by 25 per cent, contributing to a record CC trade deficit in that year of $1·1 billion – almost double the deficit of the previous year. In 1979 strict controls were once again introduced on investments, for balance-of-payments reasons.

To understand better the relationship between investments and the balance of payments, one must focus on the growth, the direction and the efficiency of investments. (Hungary's investment policy is discussed in Paul Hare's Chapter 5 of this volume, so I shall summarise only those aspects which directly influence the CC trade balance.) With respect to the growth and direction of investments, central authorities play a decisive role because of the power of their purses, even though about half of investment is decided by enterprises. The government largely funds big state investments, makes direct loans from the state budget or through the banking system, and grants subsidies to enterprises to promote projects that could not otherwise be financed.

The objective of centrally decided productive investments is almost always import substitution or increasing CMEA exports (mainly in the chemical and engineering sectors) – investments that require substantial dollar imports but contribute only marginally to dollar exports. In the manufacturing sector CC exports are provided mostly by light industry, whose development has had low investment priority until recent years (Köves, 1978, p. 113).

A good example of what appears to be poor central investment decision is the rapid expansion of the chemical industry, which in the first half of the 1970s received about a fifth of all investment funds in the manufacturing sector, more than light industry or all engineering industries combined (Balassa, 1978, p. 264). The chemical industry has a double disadvantage: it gobbles up scarce investment capital, and it requires large imports. In 1979, for example, about half of Hungary's total CC imports, 79 billion forints, comprised raw materials and semi-manufactured products (see Table 8.5), of which 37 billion forints (almost half of the total) were chemicals! And these figures do not take into account the energy-intensiveness of the chemical industry, which represents a further substantial drain on CC. These considerations suggest that it is the oil-exporting countries, not Hungary, that have a comparative advantage in building energy-based chemical industries.

Another problem is that, although local government authorities involved in investment decisions know the rules of the bargaining game with central authorities for the allocation of investments, they are not fully aware of the country's resource limits or the importance of efficiency considerations. Special interests – whether enterprises, branch ministries or local administrative organs – not infrequently have the upper hand in the bargaining, because, among other reasons, they can invoke the spectre of a costly interruption of production or service unless investment is forthcoming. The threat of a breakdown in production or service is a 'harder' argument than efficiency calculations based on costs and prices, which, it can be argued, are distorted by too many subsidies and taxes.

Another problem is a proliferation of projects, which is inefficient because the average completion time for them is much longer in Hungary than for comparable projects in Western countries. Invested capital remains unproductive longer, the technology embodied in a project and the resulting product itself tend to become obsolete sooner than planned, and completion costs rise. Especially important for CC exports is that market conditions may change, so export opportunities envisaged at the investment decision stage may not materialise.

Insufficient means and incentives for enterprises to expand CC exports. Hungary's foreign trade policy in general and exchange rate mechanism in particular were designed under the New Economic Mechanism to create an environment in which the profitability of selling on the domestic or ruble markets would be slightly better than that of selling on CC markets. For such a policy to succeed, enterprises must nevertheless produce and market commodities that are competitive on the world market. This in turn requires that enterprises have the *means* to produce such commodities and the *incentives* to expand exports to CC markets. Were these conditions satisfied in Hungary?

For enterprises to produce high quality manufactures, a necessary but not sufficient condition is access to investment resources to create or expand capacity for producing goods that are saleable on dollar markets. But enterprise profits have not been permitted to be differentiated enough for efficient enterprises to be able to expand CC exports rapidly. The Deputy Prime Minister of Hungary pinpointed the problem:

There is still considerable pressure on planning and economic regulation to ensure that largely equal opportunities for growth be given to every industry and every firm. In theory, the need to discriminate is accepted, but state bodies and even certain Party organizations and trade unions, endeavor to establish special conditions which equalize the chances for growth, regardless of work performance. Specific subsidies and an insufficiently tight incomes policy mean that firms are not compelled to improve their efficiency ... At the same time, enterprising firms that performed well did not receive the help that was their due, since excess support for firms which performed poorly or were even in the red, took up the available financial resources. (Huszár, 1979, p. 17)

As important as having limited means to expand capacity to produce for the CC market is the problem of *insufficient incentives*. Even enterprises that could export more to CC markets find that it is easier to sell on the much less demanding domestic or ruble markets. Firms are not compelled to seek dollar revenues, because accept ble earnings (which for all practical purposes can increase only modestly in any given yea because of the high marginal-tax rate) can be generated without devoting a great deal of effort to reach Western markets. Strong incentives to orient towards the domestic and CMEA markets and weak incentives to orient towards dollar markets are really two sides of the same problem.

3   Policies and prospects for reducing the convertible currency trade deficit

(a) *Overview*
Compared with the other CMEA countries, in Hungary there is a remarkably open, objective and widespread discussion of the economic problems both in the economic literature and in the popular press. There is also a growing consensus among economists and top political leaders about the general direction in which the solution to the problems must be found. The consensus can be paraphrased as follows:

It is no use complaining about the growing economic difficulties that we face because of the deteriorating external environment; fundamentally, there is nothing that we can do to change the external situation. Our country's small size and poor resource endowment preclude the option of reducing international economic interdependence. Our only hope lies in ourselves; we must face up to the new realities and adjust to them by tightening our belts and by fundamentally improving the efficiency of our economic system.

Hungary realises that the deteriorating CC trade balance is the single most important economic problem that must be solved. To be sure, the need to improve the CC trade balance has been on the agenda of all the Eastern European countries for decades; what is new in Hungary is that tackling this problem has become a top priority. This in turn requires a new way of thinking about economic performance, subordinating quantitative growth to the CC balance of payments (Bíró, 1979, p. 60).

What is Hungary doing, and with what chance of success, to improve its CC trade balance during the 1980s? Three closely interconnected sets of decisions have been taken: (1) lowering the growth rate; (2) further economic reforms in the spirit of the New Economic Mechanism; and (3) tighter monetary and fiscal policies and increased differentiation among enterprises, based on profitability and CC export potential. These will now be discussed in turn.

(b) *Lowering the growth rate*

The single most important measure to improve the CC trade balance is the reduction of planned growth rates for 1979, 1980 and for the 1981−5 five-year plan. The 1979 plan, for example, fixed the growth of national income produced at 3−4 per cent and earmarked the greater part of the increase for net exports. Hungary has a high income elasticity of demand for CC imports. For example, when national income grows at 5−6 per cent, the elasticity is 2 (i.e. each 1 per cent growth requires a 2 per cent increase in CC imports); at 3−4 per cent growth rates, the elasticity is in the 1·3−1·5 range (Bíró, 1979, p. 60). Slower growth rates will thus reduce the volume of imports and make more resources available for exports.

Early targets for the 1981−5 five-year plan aim for a 30 per cent growth of produced national income versus a 23−5 per cent increase in absorption, the difference to be channelled to net exports, mainly to the dollar area. These targets imply an approximately 5 per cent annual growth of produced national income for 1981−5, which will be difficult to achieve if, as expected, the country faces a continued deterioration in its terms of trade, due to: rising energy prices; stagnating supplies from the CMEA of raw materials, energy and material-intensive semi-manufactures; and increased competition and protectionism on the world market. The achievement of a 5 per cent growth rate without further heavy CC borrowing will require skilful economic policies, including the successful implementation of the new reform measures.

Even if the planned production targets can be achieved, it remains to be seen whether the leadership will be able to hold incremental absorption (i.e. consumption plus investment) significantly below 5 per cent (or whatever rate of production increase is achieved). It has been exceedingly difficult in all Eastern European countries (and also in the West) to check the strong pressures on resource utilisation. Vested interests in Hungary want a minimum of 5–7 per cent annual growth in absorption, in order to better the standard of living, to invest more for technological progress, to secure CMEA imports in order to improve infrastructure, and so on.

(c)   *Further economic reforms*

An inter-related set of reform measures was introduced during 1979–80. A key is reforming the price system. One objective of price reforms is to eliminate the anomaly of the wholesale price level's being higher than the retail price level. One undesirable consequence of this is that a large share of exports must be subsidised, thereby channelling the energies of enterprise-managers into bargaining about subsidies rather than striving for more exports. Furthermore, across-the-board export subsidies are illegal under GATT rules, whereas reimbursing the exporters for taxes levied on consumption (e.g. a value-added tax) does conform to GATT rules. A further adverse result of the wholesale versus retail price-level anomaly is that heavily subsidised consumer prices tend to worsen the CC trade balance, because some of the most heavily subsidised food products have to be imported (e.g. feedstuffs to produce meat) or could be exported for CC. A still further undesirable consequence of the anomaly is that it prevents the unification of the commercial and tourist exchange rates, distorting calculations and providing an obstacle to achieving the limited convertibility of the forint.

A partial solution to the price level anomaly lies in increasing retail prices – a politically difficult move. The retail price increases implemented on 1 July 1979 have gone a long way towards abolishing subsidies on consumer products and adjusting relative prices to those prevailing on the world market. (At the same time wages, pensions, family allowances and other transfer payments were increased substantially, so that approximately 75 per cent of the revenue generated by the higher prices is being rechannelled to the population.) The resulting change in consumption patterns is expected to improve the CC trade balance by freeing more agricultural products for export. Paradoxically, while the Western press tends to chide any Eastern European country when it raises retail prices for its inability to escape inflation, not only do price increases of the Hungarian type make good economic sense, but in addition their successful implementation is a sign of the government's political strength.

A further correction of the price level anomaly is to reduce wholesale prices, since they embody such exceptionally high fiscal charges. The wholesale price reform introduced on 1 January 1980 set domestic price relatives on the basis of world market prices, which increased the price level, and abolished the charge on assets, which decreased the price level. The net outcome was a small further closing of the gap between the commercial and the tourist proxy exchange rates, from 75 per cent to about 60 per cent. The primary objective of the price reform was to provide better orientation for a structural policy that augments the export potential (Biró, 1979, p. 61). These measures should help to improve the CC balance of payments by forcing enterprises to economise on expensive imports and by giving a clearer picture of the real cost of exports.

There is a discussion about the desirability of making further adjustments in exchange rates, perhaps upvaluing the forint *vis-à-vis* the ruble to discourage exports to CC areas. The expectation is that, after tighter monetary and fiscal policies have increased the price elasticity of Hungary's export supply to both areas and the price elasticity of import demand from the dollar region, exchange rate adjustments would have an appreciable impact on the CC trade balance. Moreover, now that the consumer prices are no longer subsidised heavily, the tourist exchange rates will also be easier to adjust to stimulate tourism, thus generating more CC.

(d) *Tighter monetary and fiscal policies and increased differentiation among enterprises*

A tax reform is to be introduced along with the wholesale price reform. The dual aim of changing the tax structure is to reduce the *level* of taxation in the production sector (shifting taxation to consumption) and to lower the *rate* of enterprise profits in order to bring their self-financing capability, especially regarding investments, more into balance with the economy's real resource potential. Tighter monetary and fiscal measures as well as the price reforms are intended, on balance, to lower slightly the cost of production in state industry (making it possible to reduce the gap between the commercial and tourist exchange rates), to reduce the number of new investment projects that can be started by enterprises (whose explosive cyclical growth has been a major cause of the CC trade deficit), and to create a more restrictive macroeconomic environment in order to compel firms to improve their performance. 'The essence of this compulsion is to make sales at home more difficult by moderating domestic purchasing power. This, as well as the planned regulation of non-hard currency exports, will prompt firms to increase exports to capitalist countries' (Huszár, 1979, p. 19). 'Regulating' non-hard currency exports means restricting them to the limits defined by interstate agreements. This may mean stagnation, in some cases even a decline, in production for some firms, which will seek special state support. The intention is to reject such requests.

One of the key factors that will determine the outcome of the new policy on the CC balance of payments is: will there be increased differentiation among enterprises based on profitability and CC export potential? Policy statements assert that this will indeed be so. After the price and fiscal reforms enterprise profitability, excluding subsidies and tax concessions in order to obtain a clearer picture of performance, once again is intended to be the principal guide to resource allocation. Efficient well-managed enterprises, especially those which can generate additional CC exports, are to be encouraged to expand rapidly; others are slated to stagnate and in some cases to discontinue operations.

A key instrument of this policy is the National Bank's special investment-credit programme to promote the expansion of export-oriented industries. Begun in 1976, credits under this programme are distributed on the basis of tenders among Hungarian firms and co-operatives that can repay the credit within three to five years out of the CC foreign-exchange earnings generated by the additional exports. Enterprises obtain credits on favourable terms in forints, for which they may purchase from the National Bank any currency needed to import investment goods. The bank finances the increased demand for CC by raising medium- and long-term syndicated credits on the Eurocurrency market (Fekete, 1979, pp. 12–13). Between 1971 and mid 1979 the bank had borrowed, to support this programme and other foreign-exchange needs, a cumulative total of $315 million via bonds and notes and $2·3 billion via syndicated loans and placements on the Eurocurrency market, with practically the full amount still outstanding in July 1979 (Hungarian National Bank, 1979, p. 10).

Investment credits granted by the National Bank to mid 1979 under this programme amounted to 49 billion forints (about $1·4 billion), supporting, for example, the expansion of the output of engines and chassis for buses and lorries, light bulbs, machine tools, pharmaceuticals and insecticides, truck tyres, agricultural machinery, various branches of the aluminium industry, fine metallurgy and agricultural processing plants. The bank estimated that by 1980 projects supported under this programme would be able to generate approximately $850 million in additional CC exports (Hungarian National Bank, 1979, p. 8). To be sure, a portion of this sum may well be exports that would have materialised in any case but are attributed by the borrowing enterprises to this special programme. In any event, it has been decided that:

> ... during the remaining years of the current Five Year Plan (1976–80) and during the period of the next Five Year Plan (1981–85), the major share of investment credits to be granted by the Bank will be allocated primarily to export-oriented sectors ... Elsewhere, a diminution is envisaged. (Hungarian National Bank, 1979, p. 8)

If, in Hungary's new lower-growth environment, some enterprises will be given the resources to expand rapidly because they are profitable and have excellent CC export potential, other enterprises will have to stagnate or must bear a loss. Until recently there were no such enterprises, because manifold and individually tailored subsidies prevented losses from occurring. Repeated high-level policy declarations during 1979 stated that enterprises will increasingly be allowed to incur losses, which are to be covered initially from their reserve funds and depreciation allowances and temporarily by bank loans. It is hoped that this will immediately reduce the funds available for expansion and put unprofitable enterprises on notice that they must solve their problems. If unsuccessful, they will be closed down or merged with other enterprises.

Implementing such policies is essential, because in Hungary's over-full employment economy this is the only way to rechannel manpower and other real resources in order to permit the expansion of profitable firms. An inevitable corollary of such a policy is increased differentiation of personal incomes, with compensation linked closely to performance.

If implemented purposefully and without many exceptions, this new policy will improve the CC trade balance. Enterprises will be forced to economise on inputs, to seek new opportunities for CC exports, and to become more efficient and market oriented. But effective implementation will not be easy. Is Hungarian society prepared to accept a widening differentiation of personal incomes and enterprise fortunes, which would raise difficult ideological problems and, perhaps more importantly, disturb vested interests? The success of Hungary's new economic policy with respect to the CC trade balance may well be decided by what happens when a delegation from an enterprise about to be closed down, led by the local Party secretary, confronts the planners with arguments like:

Can you be certain that distortions in economic calculations and administrative intervention at one or more points in the production process are not really responsible for our firm's profit performance? More importantly, our people have been working at this enterprise for twenty-five years; they are honest and support fully the country's political system. Are you going to refuse to give them money to keep on working and expanding?

The advice of nearly all Hungarian economists as to what should be done in such situations, and the statements of today's top political leaders on how such situations will be resolved, unequivocally favour economic efficiency over political expediency. It will be interesting to watch as events unfold during the first few years of the 1980s.

Appendix: Comparison of Different Sets of Official Trade Statistics and Alternative Trade-Share Calculations

(a)   *Trade series in forints*
Table 8.6 shows two sets of official statistics for total trade and trade settled in rubles and dollars (i.e. CC) for 1977.

Table 8.6   *Foreign trade statistics, 1977 (billion forints).*

		Imports			Exports	
Source	*Total*	*Settled in rubles*	*Settled in dollars*	*Total*	*Settled in rubles*	*Settled in dollars*
Statistical yearbook	267	123 (46%)	144 (54%)	238	120 (50%)	118 (50%)
National Bank	264	n.p. (46%)	n.p. (54%)	244	n.p. (50%)	n.p. (50%)

Note: n.p. = not published.

Sources: *Külkereskedelmi Statisztikai Évkönyv* (1977), p. 10; and Hungarian National Bank (1979), p. 26.

Trade reported in the statistical yearbook shows imports c.i.f. (which adds to the purchase price hypothetical transport and related costs to bring imports to the Hungarian border) and exports f.o.b. (which subtracts from the sales price hypothetical transport and related costs to deliver exports from the Hungarian border to the point of sale; (*Külkereskedelmi Statisztikai Évkönyv*, 1977, p. 6). The figures reported in official publications of the National Bank apparently show imports and exports on the basis of contract prices (i.e. actual cost of imports at point of purchase and actual revenue from exports at point of sale. This can be deduced on the basis of information provided on transport costs in the yearbook (*Külkereskedelmi Statisztikai Évkönyv*, 1977, p. 11).

A further possible difference between the two series may be that the statistical yearbook's figures are based on customs documents, while the National Bank's data are based on financial settlements, irrespective of whether customs clearance has been made in the given year or not.

Both sources derive forint figures by converting the foreign currency spent on imports or earned on exports at prevailing commercial exchange rates. The statistical yearbook states that for exports the exchange rate is that at which the National Bank *buys* foreign exchange, for imports the rate at which the bank *sells* foreign exchange (*Külkereskedelmi Statisztikai Évkönyv*, 1977, p. 6). It is not known whether the National Bank uses the same or a 'unified' exchange rate to report trade figures in forints.

(b) *Trade series in rubles and dollars*
Table 8.7 shows two sets of official figures in foreign exchange for trade settled in rubles and dollars for 1977.

Table 8.7 *Foreign trade statistics, 1977 (million units).*

Source	Total	Imports Settled in rubles	Settled in dollars	Total	Exports Settled in rubles	Settled in dollars
Statistical yearbook	n.p.	n.p.	n.p.	n.p.	n.p.	n.p.
National Bank: trade summary	n.p.	3,500	3,452	n.p.	3,439	3,034
Balance of payments	n.p.	n.p.	3,047	n.p.	n.p.	2,685

Note: n.p. = not published.

Source: Hungarian National Bank (1979), pp. 26 and 29.

The only foreign-exchange series published are those reported by the National Bank. The difference between the two dollar series is apparently the inclusion of transport and related costs on imports and similar revenues on exports in the 'trade summary' series and the exclusion of the same in the 'balance-of-payment' tabulations, which show the net balance on freight and insurance as a separate item.

(c) *Estimating trade flows and trade shares in dollars*
Any detailed analysis of Hungary's foreign trade must rely on data published in the statistical yearbook, which, as noted, reports forint series only. Forint figures are obtained by converting ruble- and dollar-(i.e. CC-) denominated trade at the official exchange rates prevailing at the time the transaction was recorded. Trade shown in forints can thus be reconverted into rubles or dollars at the same rates. Actually, precise conversion on the basis of information published in the statistical yearbook is not possible for any year in which the exchange rate changed other than at the year's end, because it is not known which transactions were converted into forints at which exchange rate. A reasonably accurate approximation, however, can be made on the basis of some average exchange rate.

The question is: how can trade flows settled in rubles and in dollars be brought to a common denominator; that is, how can the dollar equivalent of trade settled in rubles be obtained? There is no fully satisfactory method, mainly because prices in any CMEA country's ruble and dollar trade differ, in some years and for some commodities by substantial margins. (Marer, 1972, discussed this problem.)

One approach is to convert ruble-denominated trade shown in forints first back into rubles (at the official forint/ruble rate) and then into dollars at the official (and largely arbitrary) ruble/dollar rate set by the USSR. The justification for this approach is that, since the point of departure for trade settled in rubles is an agreed-upon historical *dollar* world-market price, which is then transformed into accounting rubles at the official ruble/dollar rate, this approach simply reverses the steps that were taken to obtain the forint value in the first place. It should be noted, however, that, while trade settled in dollars is valued at *current* world prices, trade settled in rubles is valued at *historical* world-market prices, so there is no common basis of valuation of the underlying trade flows. Be that as it may, this is the approach followed by Brown and Tardos (1980) and in presenting dollar figures in Table 8.2.

An alternative approach is to argue that price level differences between Hungary's ruble versus dollar trade are measured accurately by the forint/ruble versus forint/dollar exchange rates. It is thus possible to accept the forint figures as common denominators and calculate trade shares on that basis, as does the National Bank in its publications and I have done for trade share calculations presented in Table 8.5. Accepting this approach, Hungary's total or ruble trade in forints can be converted into dollars at the current forint/dollar rate. This procedure yields a higher share for dollar trade in the total than does the alternative approach.

Acknowledgement: Chapter 8

I am pleased to acknowledge the role of the editors of this volume in commissioning this study and in improving the substance as well as the style of presentation. I alone, of course, am responsible for the views expressed.

References: Chapter 8

Külkereskedelmi Statisztikai Évkönyv (Budapest: Központi Statisztikai Hivatal, various years).
Magyar Statisztikai Zsebkönyv (Budapest: Központi Statisztikai Hivatal, various years).
Statisztikai Évkönyv (Budapest: Központi Statisztikai Hivatal, various years).
Statisztikai Havi Közlemények (Budapest: Központi Statisztikai Hivatal, monthly).

Balassa, B. (1978), 'The economic reform in Hungary: ten years after', *European Economic Review*, vol. 11 (3), pp. 245–68.

Beke, K., and Hunyadi, L. (1977), 'A magyar export importanyag tartalma' (The material import content of Hungary's export), *Külgazdaság*, vol. 21 (7), pp. 494–506.

Biró, G. (1979), 'An economic policy for the eighties', *New Hungarian Quarterly*, vol. 20 (Autumn), pp. 59–64.

Bornstein, M. (1977), 'Price formation models and price policy in Hungary', in A. Abouchar (cd.), *The Socialist Price Mechanism* (Durham, NC: Duke University Press).

Brown, A., and Marer, P. (1973), 'Foreign trade in the East European reforms', in M. Bornstein (ed.), *Plan and Market* (New Haven, Conn.: Yale University Press).

Brown, A. and Tardos, M. (1980), 'Transmission and responses to external economic disturbances: Hungary', in E. Neuberger and L. Tyson (eds), *Transmission and Response: Impact of International Economic Disturbances on the Soviet Union and Eastern Europe* (Oxford: Pergamon Press). The page numbers cited refer to a manuscript copy.

Csikós-Nagy, B. (1979), 'East–West trade and prices', *Marketing in Hungary*, 1st quarter, pp. 5–10.

Erős, Gy. (1977), 'Az infláció egyes valutapolitikai összefüggései' (Selected aspects of the relationship between inflation and foreign exchange policy), unpublished Ph.D. dissertation, Karl Marx University of Economics, Budapest.

Fekete, J. (1976), 'Exchange rate policy in a planned economy', *New Hungarian Quarterly*, vol. 17 (Autumn), pp. 56–60, Number 63.

Fekete, J. (1977), 'A tervszerű devizagazdálkodás néhány kérdésről a magyar tapasztalatok alaján' (Concerning some questions of foreign exchange-planning on the basis of Hungarian experiences), *Pénzügyi Szemle*, special supplement, vol. 21 (5), pp. 65–73.

Fekete, J. (1979), 'Indebtedness of the socialist countries as seen from Hungary', *Marketing in Hungary*, 1st quarter, pp. 11–13.

Gadó, O. (1976), *The Economic Mechanism in Hungary: How It Works in 1976* (Budapest: Akadémiai Kiadó).

General Agreement on Tariffs and Trade (GATT) (1969), 'Questions by GATT, and answers by the Hungarian Government', following submission of the Hungarian government's 'Memorandum' (1969), GATT Document 3426(nd).

Holzman, F. D. (1979), 'Some systemic factors contributing to the convertible currency shortages of centrally planned economies', *American Economic Review*, vol. 69 (2), pp. 76–80.

Hungarian government (1969), 'Memorandum of foreign trade', official statement by the government of Hungary for GATT, prepared in connection with Hungary's application for GATT membership (December).

Hungarian National Bank (1979), 'Information memorandum', Budapest (28 September); issued in connection with US $250 million medium-term Euro-currency loan.

Hungarian National Bank (1980), 'Information memorandum', Budapest (1 April); issued in connection with a second US $250 million medium-term loan.

Huszár, I. (1979), 'The economic equilibrium and the foreign trade balance', *New Hungarian Quarterly*, vol. 20 (Spring), pp. 16–22.

Kohn, M. J. (1979), 'Soviet–East European economic relations, 1975–78', in Joint Economic Committee, *Soviet Economy in a Period of Transition* (Washington, DC: US Government Printing Office).

Kolarik, W. F. (1979), 'Statistical abstract of East–West trade finance', in Joint Economic Committee, *Issues in East–West Commercial Relations* (Washington, DC: US Government Printing Office).

Köves, A. (1978), 'Integration into world economy and direction of economic development in Hungary', *Acta Oeconomica*, vol. 20 (1–2), pp. 107–26.

Kramer, J. C. (1979), 'Hungary: preparing a new effort to reform the economy', US Department of State, Washington, DC (August).

Külgazdaság report (1979), 'Gazdasági együttmüködésünk a szocialista országokkal' (Economic co-operation with socialist countries), vol. 23 (5), pp. 3–11.

Marer, P. (1972), *Postwar Pricing and Price Patterns in Socialist Foreign Trade, 1946–1971* (International Development Research Centre, Indiana University).

Marer, P. (1977), 'Economic performance, strategy and prospects in Eastern Europe', in Joint Economic Committee, *East European Economies Post-Helsinki* (Washington, DC: US Government Printing Office).

Marer, P., and Montias, J. M. (1980), 'The theory and measurement of East European integration', in P. Marer and J. M. Montias (eds), *East European Integration and East–West Trade* (Bloomington: Indiana University Press 1980).

Portes, R. (1977), 'Hungary: economic performance, policy and prospects', in Joint Economic Committee, *East European Economies Post-Helsinki* (Washington, DC: US Government Printing Office).

Portes, R. (1978), 'Exchange rate policy in Hungary between 1972 and 1976', paper presented at the Fourth US–Hungarian Economics Seminar, Budapest (mimeo.).

Snell, E. M. (1974), 'Eastern Europe's trade and payments with the West', in Joint Economic Committee, *Reorientation and Commercial Relations of the Economies of Eastern Europe* (Washington, DC: US Government Printing Office).

Taylor, K., and Lamb, D. (1979), 'Communist exports to the West in import sensitive sectors', in Joint Economic Committee, *Issues in East–West Commercial Relations* (Washington DC: US Government Printing Office).

Wolf, T. (1978), 'Exchange rate adjustments in small market and centrally planned economies', *Journal of Comparative Economics*, vol. 2 (3), pp. 226–45.

Zoeter, J. (1977), 'Eastern Europe: the growing hard currency debt', in Joint Economic Committee, *Eastern European Economies Post-Helsinki*, (Washington, DC: US Government Printing Office).

Chapter 9

The Role of the Exchange Rate in Hungary's Adjustment to External Economic Disturbances

1 Introduction

It is generally accepted that a recognition of the necessity for a direct link between external and internal prices was one of the cardinal concepts of the Hungarian economic reform introduced in 1968. It was thought necessary to introduce a uniform coefficient for the conversion of foreign prices into forint prices. Although very few people believed in the feasibility of an internationally acknowledged (I do not want to say convertible) exchange rate, most of the experts conceived of this coefficient as having similar economic effects on the domestic economy. The distinguishing feature of a coefficient rather than an exchange rate can be taken to be that the latter influences the activity of enterprises, while the former is only an accounting technique, having no consequence other than indirectly influencing bonuses. I shall therefore generally use the expression 'exchange rate' in what follows.

In the debate about the principle of the exchange rate system, the more theoretically minded economists argued for an equilibrium or marginal rate, while those who were in, or closer to, the administration opted for a rate calculated on the basis of average export costs. Not surprisingly, the latter policy was the one that was adopted.

Alan A. Brown and Paul Marer (1973, p. 177) wrote that it would be interesting to compare the Hungarian methodological debate on foreign-trade price-coefficient calculations with the purchasing-power parity doctrine; István Lakos and Gabor Obláth (1978) further elaborated the comparison. However, it is not right to see the 'average coefficient', as it is termed in Hungary, as an exchange rate based on purchasing parity, although many of its adherents did argue in terms of the relative purchasing power of the forint. The difference between the Hungarian coefficient and Cassel's exchange rate is that the former supposes different relative prices in the two countries, while the latter does not. The subject of the debate between Cassel and his opponents has been whether purchasing parity is a causal determinant of the exchange rate or an always fulfilled condition (Schneider, 1968). On the other hand, the Hungarian 'average coefficient' leads to a situation where the average cost of the export bill is calculated with domestic relative prices different from foreign relative prices. A substantial part of the export bill calculated with this coefficient must therefore be unprofitable for enterprises, unless there is some form of budgetary intervention.

Nevertheless there are some parallels between the Hungarian case and the situation that is found in modern tests of the purchasing-power parity doctrine. These tests avoid the problem of the tautological nature of purchasing power parity by comparing various domestic packages of goods, or similar bundles with different domestic prices. In either case there are many possibilities for not only different quantity weights but also different relative prices. The difference in test cases is caused by aggregation, quality, protectionism, subsidies, taxes, transport and selling costs, payment conditions, and so on.

However, in the Hungarian case the relative price differences are not caused only by these real costs, the variety of goods and divergences in state fiscal regulations. The difference in relative prices is already manifest on a theoretical level, as a consequence of regarding the average cost of producing a unit of exports as the proper cost (i.e. the exchange rate of a unit of the foreign currency), while the cost and price of each unit of exports are determined by special Hungarian conditions, so that the domestic price of almost every product is different from its foreign price multiplied by the exchange rate (although world market prices have had some influence on domestic prices since the introduction of the New Economic Mechanism).

The conditions determining domestic prices are the result of the policy of maintaining full employment of all factors of production in combinations established both by past directive planning and by the present ideas of planners (formulated in real terms). Under these conditions the practice of cost-plus pricing, and many instances of income transfer between enterprises, have survived beyond the reform. At the same time world market prices make their effects felt both directly through the prices of manufactured imports and indirectly by central decisions about the prices of some materials.

In these circumstances the volume of exports needed by the country can be made profitable for all exporting enterprises in two ways. One is by using an exchange rate at the level of the marginal export cost; in this case many of the exporters would earn variable rents over their profits. The other is by using a lower rate, with the budget compensating exporters whose costs are higher than the price given by the exchange rate. As has been noted above, the latter course was adopted in Hungary.

From our point of view, the most important consequence of the average principle is its ability to create a stable monetary and fiscal environment around each enterprise. In reality, it was not the average principle that made this possible; on the contrary, the need for a stable environment was responsible for the application of this principle. The decision was also influenced by the assumption that the marginal rate was higher and would thus stimulate inflation.

2 Exchange rates and devaluation: price effects

I must briefly point here to the parallel between this fear of the inflationary effect of a marginal rate and the pessimistic attitude to devaluation. This digression will also serve as a point of reference for later discussion of my central topic. Most of the economists who suggested a marginal rate thought that it would be introduced in conjunction with a reformed price system. Thus, for them the problem of inflation did not even emerge. They were dealing with relative prices that could fit in with any absolute price level.[1] Nevertheless, the parallel exists in as much as external equilibrium has to be achieved after the changeover. To this extent the situation is identical to that after a devaluation. In both cases the prices of exportable goods, of imported products and of goods that are substitutable for such products (i.e. the prices of the foreign trade sector) have to be increased relative to those of other goods (i.e. the prices of the domestic sector). If price increases have an inflationary effect, it depends on what happens to other prices. If the monetary authorities are able to enforce a stable quantity of money, and if the velocity of circulation does not increase, prices in the domestic sector must decline to match the increases in the prices of the foreign trade sector. This inevitably has social consequences, which will be touched upon later.

Before discussing the real side of the adjustment process, I must comment on price changes. Let us postulate an economy with perfect competition, with fully utilised capacity and in equilibrium at the enterprise level. Price increases in the foreign trade sector result in a situation in which prices of exports and import substitutes include various amounts of differential rent (i.e. short-run profit). With a stable quantity of money and with an invariable velocity of circulation, this must cause a decrease in all other factor incomes.

On the other hand, where differential rents in prices are widespread occurrences, price increases and decreases lead to a general rearrangement of these rents. For example, a monopolistic producer of a domestic good has to decrease its price and to be satisfied with less monopolistic profit, because its customers have less demand for this product if they spend more on imported goods to which they are accustomed. Only the balance of all rent rearrangements will influence factor incomes.

If an economy with directive central planning, with accounting in equilibrium prices and without any automatic mechanism for resource transfer to more effective occupations is transformed into an economy with indirect controls that has relinquished the disjuncture between domestic and external prices, new prices must include an element of differential rent. If this country does not want these rents to lead to income differentials nor wants to rely on automatic capital transfer for the purpose of the elimination of rents, the direct linking of external and internal prices must be modified. Let us suppose now that our country solves this problem by 'nationalising' (i.e. taxing away) rents. In this case a devaluation results in rearrangements of the tax burden among enterprises, and the balance will affect factor incomes in a way similar to the case mentioned above.

The other extreme possibility is that prices do not include differential rents, which simply do not exist. The exchange rate is fixed at the cost level of the most efficient product, and all the others get state compensation. A devaluation rearranges the distribution of the compensation among enterprises and depresses the exchange rate. This latter will entail more compensation at the expense of factor costs.

The 'average cost rate' lies somewhere between these two extremes; there is some differential rent under the average cost, and there is compensation above it.

Let us now turn to the real rather than the financial effects. The transfer of income from the domestic sector to the foreign trade sector results in both the abandoning of some economic activities and the bankruptcy of some enterprises. Their specialised factors will lose their value, and their general factors will be free for use by the growing foreign-trade sector. Those activities which turn out to be unprofitable because of more expensive imports belong to a special category of abandoned activities. There must be some adjustment in final consumption as well. I do not want to deal here with the various adjustment mechanisms that regulate these changes, since they are considered fully in the literature on the economic reforms.

Concluding this generalising digression, I want to stress that the transfer of resources does not occur instantly and is not without costs. There are vested interests resisting the changes necessitated by the income transfer. In modern societies there are methods by which these interests can, through their own efforts or in other ways, put pressure on governments or on central banks. The main cause of inflation is that no administration can ignore these interests, and therefore the tight monetary policy needed for successful devaluation is not implemented. (Incidentally, I should point out that the strict suppression of inflation is not always socially desirable; in addition, it is not always possible to distinguish between opposition to change that stems from a struggle over the distribution of a stable income and opposition to something new that might ultimately increase the income of society as a whole.)

3 The average coefficient and a stable environment for enterprises

I began my digression from the 'average coefficient' (i.e. the Hungarian exchange rate) after indicating that it makes possible the creation around each enterprise of a custom-built monetary and fiscal environment. In fact, the causation is the reverse; the acceptance of the average principle was a consequence of the fact that the government wanted to maintain stable surroundings for the enterprises. It did not want to expose them to the vagaries of the market.

The purpose of such an environment has been manifold. First, there was the desire to facilitate a gentle transition from the old system to the new. Secondly, the very possibility of special central forms of intervention encouraged central authorities and enterprise-managers to think and operate in real terms. Thirdly, it seemed necessary to eliminate the possible wider differences in personal incomes. Fourthly, the above-mentioned monetary and fiscal measures would make it easier to smooth out differences in prices, regulations and usages in Hungary's trade with countries of the Council for Mutual Economic Assistance (CMEA) and with other countries too. As stated by Lakos and Obláth (1978), the 'average coefficient' suits the character of the economic mechanism, combining elements of direct and indirect controls. In other words, it seemed well suited to the regulated market that was to be introduced.

The consequences of creating stable surroundings for enterprises were not thought through, because the authors of the reform did not trust the market mechanism, especially its long run effects. Because of this they did not regard it as mistaken to permit direct budgetary intervention. They were accustomed to thinking in natural units and trusted their own capacity to correct the errors of the market mechanism. They believed, for example, that, if a price or the exchange rate provided misinformation, they would be able to correct the economic process while taking the situation of the industry or of the economy as a whole into account as well (Kozma, 1974b).

Leaving more or less intact the system of cost-plus pricing, with low prices for raw materials and agricultural products, five methods have been employed to create a stable environment for enterprises. First, there are such special budgetary devices as customs duties, import and production taxes, import subsidies and 'state export refunds'. These latter are fixed as an extra percentage over the exchange rate of the dollar or the ruble and have the same value for all the various exports of an enterprise. In practice, most enterprises within the same branch of the economy have the same rate of refund. Secondly, there are the exemptions from general taxes that have been granted in varying degrees and in various forms to many enterprises. Thirdly, there is the obligation to create or use some business assets as reserve funds. This becomes a distinct method when the budget has to subsidise some enterprise funds or one enterprise has to contribute to the fund of another. Fourthly, the investment system has a role in stabilising the position of the enterprise. Fifthly, organisational measures are used.

I shall not deal here with the issue of how this system influences the efficiency and transparency of the economy. In addition, it is well known that the need for, and possibility of, a bargain's being struck between enterprises and the representatives of the state budget in itself creates a comfortable situation for enterprises. Neither this multiplicity of forms of budgetary intervention aimed at creating a stable environment nor the informal interventions of the authorities, however, invalidates the rules of the game of pursuing profit. They simply make the rules slightly blurred and differentiated. For example, the state export refund (which is not an export subsidy in the strict sense of the term but a compensation for the loss of differential rent) simply alters the forint value of a unit of foreign exchange for a particular enterprise or for a branch. It does not directly subsidise the export of a particular product. It is in fact a multiple exchange-rate system.

The state export refund enables the central authorities to rank enterprises according to their export efficiency. This differentiates it from most of the other measures mentioned above. Operationally, this ranking is based on the refund–revenue ratio in their exports. But it disregards price and tax distortions and the costs of increasing exports.

The situation is complicated by other factors, however. There are considerable differences between the requirements of the domestic, socialist and Western markets, and these are not fully expressed by exchange rates and prices. It is generally believed that it is easier for Hungarian enterprises and for the economy as a whole to increase sales on domestic and socialist markets than on Western ones. Essentially, this is a consequence of the production share of each of these markets. Because of the immense importance of domestic and socialist markets, enterprises have adapted themselves fully to meeting the requirements of these markets. The inconvenience of serving Western markets creates additional costs, which the enterprises are not allowed to reflect in their price bargain with the authorities, and the authorities do not take such costs into account when calculating the exchange rate. These 'invisible extra costs' are not matched by commensurate 'invisible' benefits (e.g. appreciation by higher authorities, the possibility of official foreign travel).

The above-mentioned characteristics of the price system and the absence of plan directives necessitate regular formal or informal intervention by the central authorities into enterprise business activities. In addition, most investment decisions are taken by the central authorities; even investment financed by enterprise funds is more successful if it is linked with the realisation of central decisions. Therefore, the influence of export earnings alone should not be expected to lead to a major shift towards a more efficient export composition or to a large increase in the value of exports at the enterprise level. On the other hand, because of informal expectations from above, enterprises may increase exports on occasion even if this is not an efficient choice.

I shall conclude this section with a few words about imports. As Brown and Tardos (1978) stated:

> Saving on imports was practically not promoted (except during a short period in 1975) either by rigid administrative restrictions or by adequate increases of import costs. The falling import elasticity (during the year of 1970) may thus be explained mainly by the fact that the economic units accepted moral suasion by central authorities.

I might add that the necessity for moral suasion perhaps contributes paradoxically to the low price elasticity of import demand and to the fact that changes in imports seem to be correlated more closely with investments than with exchange rate movements. (Generally low cost-consciousness is also a contributing factor.) The reason for this is that larger investments have to be approved by the authorities, or at least managers are expected to consult their superiors about them. Such investment decisions are not changed if the planned imports subsequently become more expensive. On the other hand, in the case of unapproved decisions adopted independently by enterprises, it may be that the most recent price movements are more likely to be taken into account and that import savings are recognised as such by higher authorities However, this is only a tentative hypothesis.

4 Exchange control since 1973

I have outlined briefly the most important characteristics of the Hungarian New Economic Mechanism that determine its reactions to an external shock. In doing so I have referred only to those characteristics which seem important for my later exposition. Thus, I have perhaps stressed the contradiction between profit maximisation and central control too strongly. The New Economic Mechanism did free the enterprise from many constraints. The growth in exports of more complex manufactured goods to the industrially developed countries is an adequate measure of success. Exports of goods belonging to groups 54, 7 and 8 of the Standard Industrial Trade Classification (SITC), which can certainly be identified as more complex manufactured goods,[2] grew at a rate of 14 per cent per year in the last four years before the reform. In the first eight years after the reform the rate of increase was about 18 per cent per year. For 1975−6 we have no data, but the exports of these goods to all non-socialist countries grew by only about 8 per cent. In the following year, however, the increase in these exports to industrially developed countries was about 16 per cent again. It is generally believed that enterprise initiative has been an important factor in this fast growth.

I turn now to the impact of the rocketing of oil prices and later of all prices, although I do not want to present here a full history of the Hungarian economy since 1973. (For a broader and more detailed description see Brown and Tardos, 1978; and Hewett, 1980.) This followed a long period during which price increases on international markets had lagged behind the rise of domestic prices in all important trading countries with a market economy.

What we can call an exchange rate policy has changed several times since 1968. In 1969 an additional export incentive was introduced in the form of a tax rebate. This was replaced by another kind of tax rebate in 1971. In 1975 this rebate was abolished. I do not refer to these rebates, termed 'net incentives', for the sake of completeness alone; they demonstrate that aspects of the domestic price level and the budget were considered more important than the principle of controlling foreign trade by exchange-rate-like means. Similarly, at first exchange rate movements of convertible currencies were not followed, but premia were introduced for the revalued currencies. The official rate was revalued only from the spring of 1973. At the end of that year Bartha proposed an average value calculated from weighted Hungarian trade figures.

For a few months after the oil crisis, nothing happened. It was thought initially that the special enterprise reserve funds for mitigating world-market price fluctuations would be able to solve the problem. This is why these funds have often served as a framework for import subsidies since.

A few months later it could be seen that inflation abroad would increase both export earnings and the domestic price level. Some experts proposed a gradual decrease in export refunds and a curb on increases in the quantity of money, so allowing the average exchange rate to reach the marginal level. Others suggested a revaluation of the forint, which would leave the size of the refund unchanged. The policy adopted, however, was that exchange rates and domestic prices should remain unchanged and increases in export earnings should be taxed away, while imports should be subsidised. The exchange rate and prices for CMEA trade were still unchanged.

There was little public debate about exchange rate policy at that time. I can refer the reader only to the articles by Vincze (1973), Wiesel (1973) and myself (Kozma, 1974). Reading articles about the 'active exchange-rate policy' of that period, it seems that many of the authors considered this policy chiefly from the point of view of changes in the exchange rates of various convertible currencies; and even among those who did not write from this point of view, there were few who were bothered by the connection between the exchange rate and changes in relative prices.

Let us suppose theoretically that there is an external inflation, with relative price changes such that the terms of trade (in foreign currency terms) deteriorate, while the quantity and composition of exports and imports do not change because domestic prices are fixed. In this case the balance of budgetary gains from export price increases and import subsidies must be negative. But this budgetary deficit, caused by import subsidies, is different from one induced by export subsidies. The latter acts as a monetary demand against real resources, while the former can be spent only on foreign exchange borrowed by the central bank to cover the deficit in foreign currencies.

It follows from this that the policy of price-fixing is able to insulate the economy from external inflation. Nevertheless, it makes it impossible for the economy to adapt itself to the changed environment – to correct the imbalance caused by the deterioration in the terms of trade.

Naturally, the actual policy followed by Hungary after 1973 did not function exactly in the manner described above. It is impossible to follow all price movements with an export tax, an export refund or new import-subsidy rates. So, it is not surprising that from 1973 to 1974, when the big increase in import subsidies occurred, there was also an increase in the size of the export refund.

It would have been correct to abandon the policy of price-fixing. It was not sensible to finance a deterioration in the terms of trade by means of borrowing while at the same time making it impossible for enterprises to adapt themselves to the new relative prices. It was a mistake to judge the success of the policy in terms of budgetary equilibrium.

A budgetary deficit was the main reason why the Hungarian authorities changed the policy in 1975 and increased the prices of some imported goods. At the same time the effects on income of these price increases were neutralised by decreasing charges on capital, by granting exemptions from general taxes and by other special arrangements. The changes made in 1976 were more significant in form, but in content they continued the policy begun in the preceding year, and they were not so significant quantitatively apart from a big switch from import subsidies to export refunds.

In 1976 the commercial exchange rate was introduced, and the forint was revalued both against the dollar and against the accounting ruble. This time the connection with external inflation was stressed (Bartha, 1976; Medgyessy, 1977). Neither the revaluation nor the increase in producer prices was higher than in 1975. Even the change in the average domestic price of exported goods relative to the exchange rate was at the same rate as in the preceding year. But the export price index in dollar terms moved in the opposite direction from the producer price index between 1974 and 1976. Export earnings must have decreased before 1976 therefore, and this necessitated the increase in export refunds. The changes in the exemptional tax preferences played a part here as well.

It is very difficult to make a general evaluation of this policy because of the many preferences and exemptions involved. For present purposes it would be better to suppose a general increase in the credit facilities provided by the banking system, as a proxy for the policy of maintaining enterprise income through tax exemptions. In this way too it is possible that all enterprises can continue working as before or as prescribed in their plans, despite unfavourable changes in the exchange rate or prices.

Without changes in the terms of trade (or, more exactly, in relative prices) and with a balanced external account, it is theoretically possible to counteract external inflation by revaluing an exchange rate based on average costs. The standard for determining the required amount of revaluation should be stability in the level of export compensation involved and the absence of any need for import subsidies.

The situation is quite different with deteriorating terms of trade, especially if in practice the exchange rate applied to exports is not the same as that for imports. The confusion of the average costs principle and the purchasing-power parity doctrine brings its own punishment. A revaluation in accordance with the changes in import prices not only neutralises the inflationary effect but also involves a greater amount of export compensation. On the other hand, if the country revalues its currency according to export price increases in foreign terms, import prices in domestic terms will increase. In the former case, export compensation, and in the latter case higher import prices, will have an inflationary effect. Hungary chose what was probably the golden mean; export refunds rose, the domestic prices of imports increased, and import subsidies did not totally disappear either. Perhaps it should be noted that a system in which a special budgetary intervention follows every external price change indicates the re-establishment in practice of the price equalisation account (*Preisausgleich*) of the directive-planning system. It makes it impossible for enterprises to adapt themselves to the changing relative prices of the world market. Perhaps it would be more rational, given an average exchange-rate system, to revalue according to the rise in export prices, while fixing export compensation in absolute terms at the old level and taxing more heavily those export earnings which rise by more than the average. In this case the import price level in domestic terms would have to rise. An increase in the price level would force either the volume of imports to drop or the central bank to finance an unchanged volume; the outcome would depend on the balance-of-payments situation.

The role of the exchange rate in CMEA trade is secondary. Nevertheless, here also the problem of insulating against external inflation has increased since 1975, when world-market price increases spread throughout the CMEA and a yearly price revision was introduced. This raises the same theoretical problem mentioned above. The other problem is the gap between the two exchange rates: that for the dollar (the most important convertible currency) and that for the transferable ruble (the accounting unit in an area in which trade is conducted bilaterally and with obligatory quotas). As I have mentioned above with reference to the requirements of the various markets, there are costs that are not included in calculating the average costs of a dollar and a ruble. These 'invisible costs' are not the same for dollar and ruble exports. Simplifying, the change in overhead costs is not calculated if the share of the two markets alters. Moreover, the additional costs created by the need to work in a different way and to pay attention to different matters (e.g. the costs of the greater risks of better marketing) are not calculated.

5 Hungary's exchange rate policy: results

After this theoretical analysis of the various stages in Hungarian exchange rate policy, it is necessary to consider whether the exchange rate has had any effect at all on trade with the West. This question must be raised because we have seen that price effects were mostly neutralised by income measures. In addition, there are many economists who think that the real conditions of the Hungarian economy do not leave much room for changes induced by prices or exchange rates.

We would not expect total exports and imports and their balance to have been greatly influenced by exchange rate changes, because of the secondary role of the exchange rate in CMEA trade and the importance of the latter as a percentage of total trade. There have been few changes in the increase in personal consumption, and therefore changes in gross investment must have been the main factor determining the movements in the balance of trade. Investments may influence the trade balance through imports both from the CMEA and from other countries. Exports to the CMEA may be affected by the impact of investment changes more strongly than other exports, because of their different commodity composition and because of the priority given to exports

Table 9.1 Foreign trade, prices and investment, 1968–78.

	1968	1969	1970	1971	1972	1973	1974	1975	1976	1977	1978
Total balance of trade											
In valuta forints[a] (millions)	−158	+1,813	−2,214	−5,744	+1,490						
In forints (million)				−23,736	+3,065	+16,449	−24,686	−38,546	−23,524	−28,375	−59,844
Exports[b]											
Export volume:											
Socialist countries	—	—	—	113	121	114	105	107	104	115	100
Non-socialist countries	—	—	—	97	116	110	97	100	115	107	103
Export value:											
Socialist countries	109	113	108	113	121	115	110	120	99	119	99
Non-socialist countries	97	126	118	99	121	124	116	94	110	112	104
Imports[b]											
Import volume:											
Socialist countries	—	—	—	119	94	104	115	112	99	107	109
Non-socialist countries	—	—	—	114	97	101	118	98	110	111	116
Import value:											
Socialist countries	104	107	124	121	96	105	124	136	96	114	111
Non-socialist countries	97	108	142	116	100	118	159	97	99	119	115
Prices[b]											
Export price:											
Socialist countries	100	100	101	100	100	102	104	112	95	104	99
Non-socialist countries	97	107	109	101	105	113	119	94	96	105	101
Import price:											
Socialist countries	100	100	101	101	102	101	107	124	97	106	101
Non-socialist countries	98	103	106	102	103	118	135	99	90	108	99
Investment											
Changes in the investments of the socialist sector[b]	85	132	118	111	99	104	109	113	100	113	99
Volume index of gross investment (1950 = 100)	347	380	448	495	491	511	556	629	629	710	740

[a] In use up to 1972.
[b] Indices, previous year = 100.
Sources: *Külkereskedelmi Statisztikai Évkönyv* (1972, 1977, 1978); *Külkereskedelmi Árstatisztikai Adatok, 1957–1977*; and *Statisztikai Évkönyv* (1972, 1977).

for convertible currencies. Export and import volumes provide a more suitable measure of the impact of exchange rate changes than do value data.

The exchange rate has been most likely to have an effect on dollar exports, while dollar imports have been influenced more by real processes and by changes in national income. This is because, while exporting has at all times been considered meritorious, profit too has been an indicator of success. Thus it is probable that, when profit on exports has been increasing, a higher exchange rate has not acted as a brake on exports but functioned rather as an incentive to sell more for dollars. On the other hand, dollar imports have depended more on changes in national income, since changes in import prices have been neutralised in one way or another.

Examining the evidence between 1968 and 1977 (see Tables 9.1 and 9.2), we see that the changes in the total trade balance moved in parallel

Table 9.2   *Exchange rates, 1971–7.*

	Date	Valuta forints (Vft)[a] or forints (Ft)[b]	
Dollar exchange parity			
Before	23 Dec. 1971	11·74	Vft
From	23 Dec. 1971	10·8125	Vft
	27 Feb. 1973	9·7318	Vft
	9 July 1973	9·1479	Vft
	1 Jan. 1975	9·0564	Vft
	1 Mar. 1975	8·5130	Vft
	1 Jan. 1976	41·30	Ft
	23 Mar. 1976	41·70	Ft
	21 Mar. 1977	41·20	Ft
	25 July 1977	40·60	Ft
Ruble exchange parity			
Before	1 Jan. 1976	13·044	Vft
From	1 Jan. 1976	35·00	Ft
Dollar exchange rate weighted by trade values			
Until	1971	11·74	Vft
	1972	10·81	Vft
	1973	9·391	Vft
	1974	9·15	Vft
	1975	8·59	Vft
	1976	41·57	Ft
	1977	40·9212	Ft

[a] In use up to 1972.
[b] Commercial exchange rate.
Source: *Külkereskedelmi Árstatisztikai Adatok, 1957–1977.*

with fluctuations in the rate of investments, except in 1969, 1971 and 1975. Changes in ruble imports followed investments even more closely. Dollar imports moved in the same direction, except in 1975 and 1976.

Changes in exports to CMEA countries fluctuated in a direction contrary to investment changes until 1974. Dollar exports too changed in the expected direction, except in 1971 and 1973. On the other hand, it is possible that the decline in the rate of export increase in 1970−1 and 1974−5, as well as the higher rates in 1972, 1976 and 1977, were partly the result of changes in the difference between the exchange rate and the average domestic price of exports of the preceding year.[3] In 1970 the rise in dollar exports was halted when investments fell, but they remained at a high level. In 1974 the decline in the rate of export increases was too early in relation to the investment cycle. Investments were rising again in 1977, after the curb in the previous year, but dollar exports increased nearly as much as in 1976. The higher level of domestic prices for exports, in relation to the exchange rate in 1976, may have been a factor in this increase in exports. We would be justified in comparing the exchange rate of the previous year and the investment change of the same year to trade fluctuations. After all, the exchange rate influences decisions, while the correlation between investment and foreign trade is an *ex post* relationship. (Needless to say, a significant part of the contracts of a given year are signed in the previous one.)

On the basis of these data, we cannot decide whether the exchange rate has had any role in regulating foreign trade (I would even be suspicious of the results of an opinion poll of chief accountants or managers). But it is certain that the profit motive has played a part in rational decisions, even if there have been factors limiting its effectiveness.

A more interesting question is whether the exchange rate *may* have had a more decisive role than it in fact has had. This problem brings us back directly to the discussion of whether a marginal or an average rate is better suited to expressing the values of foreign currencies. The difference is not simply the level of the exchange rate. Therefore, neither Wiles (1974) nor Portes (1977, 1978) was correct to write that the forint was overvalued in 1968 or that it would have been better to revalue the forint after 1973.

An exchange rate based on average costs is not suitable for macro-economic policy. It is better than the price equalisation account (*Preis-ausgleich*), since it makes it both necessary and possible to aim at a more efficient export policy for enterprises. However, it cannot function without export compensation, and this not only makes the export policies of enterprises inefficient from a macroeconomic point of view but also inevitably results in enterprises' becoming less interested in costs and profit. An average-cost exchange rate therefore results in price elasticities of import demand and of export supply that are lower than they would otherwise be. The average principle itself has surely been a contributing factor to 'the main obstacle to expanding hard currency exports' mentioned by Portes (1978). It is correct that an exchange rate policy cannot achieve its aim without a matching internal monetary and fiscal policy. But it is similarly true that a corresponding exchange rate is required if efficiency in the international division of labour is to act as a parameter on domestic efficiency.

The export successes of the first years of the reform were the result of the greater possibilities created by the reform itself and of moral and monetary incentives over and above the exchange rate. I do not understand how an exchange rate can be undervalued, if a large proportion of exports would not be achieved without a state export refund. Given the deteriorating terms of trade and the existing type of exchange rate, there were two possibilities: a lesser revaluation of the exchange rate combined with import subsidies, or a greater revaluation accompanied by a bigger export refund. The former would have made the enterprises even more indifferent to import costs; the latter would have caused higher prices because of the increase in the quantity of money. A revaluation of the forint therefore would not have succeeded in insulating the economy against imported inflation unless the exchange rate had been marginal.

However, after the increases in energy and raw material prices, the domestic price level could only have remained unchanged, even with a marginal exchange rate, if the nominal costs of manufacturing had fallen (not very probable) or perhaps if the quantity of energy and materials consumed had also decreased. Moreover, the correction of an imbalance further entails changes in accustomed production processes and consumption patterns, by abstaining from the use of certain imports in the short run and by inventing new methods in the long run. Adaptation takes time, and it is not therefore irrational to make the first phase of the change less painful by a little credit-created inflation, while allowing prices to inform producers and consumers of the changed conditions.

In conclusion, I would stress that supporters both of a marginal and of an average exchange rate do not disagree on the choice between two different levels of exchange rate. Nor do they disagree on the possibility of correcting the imbalance directly and solely on the basis of this choice. Some economists (e.g. Balázsy, 1978; Szakolczai, 1972; Szakolczai and Bárány, 1975) have argued, without any reference to changes in the real sphere or in the balance of trade, that a marginal rate could be introduced by reducing the 'pure income elements' (i.e. capital incomes, rents, profits, taxes) in prices or by abolishing the practice of paying taxes only in order to get subsidies (or vice versa). They have proposed a marginal *and* lower rate for the sake of rationality. But they agree with me and with other economists that in a more rational and more transparent economy there would be more room for further measures, which could make management more effective and more enterprising, investment decisions more profit-oriented and profits more suited to expressing efficiency.

We also think that changes of this nature in the methods of economic management, both at enterprise and national levels (perhaps together with matching organisational measures), would lead to a real increase in both national income and the standard of living, as well as to a more satisfactory long-term balance of trade.

Acknowledgement and Notes: Chapter 9

I am grateful to M. Marrese and M. Tardos for helpful comments on an earlier version of this chapter.

1   Naturally, different price relativities may have a differential impact on the standard of living of groups with different income and consumption patterns. This is the only real substance in the argument against a radically new price system.
2   The SITC categories referred to are as follows:
    54 Medicinal and pharmaceutical products (an Hungarian specialism)
     7 Machinery and transport equipment
     8 Miscellaneous manufactured articles.
3   The exchange rate is based on the average costs of a unit of export earnings estimated on the basis of a certain previous year, although this rate is later revalued according to movements on the foreign exchange markets and in relative purchasing power. The average domestic price of exports is the sum of the real domestic prices of exported goods in the given year divided by the foreign exchange revenue. Export products that are not sold on the domestic market are priced proportionally to similar goods marketed domestically.

References: Chapter 9

Külkereskedelmi Árstatisztikai Adatok, 1957–1977 (Budapest: Központi Statisztikai Hivatal, 1978).
Külkereskedelmi Statisztikai Évkönyv (Budapest: Központi Statisztikai Hivatal), various years.
Statisztikai Évkönyv (Budapest: Központi Statisztikai Hivatal), various years.

Balázsy, S. (1978), 'A keresetszabályozás "megoldhatatlan" dilemmája' (The 'unsolvable' dilemma of regulating earnings), *Közgazdasági Szemle*, vol. 25 (2), pp. 154–73.
Bartha, F. (1973), 'A nemzetközi pénzügyi válság és a külkereskedelmi árszorzó' (The international monetary crisis and the foreign exchange rate), *Külgazdaság*, vol. 17 (12), pp. 885–96.

Bartha, F. (1976), 'Az aktiv árfolyampolitika szükségességéről' (On the need for an active foreign-exchange policy), *Külgazdaság*, vol. 20 (5), pp. 357–63.

Bornstein, M. (ed.) (1973) Plan and Market (New Haven, Conn: Yale University Press).

Brown, A. A. and Marer, P. (1973), 'Foreign trade in the Eastern European reforms', in Bornstein (1973).

Brown, A. A., and Tardos, M. (1978), 'The impact of global stagflation on the Hungarian economy', Kennan Institute for Advanced Russian Studies, Paper 45 (September).

Kozma, G. (1974a), 'Külföldi áremelkedések és belföldi árszinvonál' (Foreign price increases and the domestic price level), *Világgazdaság*, vol. 6 (37), supplement.

Kozma, G. (1974b), 'Az új gazdaságirányitási rendszer hatása a tőkés országokkal folytatott külkereskedelemre' (The effect of the new system of economic management on trade with capitalist countries), in *Tanulmánykötet a Nemzetközi Munkamegosztás Kérdéseiről* (Textbook on Questions of International Division of Labour) (Budapest, mimeo.).

Hewett, E. (1980), 'The Hungarian economy: lessons for the 1970s and prospects for the 1980s in Joint Economic Committee, *East European Economic Assessment: A Compendium of Studies* (Washington, DC: USGPO).

Lakos, I. and Obláth, G. (1978), 'A külkereskedelmi árszorzóról' (On the foreign-trade price multiplier), *Külgazdaság*, vol. 23 (8), pp. 19–29.

Medgyessy, P. (1977), 'Az aktiv árfolyampolitika és az exportösztönzés' (Active foreign-exchange-rate policy and the stimulation of exports), *Gazdaság*, vol. 11 (2), pp. 65–79.

Portes, R. (1977), 'Hungary: economic performance, policy and prospects', in Joint Economic Committee, *East European Economies Post-Helsinki* (Washington, DC: US Government Printing Office).

Portes, R. (1978), 'Exchange rate policy in Hungary between 1972 and 1976', paper presented at the Fourth US–Hungarian Economics Seminar, Budapest (mimeo.).

Schneider, E. (1968), *Zahlungsbilanz und Wechselkurs* (Tübingen: Siebeck).

Szakolczai, Gy. (1972), 'Importillék vagy devizaszorzómódositás' (Import tax or modification of the foreign exchange rate), *Külgazdaság*, vol. 16 (7) pp. 522–38.

Szakolczai, Gy., and Bárány, B. (1975), 'A termelés reális költségei és az árszintproblémak' (Real costs of production and price level problems), *Közgazdasági Szemle*, vol. 22 (11 and 12), pp. 1291–311 and 1406–25.

Vincze, I. (1973), 'Külkereskedelmi árak-pénzügyi szabályozás' (Financial regulation of foreign trade prices), *Figyelő*, vol. 17 (30), p. 3.

Wiesel, I. (1973), 'Az importált infláció' (Imported inflation), *Figyelő*, vol. 17 (31), p. 3.

Wiles, P. (1974), 'The control of inflation in Hungary: January 1968–June 1973', *Economie appliquée*, vol. 27 (1), pp. 119–47.

Part Six

Agriculture

Chapter 10

The Evolution of Hungary's Agricultural System since 1967

1 Introduction

Although Hungarian agriculture has developed considerably since 1968, it is inappropriate to attribute this change uniquely to factors inherent in the New Economic Mechanism itself. The face of Hungarian agriculture has changed immeasurably since 1968, but the economics of it and the importance of non-economic considerations to its development have not, while the motivating force behind these facial changes cannot be attributed unambiguously to the New Economic Mechanism. The influx of modern Western technology into cereal production after 1968 was, it is true, in part due to a local-level managerial initiative, which was made possible by a market-determined investment policy. Similarly, the leniency adopted *vis-à-vis* small-scale private agriculture was perhaps possible only in an atmosphere where market forces generally were encouraged, while a less consumer-oriented policy might have limited agriculture's share of the national budget. However, the policy itself of improving the technological structure of agricultural production while using small-scale private agriculture as a complement to it was not new and would presumably have continued irrespective of the reform.

However, these issues are imponderables. Rather than involve itself in an attempt to weigh up the success or failure of the New Economic Mechanism in agriculture, this chapter will adopt a different approach. In two introductory sections some statistics for agricultural performance since 1968 are considered (section 2), and the degree of operational autonomy enjoyed by the co-operative farm in this period is discussed (section 3). The co-operative rather than the state farm has been chosen because of its very much greater importance within agricultural production. Section 4 considers how the development of the 'closed production systems' reflects continued scarcity on the capital goods market, while the final two sections examine how non-economic factors have had considerable importance in relation to co-operative farm mergers (section 5) and in the policy towards the small-scale private sector (section 6). These latter sections thus illustrate concretely the co-operative's scope for autonomous action since 1968 and the sorts of non-economic influences that continue to affect it.

2 Agricultural performance

Agriculture's relative importance in the economy as a whole declined between 1968 and 1976 (Table 10.1). By 1976 agriculture's share of both gross and net production within the economy had fallen quite significantly, although its importance for exports continued. Unfortunately, the statistics illustrating this tendency are not available for each year since 1968, but agriculture's share of gross national production fell from 17·4 per cent in 1965 to 16·3 per cent in 1970 and 15·1 per cent in 1976, while its share of net production showed a more marked fall from 21·9 per cent in 1965 to 18·6 per cent in 1970 and 14·8 per cent in 1976.

Table 10.1 *Agriculture's share in national production, in exports and in the active population, 1960–76 (%).*

Year	Gross production[a]	Net production[a]	Exports[b]	Active earners in agriculture
1960	20·3	26·4	22·1	37·3
1965	17·4	21·9	23·2	27·4
1970	16·3	18·6	22·8	24·0
1971	16·4	18·7	23·7	23·3
1972	16·3	18·4	23·0	22·7
1973	16·4	18·3	24·2	21·9
1974	16·1	17·4	24·2	20·9
1975	15·9	16·4	22·6	20·4
1976	15·1	14·8	23·1	19·9

[a] In 1968 prices.
[b] Including food-supply industry products.
Source: MSZs (various issues).

The share of agriculture and food industry products together within national exports, however, remained fairly constant during this period, forming 23·2 per cent of exports in 1965, 22·8 per cent of exports in 1970 and 23·1 per cent of exports in 1976 (Table 10.1). Workers in agriculture also continued to decline as a proportion of the total active population, although the drop was not as spectacular as the 10 per cent drop between 1960 and 1965 – the years of collectivisation and immediately after – and they continued to represent a larger proportion of the population than did their contribution to either gross or net national production. Thus, in 1965 27·4 per cent of the active

Table 10.2   *Gross and net production indices within agriculture,*
1960–76 (1950 = 100).

Year	Gross production	Material costs	Net production	Net turnover
1960	120	150	102	115
1965	127	176	99	144
1968	145	206	109	177
1969	155	210	123	198
1970	146	229	98	184
1971	160	248	108	213
1972	164	256	111	228
1973	175	272	119	245
1974	181	294	116	254
1975	185	300	117	260
1976	178	—	—	—

Source: MSZs (various issues); and Fazekas (1976), p. 292.

Table 10.3   *Yearly average growth of gross production, 1951–76 (%).*

Year/period	Crop production	Animal husbandry	Together
1951–55	4·4	1·7	3·4
1956–60	−0·5	1·6	0·4
1961–5	0·2	2·5	1·2
1966–70	1·9	3·9	2·8
1971–5	5·9	3·7	4·8
1976	−5·0	−1·0	−3·0

Note: Based on 1968 prices.
Source: MSZs (various issues).

population worked in agriculture, while in 1970 the figure was 24·0 per cent and in 1976 it was 19·9 per cent (Table 10.1).

Turning from agriculture within the national economy to agriculture taken on its own, we see that, while gross production rose quite quickly between 1968 and 1976 (especially after 1970), net production grew more slowly because of the increasing size of material costs (Table 10.2 and Table 10.3). Taking 1950 as a base, the index of gross production rose from 145 in 1968 to 155 in 1970 and 185 in 1975, while that for net production dropped from 109 in 1968 to 98 in 1970 and then rose again to 117 in 1975, with material costs registering 206, 229 and 300 in the same years. Net turnover, on the other hand, increased more markedly, from 177 in 1968 to 184 in 1970 and 260 in 1975.

Output trends alone say very little about the profitability of agriculture (Table 10.3), since the latter is also dependent on prices. These

Table 10.4   *Price indices, 1967—76.*

Year	State producer prices	Market producer prices	Producer selling prices
1958 = 100			
1967	130·5	138·3	131·0
1968	142·7	143·8	142·4
1969	143·2	136·6	140·5
1970	154·1	141·7	149·6
1971	158·1	150·4	154·2
1972	161·7	153·3	156·8
1973	174·5	159·8	168·4
1974	177·3	169·7	171·7
1970 = 100			
1970	100·0	100·0	100·0
1975	115·4	121·3	115·8
1976	128·2	143·9	129·0

Source: MSZs (various issues).

increased considerably between 1968 and 1976 (Table 10.4). State producer prices in 1975 were 15·4 per cent higher than they had been in 1970, and 1970 prices had increased 8 per cent over those of 1968 and 18 per cent over those of 1967. Market producer prices showed a slightly sharper increase. The 1975 prices were 21·3 per cent higher than those of 1970, while prices in 1970 represented a 1·4 per cent rise over 1968 and a 2·5 per cent rise over 1967. Producer selling prices, on the other hand, rose less steeply. The 1975 prices were only 15·8 per cent up on those of 1970, while the 1970 level was 5 per cent higher than in 1968 and 14·2 per cent higher than in 1967 (Table 10.4). In 1976 agricultural prices again increased, so that state producer prices, market producer prices and producer selling prices were 128·2, 143·9 and 129·0 per cent respectively of their 1970 value. As we shall see, however, price changes had little effect on either agricultural branch or overall agricultural profitability.

Within agriculture there were wide discrepancies according to sector (Table 10.5). While overall both gross and net production value grew between 1968 and 1976, the latter the more slowly, the net production value of animal husbandry on both the state farms and the communal part of co-operatives became progressively negative and was only made positive overall by the contribution to the national economy of the animal husbandry of the household plot. Only in 1976, when the policy in animal husbandry was switched from building large complexes to improving the quality of the stock (*TRHGy*, 42/1975 (XI.15) 22-27SS), did the size of the loss begin to diminish on the state farms at least.

Table 10.5   *Gross and net production per hectare of agricultural land, 1961–76 forints.*

Year/ period	Gross production Crop production	Animal husbandry	Together	Net production Crop production	Animal husbandry	Together
Socialist sector including household plots						
1961–5	6,798	5,208	12,006	4,515	1,678	6,193
1966–70	8,034	6,054	14,088	5,203	1,535	6,738
1971–5	9,465	7,456	16,921	5,750	1,319	7,069
1970	7,560	6,626	14,186	4,394	1,651	6,045
1971	8,469	7,070	15,539	5,099	1,594	6,693
1972	9,012	6,960	15,972	5,580	1,269	6,849
1973	9,790	7,286	17,076	6,101	1,278	7,379
1974	9,888	7,926	17,814	6,055	1,174	7,229
1975	10,177	8,050	18,227	5,923	1,276	7,199
1976						
State farms						
1961–5	6,712	5,388	12,100	3,553	417	3,970
1966–70	8,521	6,386	14,907	4,069	− 25	4,044
1971–5	10,620	7,760	18,380	4,781	− 242	4,539
1970	8,556	7,178	15,734	3,270	164	3,434
1971	9,388	7,317	16,705	3,549	398	3,947
1972	10,297	6,865	17,162	4,370	− 208	4,162
1973	11,063	7,468	18,531	5,134	− 197	4,937
1974	10,922	8,587	19,509	5,441	− 769	4,672
1975	11,471	8,608	20,790	5,452	− 450	5,002
1976	10,769	8,982	19,750	—	—	3,672
Agricultural co-operatives (communal land)						
1961–5	5,753	2,214	7,967	3,595	168	3,763
1966–70	6,742	3,169	9,911	4,046	8	4,054
1970	6,061	3,612	9,673	3,124	37	3,161
1971	7,227	3,761	10,988	4,143	− 63	4,080
1972	7,733	3,792	11,523	4,523	− 163	4,360
1973	8,500	3,936	12,436	4,968	− 254	4,714
1974	8,704	4,377	13,081	4,932	− 207	4,725
1975	8,957	4,331	13,289	4,739	− 365	4,374
1976	8,505	4,579	13,084	—	—	5,975
Agricultural co-operatives and household plots						
1961–5	6,645	4,607	11,252	4,438	1,433	5,871
1966–70	7,678	5,438	13,116	5,028	1,258	6,326
1970	7,050	5,925	12,975	4,157	1,346	5,503
1971	8,105	6,222	14,327	5,065	1,216	6,281
1972	8,630	6,123	14,753	5,497	962	6,846
1973	9,303	6,416	15,719	5,852	994	6,846
1974	9,492	6,921	16,413	5,800	1,021	6,821
1975	9,692	6,802	16,494	5,547	863	6,410
1976	9,199	6,509	15,708	—	—	5,421

Note: Based on 1968 prices. From 1978 onwards the source uses 1976 prices. The 1976 figures given are the only ones available based on 1968 prices.
Source: *MSZs* (various issues).

Table 10.6   *Increases in specific crop production in various periods between 1961 and 1976 (%).*

Crop	1966−70 over 1961−5	1971−5 over 1966−70	1975 over 1968	1976 over 1968
Wheat	48·9	42·6	19·2	53·2
Rye	− 17·4	− 23·7	− 38·8	− 34·6
Barley	− 12·8	− 3·8	− 22·6	− 17·3
Oats	− 25·9	1·3	27·7	27·7
Maize	20·8	46·6	88·0	34·8
Sugar beet	2·7	− 2·5	17·8	13·6
Tobacco	4·6	− 26·0	− 37·0	− 29·6
Sunflowers	− 13·0	43·0	59·8	93·8
Potatoes	2·4	− 23·2	− 0·1	− 14·5
Vegetables	17·2	3·1	− 4·4	2·2
Grapes	20·0	6·1	− 2·6	− 11·1
Fruit	27·6	13·2	34·4	47·0

Note: Percentages calculated by the author.
Source: *MSZs* (various issues).

At the same time, within crop production there have been considerable fluctuations in the total production of certain crops (Table 10.6). These changes both reflect the profitability of the various crops (for management has had autonomy as to what to grow) and, where the fluctuations have been wilder, changes in aid as well as changes in policy towards small-scale agriculture. Thus, wheat and sunflowers have become more widespread, with a profit of 8,300 forints and 7,800 forints per hectare respectively in 1977 (*Figyelő*, 1977, no. 19), while rye, barley and, to a lesser extent, oats and potatoes have been on the decline. The decline of rye and barley has become less pronounced; that of potatoes has become more so. Vegetables, fruit and grapes have all been on the increase, although the fall in 1975 was probably due to the attack on private agriculture of that year. Maize is a special case, its role as fodder ensuring its continued production despite falling profitability (*Figyelő*, 1977, no. 19). Sugar beet has shown a fairly stagnant picture, although the apparent increase in both 1975 and 1976 probably reflects the success of the government's policy in those years to aid sugar beet production.

The major contributor to these global figures has been the agricultural producer co-operative (referred to as agricultural co-operative unless there is danger of ambiguity; Table 10.7). The agricultural producer co-operatives are by far the largest sector in Hungarian agriculture. In 1977 they covered 78 per cent of agricultural land and 63·7 per cent of all land in Hungary (*MSZs*, 1978), while the ratio was

Table 10.7 *Percentage of gross and net production from state farms and from agricultural producer co-operatives, 1971–7.*

Year/ period	State farms	Agricultural producer co-operatives (communal land)	Agricultural producer co-operatives (including household plots)
Gross production:			
1971–5	14·0	46·8	67·6
1976	14·9	47·7	64·5
Net production:			
1971–5	8·4	39·0	67·8
1976	8·9	38·3	61·2

Note: Based on 1976 prices; percentages calculated by the author.
Source: MSZs (1978).

substantially the same in 1968 (Fazekas, 1976, p. 294). Their share of overall gross and net production and of gross production within the major production branches throughout the 1970s was roughly in line with the latter of these figures, as Table 10.7 shows. Besides the state farm sector, the remaining producers in Hungarian agriculture are the specialised co-operatives and the small-scale private sector. In 1977 there were ninety-eight specialised co-operatives, compared with 243 in 1970 and 144 in 1975 (*MSZs*, 1978, p. 16). Total value added for this sector in 1975 was 752 million forints, 2·6 per cent of that achieved by the agricultural producer co-operatives (*MSzGSzT*, 1976, pp. 98 and 121), while their profit in the same year, 269 million forints, was also 2·6 per cent of that realised by the agricultural producer co-operatives. These ratios were substantially the same in 1971, at 2·1 per cent of value added and 1·9 per cent of profit (*MSzGSzT*, 1976, pp. 98 and 121). The small-scale private sector consists of the auxiliary plots owned by state farm, industrial worker and employee households. As the figures for the specialised co-operatives show, these small plots make up the bulk of the difference between total production and that provided from the state farm and agricultural producer co-operative sectors (Table 10.7).

The figures that most warm the hearts of those involved with agriculture in Hungary are those for the yields of certain crops, mainly wheat and maize, in the last few years (Table 10.8). The figures for 1976, which in general were poorer than those for 1975, show that Hungary's yield was above the average of the European Economic Community (EEC) for wheat and roughly on a par with it for maize and barley. Maize suffered disproportionately in 1976, however, and its 1975 yield was well in advance of the EEC average. Yields in other crops (e.g. rye) were considerably below the EEC average. In relation to the other countries of the Council for Mutual Economic Assistance (CMEA),

Table 10.8   Yields of certain crops in Hungary and elsewhere, 1976
(q/ha).

Area/Country	Wheat	Rye	Barley	Maize	Sugar beet	Potatoes
World	17·7	16·8	20·3	28·3	314	136
CMEA (excluding Romania)	18·4	18·6	21·6	34·1	263	141
Bulgaria	39·7	12·0	34·0	41·3	332	119
Hungary	38·8	16·8	32·7	38·1	305	121
GDR	35·6	24·3	36·0	22·1	191	114
Poland	31·4	23·6	29·9	44·0	272	203
Soviet Union	16·3	15·5	20·3	30·6	266	120
Czechoslovakia	37·6	30·1	33·8	36·0	244	176
Yugoslavia	34·7	13·8	22·3	38·4	440	91
EEC	35·3	30·6	33·8	45·3	394	221
Belgium	45·9	31·3	41·6	—	505	242
UK	38·3	25·0	35·7	—	301	216
Italy	26·8	20·9	27·7	55·9	420	179
Netherlands	54·4	30·6	42·8	—	467	297
France	37·6	24·8	30·3	38·4	363	166
FGR	41·1	31·7	37·4	46·8	409	236
Canada	21·1	17·4	23·8	54·4	362	229
USA	20·4	13·0	24·0	54·9	446	282
Finland	29·8	27·3	30·7	—	226	180
Japan	23·9	—	26·2	—	468	230

Source: MSZs (1978).

Hungary's yields were higher than the average for wheat, barley and
maize, but lower for potatoes and rye. The boast that Hungary is now
in the world league for certain crops is not without foundation. In 1975
only Italy, the USA, West Germany, Canada and Czechoslovakia had
better yields per hectare (*MSZs; MSzGSzT*, 1978).

3   The co-operative–government relationship

Control of Hungarian agricultural producer co-operatives has taken
an indirect form since October 1956,[1] and the reforms of 1967 and 1968
in agriculture were aimed not so much at decentralising control as at
providing the co-operatives with the legal and financial basis necessary
for really autonomous action (*TRHGy*, 1967 évi III Tv). Since control
is indirect and production in agriculture is not restricted to a single
good, it may be expected that the agricultural producer co-operative
has a greater scope for autonomous action than is the case for industrial enterprises. To some extent this is the case, as will become

apparent below, but it is only true with a number of important provisos, which must first be made.

First, agricultural prices are low in relation to production costs, and despite price increases both before and since 1968 they have remained so. In 1966 there were producer price rises of 9–10 per cent followed by further rises of 8–9 per cent in 1968 (Hegedüs, 1971, p. 802), and in 1967 repayments of 60 per cent of outstanding credits were cancelled (László, 1970), while the price rises from 1968 onwards have already been discussed in section 2. However, the unfavourable price relationship in agriculture has persisted, so that, for example, Mrs Szabó found that, while social net income in the economy as a whole was around 50 per cent of value added between 1968 and 1974, in agriculture it was much lower at 20–4 per cent (Szabóné Medgyesi, 1976, p. 1215). Only in wheat and maize production was profitability considerable, and this has been achieved despite continual increases in the prices of industrial goods and fertilisers over the period (Szabóné Medgyesi, 1976, p. 1222).

Secondly, as non-economic criteria have gradually been reintroduced into agricultural investment decisions and the allocation of investment aid over the period since 1968, so the scope for autonomous action by the co-operatives has become restricted, and *de facto* control by the centre has been reintroduced. Between 1968 and 1970, while the government encouraged construction projects, no official priorities for investment existed. Decisions were made primarily on the basis of future profitability. The mushrooming of construction projects reflected in Table 10.9 contributed towards a general crisis of over-investment (Portes, 1972, p. 647), and from 1971 onwards an increasing element of control was introduced. Since in agriculture, unlike industry, there is a multiplicity of producers, central control has to be more systematic than simply an informal understanding between enterprise and ministry (Hegedüs and Tardos, 1974). Thus, as was the case for the period 1959–66, every year since 1970 has seen the publication of a government decree setting out the projects that the government wants to encourage in the subsequent year and the aid that is forthcoming in order to help (*TRHGy*, 3004 series, 1028/1967 (IX.8); *TRHGy*, 1045/1970 (X.17) Mt sz.hat. and its modifications).

From 1970–1 investment aid was reduced (Szabóné Medgyesi, 1976 p. 1217). Direct aid in the form of subsidies was restricted to the building of roads linking co-operative farms with the public highway and to forest plantation (Szabóné Medgyesi, 1976, p. 1217), while more emphasis was put on price support as a form of indirect aid (Szabóné Medgyesi, 1976, p. 1218). At the same time, within the individual co-operative's budget the role of price support itself diminished in favour of self-generated finance and the use of credit (Table 10.9).

Not only was overall aid cut, but also aid for projects other than

Table 10.9   *Agricultural producer co-operative investment: volume, source and composition, 1968–75.*

	Volume in milliard forints (1968 prices)	*Proportion of all investment in socialist agriculture (%)*	*As % of 1968 level*	*Composition of investments (%)*		
				Construction	*Machines*	*Other*
1968	7·3	77	100	63	22	15
1969	9·3	76	127	66	23	11
1970	10·8	70	148	63	29	8
1971	10·2	68	140	55	38	7
1972	8·3	67	114	54	39	7
1973	8·4	69	115	47	46	7
1974	9·2	69	126	46	49	5
1975*	10·6	71	145	42	52	6

	Sources of investment (%)				
	Depreciation	*Other*	*Retentions*	*Credit*	*Price support*
1968	22		24	14	40
1969	20		27	11	42
1970		46		16	38
1971		52		16	32
1972		58		15	27
1973		60		21	19
1974		61		19	20
1975*		64		17	19

* Preliminary data
Source: Fazekas (1976), p. 244.

supported ones became more difficult to obtain. Price support for other projects, especially those including construction, was not automatic as it was for supported ones. In 1974 a system was introduced whereby a certificate had to be drawn up for all non-listed investments, which had to include details of, and justifications for, the project and then had to be presented to the county's executive committee. In the case of projects involving construction, this certificate had to be submitted to the Hungarian National Bank (*TRHGy*, 4/1974 (VIII.7) OT PM MÉM). In 1976 the procedure was revised, so that fewer projects received automatic aid, and very complex conditions established the types of project that could be considered, on a competitive basis for further aid (*TRHGy*, 42/1975 (XI.15) PM MÉM). Further regulations specified that for construction projects a deposit of 500,000 forints had to be made in the National Bank (*TRHGy*, 6/1975

(XII.17) OT PM MÉM). Aid for non-encouraged projects, then, was relatively difficult to obtain, and in addition such aid would often be cut towards the end of each year as investment funds became exhausted (*TRHGy*, 26/1975 (VI.30) PM MÉM; *TRHGy*, 19/1977 (X.3) PM).

The agricultural producer co-operative thus could generate only limited funds for investment because of the relatively low level of agricultural producer prices, and it found aid available only for government-approved projects. Faced with this situation, either management could ignore government policy entirely, concentrate on the more profitable branches and continue to make a slowly increasing profit; or it could follow government policy but strive to generate a sufficiently large surplus in profitable branches to cover any loss that following government policy might entail; or it could follow government policy unquestioningly and run at a loss. Although the first policy may have appeared attractive, it carried with it the danger that by ignoring present government requests the co-operative might lose its future 'creditworthiness'. Thus, the majority response seems to have been the second of the three. Generally, cereal production was expanded to compensate for other and less profitable crops and for animal husbandry. Gross production in the areas that were given government support, and yet remained relatively costly, increased more slowly than that in the more profitable areas that received no government support (Szabóné Medgyesi, 1976, p. 1222).

Although the co-operative farm has somewhat greater, if still restricted, autonomy of decision-making in relation to capital goods, to some extent it is more restricted than state industry in relation to labour. The agricultural producer co-operative has a fixed labour force, and its management is under some obligation to provide all these workers with employment. Much has been made of this obligation in the literature on co-operative agriculture (e.g. Donáth, 1977, p. 121; Filla and Kalocsay, 1972, p. 13), and this is why for co-operative agriculture the economic indicator that is used for most purposes is value added rather than profit. However, it appears that in reality the restrictions imposed by this employment obligation are not so great. Clearly, the agricultural producer co-operative does have a stronger obligation to its members than a state enterprise has to its workers. However, it also has the possibility of offering them self-employment on their household plots if the co-operative cannot offer them regular work, while co-operative practice in relation to the 'ancillary industrial enterprise' reveals that the increase of profit rather than the provision of employment has been the motivation behind these ventures.

Thus, widows and pensioners[2] on the co-operative – members for whom the co-operative may be assumed to have problems in finding employment – are exempted from income tax on their household plot (*TRHGy*, 51/1968 (XI.24) Korm sz.r.3.§ b); *TRHGy*, 36/1976 (X.17)

MT 2.§ a)), while many co-operatives provide such members and their plots with the usual services of ploughing and tilling at a reduced rate or for nothing, depending on the policy of the farm. Although this latter provision is a drain on co-operative finances, it is marginal and less costly than providing uneconomic full-time employment. As for the history of 'ancillary enterprises', the rationale of which has been to provide 'off-season' employment for members, a study by Lukács V. Nagy (1973) found that the aim of the ancillary enterprises was to increase income generally and that the majority of those working them were not the less employable co-operative members but outside employees. The co-operative farm clearly has a less flexible labour force than the industrial enterprise. Its initial size bore no relation to production requirements. The farm has continued responsibility towards its members beyond retirement, but the economic burden of these ties can be exaggerated.

4   Closed production systems[3]

The history of 'closed production systems' – or 'industrial-type production systems', as they are termed in Hungary – is that of a local level initiative on an admittedly privileged state farm, which became institutionalised and was gradually incorporated into the system of administering the allocation of capital goods to co-operatives. Industrial-type production systems are the brainchild of Róbert Burgert, Director of the Bábolna State Farm. Their origins go back to his decision, after taking over the farm in 1960, to realise his dream of establishing chicken-farming on an industrial basis. He succeeded in this with the help of West German co-operation, and in 1963 a number of agricultural producer co-operatives were encouraged to take over the system that he and his technical experts had devised, agreeing to pay back to Bábolna a percentage of their surplus product for the privilege. He then turned his attention to pig-farming, but with less conspicuous success.

His experience with both products led him to realise that it was of little use organising animal husbandry on an industrial basis if there was no industrially produced fodder available. Thus, after experimenting with various fodders, he decided on maize, and in 1969 Bábolna bought the Corn Production System (CPS), modified to suit Hungarian conditions, from the Americans (Burgert, 1974; Tiszáné Gerai and Meszticzky, 1977b, p. 606). This Bábolna could afford to do with a two-year foreign-exchange credit from a sympathetic head of the Foreign Trade Bank and a government credit policy that still approximated to the original ideals of the New Economic Mechanism, where projected profitability rather than administrative preferences was the determining factor.

After an exceptionally successful first year of operation in 1970, which enabled it to repay the two years' credit in full (Burgert, 1974), Bábolna initiated the same sort of affiliation policy for maize as it had for chickens previously. In 1971 six state farms and four agricultural producer co-operatives joined the maize system, run on the same basis as the previous chicken system (Burgert, 1974). Between 1972 and 1973 three further agricultural producers followed Bábolna's lead and set up their own systems: the Baja State Farm (BKR), the Szekszard State Farm (KSZE) and the Nádudvar Agricultural Co-operative (KITE) – the biggest agricultural producer co-operative in Hungary, whose chairman is President of the National Co-operative Council. Of these, Nádudvar's KITE was the only one that started out with systems for more than one crop. On 31 March 1973 the Bábolna system reorganised itself and, combining itself with a total of thirty-four state farms, thirty-six agricultural producer co-operatives and the Intercooperation Trade Development Company, created the Bábolna Industrial Maize Production System (IKR) as a joint enterprise, with a capital of 474 million forints, 154 tractors, 157 combine harvesters and 126,000 hectares of land. By 1975 the IKR farmed 243,329 hectares of land and had even spread across national boundaries to Odessa, Slovakia and Yugoslavia (Burgert, 1974, p. 55). By that same year the KITE had become the second biggest, with 197,286 hectares of land under agricultural production spread over 275 farms. By 1977 the number of farms belonging to the KITE was 318.

Overall, in 1975, 963 agricultural enterprises participated in one system or another; 231 belonged to two systems, 57 belonged to three and 30 belonged to four. System-based production took place on 20 per cent of the arable land where large-scale farming was dominant, and 7 per cent of wheat, 68 per cent of rice, 56 per cent of maize, 40 per cent of sugar beet, 37 per cent of sunflower, 59 per cent of soya, 26 per cent of potato and 7 per cent of lucerne production took place within systems. On top of this there were twenty systems in vegetable, fruit and grape production, occupying 18,090 hectares and involving seventy-nine agricultural producer co-operatives and two state farms. In animal husbandry there were ten industrial production systems, numbering 677 members, of which 421 were agricultural producer co-operatives.

There have been two recent innovations within the framework of the closed production systems, aimed at greater integration. First, a county set of systems, including a range of crops and with a headquarters at Rákóczifalva, has been set up in Szolnok county in order to cope with the problems associated with the wide dispersal of most systems throughout the country. IKR after all now operates on farms in every county in Hungary, while KITE operates in twelve of the total of nineteen (Tiszáné Gerai and Meszticzky, 1977a, p. 10). A second form of integration is the attempt to establish 'vertical' links with industry by the Tiszavar Alkaloid Chemical Factory, which began a poppy seed-growing system on 1 January 1977 with almost thirty partners.

Thus, systems have become a significant factor in agricultural production. They have also had considerable success in increasing yields. Yields of maize, for example, averaged 47·3 quintals per hectare (q/ha) within systems in 1976, while the yields for maize outside the systems averaged only 40·2 q/ha. Similarly, yields for wheat averaged 42·4 q/ha within the systems and 38·9 q/ha outside them. It is noticeable too that the years in which Hungarian agriculture reached world rankings in these crops were those when system production had become most widespread. On the other hand, yields for soya and sunflower systems have been less impressive in relation to those outside (11·6 q/ha versus 10·8 q/ha and 15·6 q/ha versus 13·6 q/ha respectively in 1976) – a fact that either reflects the novelty of the systems or casts doubt on the inherent superiority of system production.

The legal basis of the systems, however, is not uniform. The spectrum of organisational forms extends from the 'joint venture' basis of the Bábolna's IKR to the 'simple association' of Nádudvar's KITE. Both these forms have been made possible by legislation in 1970 (*TRHGy*, 1970 évi 19 tvr). While other systems operate as simple associations, IKR is the only joint venture. Between these extremes the remaining systems are based on a fee paid to the head of the system for the services provided. IKR thus involves the creation of an independent legal person incorporating the material contributions of the member farms, the distribution of the profits and the share of any losses being in proportion to the amount of capital invested in the venture by the members. Clearly, such an organisation is geared towards making a profit, as is the case with the intermediate forms of system; the most common forms, Baja's BKR and Szekszard's KSZE, act as profit-making entrepreneurs, offering the system's technology to the members for a share of the extra product that it creates. The cost of the system naturally varies from system to system and from year to year. For the KSZE the charges per quintal of produce in 1974, 1975 and 1976 were 3·66, 3·5 and 3·57 forints respectively.

On the other hand, the aim of the simple association is just to cover the costs of the services that the system chief provides. In all the systems the system chief prescribes the necessary technology and helps in its acquisition. Under the IKR the system buys the machinery for the members, while under the KITE the members have to buy the machinery themselves. Both arrangements have their advantages. The form of the simple association provides a better forum for the elaboration of a real agreement of interests between the members, while the readiness of members' farms to help each other out with problems is stronger in the joint venture format.

Despite the mushrooming of industrial production systems throughout agriculture, they are not without problems. There are problems of a financial and a technical nature as well as more structural conflicts of interest between the system chief and the member farms.

The central financial objection from member farms concerns the cost of the services charged by the system chiefs. A study based on a representative sample of seventy-three agricultural producer co-operatives and state farms found that 50 per cent of respondents thought that the fee charged was definitely too high (Tiszáné Gerai and Meszticzky, 1977b, p. 625). It seems that the systems' chiefs have recognised the justice of these complaints, for many systems either have changed their charges or are reviewing them.

Technical problems are more numerous. There are problems caused by the fact that the same system organises the production of more than one crop, compounded by the fact that the same farm, as we have seen, often belongs to more than one system, employing the services of a different system for different crops. There are further organisational problems due to the great dispersal of the systems all over the country – a problem compounded by the well-known inadequacy of communications systems in Hungary. For example, the study found one suboffice dealing with thirty-eight farms that had a telex link with only four of them, while 'the deficiencies of telephonic contacts are well-known' (Tiszáné Gerai and Meszticzky, 1977b, p. 629).

However, perhaps more important than these problems are the two more structural factors: first, the necessary conflict of interest between the system chief and the member farm; and secondly, the lack of an adequate legal framework in which such problems can be solved. The study found that, in the same representative sample, 37·5 per cent of respondents were of the opinion that there was a conflict of interest in many fields and that the conflict of interest was economic. It also found that the conflict of interest was more common in the IKR and the BKR systems of organisation. The essence of the conflict of interest lies in the fact that the system chief is interested only in the system and, depending on the basis of the system, more or less uniquely in increasing yields on system land. In contrast, the member farm chairman is interested in running his own farm; and as well as having an interest in increasing the yields of crops cultivated according to the system, he has an interest in increasing profitability per unit area of land on the farm as a whole. The profitability of the member farm, however, is of no direct interest to the system chief. This situation of conflicting interests is exacerbated by the fact that the necessary legal framework for their resolution has not evolved. Apparently, 'the problem of damage arising from negligence by the system-chief is unclear' (Tiszáné Gerai and Meszticzky, 1977b, p. 626), despite a ministerial regulation in 1976 setting out in general terms the obligations of system chiefs and the member farms (*TRHGy*, 22/1976 (VI.19) MÉM).

Despite these difficulties the systems are still exceptionally popular, and the recent debate on their future centred more on the problem of foreign trade and the need to use more Eastern European technology than on problems inherent in the nature of the systems themselves. The question that needs to be answered therefore is why farms continue to join the systems, given the problems that we have noted. The reason becomes clear if we remember the situation of the agricultural production unit in relation to the acquisition of capital equipment. Of course, the yields for those operating within the system are better than those outside it, and this must also be an attraction, but the main aim is to get hold of the sort of Western machinery that will make the already profitable branches of crop production even more profitable. Joining a system is quite simply a way of getting at the sort of sophisticated machinery that is not available on the open market. In the survey sample of agricultural producer co-operatives already mentioned (Tiszáné Gerai and Meszticzky, 1977b), 54·3 per cent of respondents gave as their reason for joining that it offered them better opportunities for acquiring materials and machinery. The need to make the branch of production profitable was the next most common response at 22·7 per cent, and only 1·6 per cent of respondents, all from co-operative farms, cited a shortage of personnel as a reason for joining. It is also of interest that the size of the professional staff of the farms had not diminished despite this new source of technical advice. In 76·77 per cent of farms, the number had remained the same, and in 20·4 per cent it had increased. For co-operative chairmen who are not members of a system, the acquisition of the type of seed or machinery that they want may well be impossible (Zam, 1977). For AGROKER (the company dealing with agricultural goods) systems have priority – a priority that was effectively made official in the legislation on systems in 1976 (*TRHGy*, 22/1976 (VI.19) MÉM).

Although their initial evolution may have been due to a lucky conjuncture of a local initiative and a credit policy (in 1969) based almost exclusively on financial considerations, systems have become incorporated into the means of administering capital goods, and joining a system has become a method by which co-operative farms can gain privileged access to that market.

5   The merger movement

A second and probably more visible change in the organisation of collectivised agriculture since 1968 was the increase in the rate of mergers between farms that took place in the mid 1970s. It is less easy to say where the initiative for this acceleration originated. Ever since the Central Committee meeting of November 1972, and more clearly since the reorganisation of the finances of some industrial enterprises in 1974, there have been signs of a gradual re-establishment of central control over the economy.[4] This might have inspired central moves in favour of a 'rationalisation' of agriculture. However, it was local government and a particular section of co-operative farm management that benefited substantially from the change, while central government was eventually obliged to introduce measures to restrict mergers of co-operative farms.

In 1961, at the end of collectivisation, there were 4,204 agricultural producer co-operatives. By 1965 the number had dropped to 3,278 and by 1970 to 2,441 (Fazekas, 1976, p. 293), while by 1976 the number had fallen to 1,598 (MSZs, 1978). The fall in numbers over the 1960s was fairly uniform at around 150 per year, except for a dramatic drop of over 480 between 1961 and 1962, attributable to rationalisation after the completion of collectivisation, and for a small drop of only ninety-seven between 1965 and 1966. The year 1970 saw an increase in the number of amalgamations, with 235 agricultural producer co-operatives ceasing to exist, but from then on there was relative stability until 1974 and 1975, when 282 and 319 agricultural producer co-operatives respectively were merged with other farms (Fazekas, 1976, pp. 230–1). Fearing that the wave of amalgamations was getting out of hand, in September 1975 the government passed a decree obliging farms to obtain ministerial permission before any further mergers could take place (*TRHGy*, 32/1975 (XI.19) MT szr). This measure slowed down the rate of mergers. In 1976 the number of agricultural producer co-operatives fell by 128 and in 1977 by a further forty-five, so that by the end of 1977 there were a total of 1,425 agricultural producer co-operatives (MSZs, 1978). The average farm in 1975 covered 3,450 hectares as opposed to the 1961 average of 966 hectares, and it spread over an average of three to four villages. The biggest farm covered 17,000 hectares in 1975, and the smallest covered only 100 hectares, and even in 1972 324 co-operatives had land in more than six villages, while only a quarter had land in a single village (Fazekas, 1976, p. 231).

It is open to question whether this acceleration in the rate of concentration of production resources was due to purely economic factors. Evidence from two sources suggests that it was not. First, it is unclear whether the mammoth production units that the mergers created are economically more viable; and secondly there is little evidence to show that the impetus came from such economic motives as the incorporation of insolvent co-operatives within their more financially secure neighbours. In fact, there are some clear indications that the impetus was non-economic in nature.

In considering the first of these cases, an article by Ferenc Donáth (1976) is instructive. Examining a number of indicators of performance for agricultural producer co-operatives, grouped according to their area, he found that:

(1) Production value per hectare does not increase with an increase in the size of the co-operatives. In fact, it decreases.

(2) Capital equipment is not more efficient in the bigger co-operatives. In fact, per unit increase in the area of the co-operative, the production value of each unit of capital equipment decreases.

(3) In the bigger co-operatives costs per unit of capital equipment do not decrease but are roughly the same as in the smaller co-operatives.

(4) Profit per hectare is smaller, investment per hectare is smaller and wages are no higher in the biggest co-operatives.

(5) Only the productivity of live labour shows a modest, although definite, trend towards improvement as the area of the co-operative increases. On the other hand, the bigger co-operatives pay less tax per unit area and have a comparatively greater share of state aid than the smaller co-operatives.

The economic advantages of the increased concentration of resources can thus be questioned. On the other hand, it can be argued that organisers of agricultural production are aware of this fact but that the reason behind mergers was the economic incapacity of one of the partners to continue alone. This is often the argument that is presented by co-operative farm chairmen when questioned on the subject. If, however, we look at the data available, there seems to be no clear link between the number of co-operatives that are insolvent and the number of mergers. While 1970, 1974 and 1975 were the years in which the number of co-operative farms merging peaked, the years when loss-making on the agricultural co-operatives was at its highest were 1970, 1971, 1972 and 1975 (*MSZs*, 1970–5). Years of high loss-making apparently did not immediately precede years where the rate of farm-merging accelerated. The size of the losses on co-operative farms in 1969 was only a fraction of that in 1970 (51 million forints compared with 851 million forints), and yet the acceleration in mergers took place in 1970, and the rate fell back in 1971. Similarly, the years immediately preceding 1974 and 1975 witnessed rather smaller losses in co-operative agriculture than was the case in 1970 and 1971 (*MSZs*, 1969–75).

There is therefore no clear sequential pattern of insolvency leading to mergers. At most it can be argued that the continued insolvency of many farms gave weight to the arguments of those who saw a solution in their incorporation into larger units. It is more instructive, while considering loss-making, that (with the exception of 1975) the years in which most co-operatives registered a loss were those in which there was most emphasis on the building of cattle shed complexes.

If we turn to non-economic factors to help to explain this increase in mergers, we can see that both local government and the professional strata within management benefited from the changes. The first point seems obvious. In a system where the only tool available to the government for influencing agricultural production is 'persuasion' via its local representatives, and in a period when recentralising trends enhance the need for such persuasion, it is much easier for the local authorities who are obliged to do the persuading to have only a small number of co-operatives to deal with. Since the mid 1970s acceleration in the rate of mergers, the average district organisation has had only 7·6 co-operatives to look after – clearly an easier task than the 17·5 of 1968. Within this total some counties are down to as few as three to four co-operatives per administrative district (Veszprém and Komáron), while Szábolcs Szatmar county has the least manageable figure: an average of 13·3 (*MSZs*, 1968, 1978). It is in the interest of local officials to 'eliminate' weak co-operatives, so that figures for their region are more impressive, and mergers are one obvious means of achieving this end.

As far as benefits to management are concerned, the first and less important point to make concerns the chairman's and other leaders' income. With the increase in size of farm, the income level of the new chairman and leaders grew, since area is one of the categories used to rank co-operatives, and it is on these rankings (among other things) that managerial incomes depend (*TJ* 1975, pp. 806–7). More importantly, however, it seems that, as a result of these mergers, the qualified agronomist stratum, which had been growing as a force within co-operative farm management since 1961, took over the chairmanship of many of the new farms. While early chairmen were local peasants, even successful middle peasants (Erdei, 1969; Kunszabó, 1974), the number of those within co-operative management with higher education grew steadily, so that by the early 1970s, with the exception of the finance-manager, the chairman was often the least qualified of upper-level co-operative managers. Thus, in 1970 only 18·3 per cent of chairmen had higher education, compared with 72 per cent of the professionals within management (Gy. Nagy, 1976, p. 16).

Within four years this situation dramatically changed. In 1974 the proportion of co-operative farm chairmen with higher educational qualifications shot up to 43·3 per cent (Gy. Nagy, 1976, p. 16), while a study of a representative sample taken in the early 1970s found that already 89·8 per cent of chief agronomists had university degrees or their equivalent, as did 31·8 per cent of chairmen (Bognár and Simó, 1975, p. 86). Qualified personnel were suddenly occupying the key posts of responsibility on the agricultural producer co-operatives. Of course, this may also have been due to a sudden inflow of qualified personnel elected as chairmen or to many existing chairmen's going in for refresher courses. It may also have been caused by existing co-operatives' voting in, for the first time, chairmen with professional qualifications. On balance, however, it seems likely that alongside these trends a major component of this increase must be explained by the assumption that in every merged co-operative it was the more quali-fied of the partner chairmen who took control. Mergers of co-operatives in these years thus contributed significantly to the rise to power of the technocratic strata within the co-operatives – a rise that was more or less concurrent with the decline in importance of work-place level and semi-autonomous decision-making by 'complex brigades'.[5]

6   Small-scale agriculture

The private sector of small-scale agriculture based on the family labour of both co-operative members and industrial workers has always been important in Hungarian agriculture. Indeed, the success of Hungarian agriculture can be explained in some measure by its pragmatic attitude to small-scale agriculture and by its attempt to integrate it both into the agricultural producer co-operative itself and, via consumer co-operatives, into the economy as a whole. However, at the 1975 Party Congress an attitude rather hostile to agriculture in general emerged. This led to a sudden breaching of this carefully integrated system, resulting in a flight from agriculture in the small-scale sector and in shortages of meat and vegetables in the following spring. One of the cornerstones of what has been called the Kádárist 'social compromise' (Kemény, 1978), namely, the maintenance of a high standard of living, was thus grievously threatened.

How is such an occurrence to be explained? Only by the ability of political considerations to outweigh economic ones and by the conniv-ance of sections within agriculture and co-operative farm manage-ment, for which the small-scale sector was either a nuisance or a threat. Government departments and expert opinion generally were persuaded of the enduring importance of the household plot. The *General Statistical Compendium* of 1972 published its first findings on the state of private small-scale agriculture. The Ministry of Agriculture and Food Supply in 1974 was presented with a report by its statistical and economic centre documenting the continued importance of the sector. However, such opinion was apparently ignored, or at least insufficient attention was paid to the sensitivity of the sector and to the sorts of signals to which it responds. In addition, co-operative farm management took no initiative to defend the household plot by tacit encouragement of the sort that it had given to sharecropping in the 1960s. It was not in co-operative farm management's interest to do so. Household plots for most co-operative managements are often regarded as an irritant that requires considerable time and promises little reward to the farm (cf. *Népszabadság*, 11 July 1975). By 1974, it is true, produce from the household plot that was marketed by the agricultural producer co-operative did count towards co-operative value added and thus towards one of the criteria on which managerial wages and bonuses are based (*TJ*, 1975, pp. 806–7), but this established only a rather mediated form of interest in household plot production, and most chairmen left the organisation of buying from private agriculture to the General Consumer and Marketing Co-operatives.

What, then, was the nature of this 'attack' on the small-scale private sector in agriculture? 'Attack' is perhaps too strong a word. The private sector apparently reacted to minor changes in prices, to the government's reneging on contracts and to a political climate unfavourable to it. The threat of adverse changes in taxation was a more effective disincentive than the actual changes that took place. The first stage in the process seems to have been the suspension of contracts for pigs fattened on household and other small-scale plots in the second half of 1974, because of EEC import restrictions (Lovas, 1975). This in itself might not have had any really serious repercussions if the politico-economic climate had favoured small-scale agriculture. However, the political climate of the Eleventh Party Congress in March 1975 gave no indication that small-scale agriculture was to be supported; indeed, it gave many a hint in the direction of a new hard line in agriculture. Moreover, the tone of the Party statements at the beginning and end of the congress showed, if anything, a hardening of the official line towards agriculture during the congress (*Népszabadság*, 15, 18 and 23 March 1975). Although there was a passing reference to the household plot in the decree passed on 23 March, the emphasis was on 'strengthening the socialist character' of enterprises and on state rather than co-operative farms. There were also attacks on profiteering and speculation, which often signified an attack on the private sector generally. Perhaps more importantly, neither Kádár's nor Németh's speech made any reference to the household plot or small-scale agriculture.

In the wake of this new political climate, the increase in the buying price for pigs promised just before the congress was reversed. It had been considered necessary in order to compensate for the fact that the natural cycle in pig production in the small-scale sector had reached a peak in 1974, so that output was likely to fall in any case (*Figyelő*, 45, 1975, p. 15). In the event, revisions in the weight limits for various qualities of pork effectively meant a small cut in buying prices (*MEME*, 26 August 1972, 19 May 1975). In addition to this reversal of price policy, a propaganda campaign was launched against excessive peasant incomes and in favour of introducing progressive taxation to combat them. Although it cannot use such phrases as 'propaganda campaign', even *Figyelő* reported that 'much has been heard' about excessive peasant income (*Figyelő*, 45, 1975). Taxation at twice the previous rate was mooted (Kemény, 1978, p. 45) but apparently not put into effect.

This combination of press campaign, threats and real inroads into the profitability of small-scale farming had disastrous results. Kemény (1978) wrote of the killing of the country's whole stock of sows in the private sector in a week. Other unofficial sources refer to 100,000 pigs' being killed in ten days. Although it is difficult to verify figures for such short periods, published figures for the period from mid 1974 to October 1975 show a huge drop. In this period 553,000 household plot pigs were killed as well as 475,000 pigs kept on other small-scale plots. This resulted in a 20 per cent drop in the pig stock as a whole and a 30 per cent drop in the number of sows kept on small-scale farms of any type (Lovas, 1975). Vegetable and fruit production also suffered (Kemény, 1978; Csizmádia, 1978, p. 78), so that both meat and vegetables had to be imported in the first half of 1976 (*Figyelő*, 25 and 31, 1976).

The government acted swiftly to meet this threat to its 'social compromise'. The Minister of Agriculture and Food Supply was replaced in July 1975, just a few days after a Central Committee statement called for help to small-scale agriculture and noted that, in the first months of the new five-year plan, the pig stock on small-scale farms had 'fallen somewhat' (*Népszabadság*, 3 and 5 July 1975). More constructively, the buying price for pork was increased in September 1975 (*MÉME*, 19 May and 29 September 1975), and this buying price continued to rise in subsequent years. In August 1976 small-scale producers were allowed the same price premium as large-scale ones for meat to be sold on a contractual basis with a buying enterprise (*TRHGy*, 28/1976 (VIII.15) MÉM AH). The following month a temporary 1 forint per kilogram was given for live fattened pigs raised on a contractual basis (*TRHGy*, 33/1976 (X.23) MÉM AH), while the following year the buying price for certain types of pork was increased (*TRHGy*, 4/1977 (VIII.1) MÉM AH; *TRHGy*, 23/1977 (VIII.17) MT).

More importantly, when the new uniform tax on all small-scale agriculture, including the household plots of members of agricultural producer co-operatives, was introduced, the threshold for taxation of 'exceptionally high incomes' was effectively increased. The basis of this part of the tax was changed to 'sales receipts' rather than income, and the threshold was increased to three times the previous income level. Since labour and capital costs are very low in this sector, this change can be taken as a considerable increase in possible untaxed income. In addition, the definition of 'regular employment' of outside labour (which also incurred extra taxation) was made less strict

(*TRHGy*, 51/1967 (XI.24) MT sz.r.; *TRHGy*, 37/1973 (XII.24) MT sz.r; *TRHGy*,36/1976 (X.17) MT sz.r.). Furthermore, the government increased investment aid to the small-scale sector. Although aid to purchase polythene sheeting for vegetable production was reduced from 30 to 20 per cent in 1976, to be increased to 40 per cent in 1977, the government introduced investment aid for the purchase of small tractors and similar machinery (*TRHGy*, 1050/1971 (XII.29) MT hat; *TRHGy*, 1010/1974 (III.6) MT hat; *TRHGy*, 1030/1975 (XI.15) MT hat; *TRHGy*, 1028/1976 (IX.16) MT hat).

In 1977 two further measures were taken to bolster small-scale agriculture. From 1 January co-operative farm members and others were encouraged to take on any areas of state or co-operative land that were not capable of cultivation on a large-scale basis. The upper limit of such land per individual was 0·6 hectares, the same as that for the household plot. Use of the land required payment, but the maximum cost was to be 50 per cent of the market price of land of a similar quality, and payment could be made in instalments spread over ten years (*TRHGy*, 6/1977 (I.28) MÉM EVM PM IM). Co-operative farm members could thus double the size of their plots and other small-scale farmers increase theirs by an even greater ratio, provided that suitable land was available and that the plots were profitable enough to realise the cost of the extra land. In addition, the government initiated a measure to stimulate the interest of co-operative farm-managers in the household plot production of their members by making the improvement of household plot or other small-scale production a criterion for which management might receive a 20 per cent bonus (*TRHGy*, 19/1977 (V.25) MÉM MÜM).

Finally, and more symbolically, the government pledged itself both to agriculture and to its small-scale sector. Although the 1975 Party Congress had played down agriculture, Kádár not only attended the Congress of Agricultural Co-operatives in December 1976 but also made a speech that was interpreted as a recognition of the importance of agriculture for the Hungarian economy. What is more, he explicitly stressed the unity of the household plot and the co-operative farm (TOT, 1977, p. 78). The Central Committee statement in March 1978 further stressed both agriculture in general and its small-scale component. The lessons of the preceding years had apparently been learned.

7 Conclusions

Four conclusions can be drawn from this examination of Hungarian agriculture since 1968. First, overall economic performance has not been startling. Net production has not shown a very great improvement since 1968, while within it animal husbandry has been dependent on the small-scale private sector in order to avoid a deficit. Government aid, it seems, has not solved the problems of low profitability due in part to low agricultural producer prices. On the other hand, cereal yields have improved significantly, while in both animal husbandry and cereals the technological basis of production has been radically transformed.

Secondly, the real autonomy of action of the majority of agricultural producers (i.e. the agricultural producer co-operatives) has remained rather restricted, despite formal autonomy. Again, this can be attributed in part to the low level of agricultural producer prices, but it is also related to the scarcity of capital goods, which have ceased to be distributed according to the logic of financial rationality alone but have become subject to a degree of administrative control from central government.

Thirdly, Hungarian agricultural co-operatives have increasingly come under the management of a professionally qualified group with training in agronomy, whose production decisions (in relation to mergers at least) have not necessarily followed the dictates of economic rationality.

Fourthly, non-economic and wholly political factors have continued to be important for agriculture during this period, from both local administration and central government levels. Perhaps, however, the limitations of political intervention were learned when the 1975 'attack' on small-scale agriculture led to shortages, threatened living standards and put a vital element of the Kádárist 'social compromise' in jeopardy.

Notes: Chapter 10

1   Compulsory deliveries were abolished by the Nagy government on 30 October 1956 (Váli, 1961, p. 293) – a policy that was then sanctioned by the Kádár government in the same year (*TRHGy*, 1956 évi 21 tvr).

2   The provision of some sort of seasonal employment for co-operative farm pensioners is considered necessary because of the low level of co-operative farm pensions, especially in the case of women. For a discussion of the differences between the levels of social benefits generally on the agricultural co-operative in industry, see Lajos Nagy (1976). In 1968 the value of the agricultural co-operative pension was less than half of that in industry. By 1975 it had risen to 63 per cent – still considerably smaller at 926 forints per month (Fazekas, 1976, p. 279).

3   Much of this section is based on Tiszáné Gerai and Meszticzky (1977a, b).

4   Cf. among other measures: the expulsion of the 'Budapest School' from their posts in 1973; the central wage increases of 1973 and 1974 (1001/1973 (I.24) MT hat; 1007/1974 (III.6) MT hat); the introduction of a centralised wage table in 1975 (6/1974 (III.22) MÜM); and changes in investment regulations (34/1974 (VIII.6) MT) in *TRHGy*.

5 For discussion of the complex brigades, see Juhász and Párkányi (1977), Kunszabó (1972, 1975), Kovács and Kunszabó (1974) and Szomolányiné Szabo (1970).

References: Chapter 10

A few official publications are referred to by means of abbreviations throughout this chapter. The following abbreviations are employed:

MÉM. Mezőgazdasági és Élelmiszeripari Minisztérium Értesitő. (Budapest: Lapkiadó Vállalat, 1972 and 1975).
MSZs. Mezőgazdasági Statisztikai Zsebkönyv (Budapest: Központi Statisztikai Hivital, 1967–76).
MSzGSzT. Mezőgazdasági Szövetkezetek Gazdálkodása a Számok Tükrében (Budapest: Termelöszövetkezetek Országos Tanácsa and Központi Statisztikai Hivatal, 1976).
TJ. Termelöszövetkezeti Jogszabályok (Budapest: Közgazdasági és Jogi Könyviadó, 1975).
TRHGy. Törvények és Rendeletek Hivatalos Gyujteménye (Budapest: Közgazdasági és Jogi Könyvkiadó, 1956 and 1967–77).

Bognár, R., and Simó, T. (1975), *A Termelöszövetkezeti Vezetök Társadalmi Mobilitása* (Social Mobility of Producer Co-operative Farm-Leaders), Szövetkezeti Kutató Intézet Közleményei 105 (Budapest).
Burgert, R. (1974), 'Ötszemközt Burgert Róberttal' (TV interview with Robert Burgert), *Valóság*, vol. 18 (9), pp. 47–60.
Csizmádia, Mrs E. (1978), 'A háztáji termelés új vonásai' (New directions of household production), *Valóság*, vol. 21 (2), pp. 78–86.
Donáth, F. (1976), 'A kollektivizált mezőgazdaság iparosodása Magyarországon' (The industrialisation of collectivised agriculture in Hungary), *Közgazdasági Szemle*, vol. 23 (6), pp. 661–78.
Donáth, F. (1977), Reform és Forradalom (Reform and Revolution), (Budapest: Akadémiai Kiadó).
Égetö, E. (1976), *Felhalmozás és Jövedelmezöség a Termelöszövetkezetekben* (Accumulation and Profitability in the Producer Co-operatives) (Budapest: Kossuth Könyvkiadó).
Erdei, F. (1969), 'A mezőgazdasági termelöszövetkezetek néhány társadalmi kérdése' (Some social questions about the agricultural producer co-operatives), *Valóság*, vol. 12 (2), pp. 74–89.
Fazekas, B. (1976), *A Mezőgazdasági Termelöszövetkezeti Mozgalom Magyarországon* (The Agricultural Producer Co-operative Movement in Hungary) (Budapest: Kossuth Könyvkiadó).
Filla, M., and Kalocsay, F. (1972), *A Munkaerö-gazdálkodás Gyakorlati Kérdései a Termelöszövetkezetekben* (Practical Issues in Labour Force Management in the Producer Co-operatives) (Budapest: Közgazdasági és Jogi Könyvkiadó).
Hegedüs, M. (1971), 'A Mezbgazdasági termelöi árak és a termelés összefüggése' (The relation between agricultural producer prices and production), *Statisztikai Szemle*, vol. 49 (8–9), pp. 800–15.
Hegedüs, Zs., and Tardos, M. (1974), 'A vállalati vezetök helyzetének

motivációjának néhány problémája' (Some problems of motivation for enterprise-managers), *Közgazdasági Szemle*, vol. 21 (12), pp. 162–73.

Juhász, P., and Párkányi, M. (1977), 'Miért nincsenek komplexbrigádok?' (Why are there no complex brigades?), in *Szövetkezeti Kutató Intézet Évkönyv* (Budapest: Közgasdasági és Jogi Könyvkiadó).

Kemény, I. (1978), 'Hol tart a társadalmi kompromisszum Magyarországon?' (Where is the social compromise in Hungary maintained?), *Magyar Füzetek*, no. 1, pp. 21–46.

Kovács, A., and Kunszabó, F. (1974), 'Nehéz taláj' (Difficult ground), *Valóság*, vol. 17 (9), pp. 38–46.

Kunszabó, F. (1972), *Sárköz* (Sarköz – a region south of Budapest) (Budapest: Szépirodalmi Könyvkiadó).

Kunszabó, F. (1974), *Elnöktipusok a Termelőszövetkezetekben* (Types of Chairman in Producer Co-operatives) (Budapest: Akadémiai Kiadó).

Kunszabó, F. (1975), 'Termelő és termelés' (The producer and the product), *Valóság*, vol. 18 (7), pp. 48–56.

László, J. (1970), 'Irányitási rendszer és termelési struktura a termelő szövetkezetekben' (Management system and structure of production in producer co-operatives), *Valóság*, vol. 13 (7), pp. 9–21.

Lovas, M. (1975), 'Kifelé a hullámvölgyböl' (Upwards from the trough), *Figyelő*, vol. 19 (45), p. 15.

Nagy, Gy., (1976), 'A mezőgazdasági termelöszövetkezetek vezetésének alapkérdései' (Basic questions of leadership in agricultural producer co-operatives), *Vezetéstudomány*, no. 4, pp. 11–17.

Nagy, L. (1976), 'Az ipari és mezögazdasági személyi jövedelmek aránya és arányos fejlesztése' (The ratio and proportionate development of industrial and agricultural personal incomes), *Közgazdasági Szemle*, vol. 23 (3), pp. 279–92.

Nagy, L. V. (1973), 'A termelöszövetkezetek kiegészitő tevékenységének hatása a munkaerő-gazdálkodásra' (The effect of the complementary activities of producer co-operatives on manpower management), *Közgazdasági Szemle*, vol. 20 (10), pp. 1210–17.

Portes, R. (1972), 'The strategy and tactics of economic decentralisation', *Soviet Studies*, vol. 24 (4), pp. 629–58.

Szabóné Medgyesi, E. (1976), 'A szabályozó rendszer sajátosságai a mezőgazdaságban' (Peculiarities of the regulator system in agriculture), *Statisztikai Szemle*, vol. 54 (12), pp. 1215–28.

Szomolányiné Szabó, J., and Kiss, Z. (1970), *A Szántóföldi Gépesített Komplexbrigád Gépesitésszervezési és Szociálpsychológiai Vizsgálata* (Organisational and Social–Psychological Examination of a Mechanised Complex Brigade in Arable Farming), Agrárgazdasági Kutató Intézet Füzetei 14 (Budapest).

Termelöszövetkezetek Országos Tanácsa (TOT) (1977), *A Mezőgazdasági Szövetkezetek III Kongresszusa* (The Third Congress of Agricultural Co-operatives) (Budapest: Kossuth Könyvkiadó).

Tiszáné Gerai, V., and Meszticzky, A. (1977a), *Tapasztalatok és Gondolatok a Szántóföldi Növénytermelési Rendszerekről* (Experiences and Thoughts about Crop Cultivation Systems), Szövetkezeti Kutató Intézet Közleményei 128 (Budapest).

Tiszáné Gerai, V., and Meszticzky, A. (1977b), 'A szántóföldi termelési rendszerek terjedésének társadalompolitikai és ökönómiai hatása az üzemi viszonyokra' (The socio-political and economic effects of the spread of crop production systems on working relationships), in *Szövetkezeti Kutató Intézet Évkönyv* (Budapest: Közgazdasági és Jogi Könyvkiadó).

Váli, F. (1961), *Rift and Revolt in Hungary: Nationalism versus Communism* (Cambridge, Mass.: Harvard University Press).

Zam, T. (1977), 'Javasoljúk a kongresszusnak . . .' (We recommend to the congress . . .), *Valóság*, vol. 20 (6), pp. 52–63.

Index

agricultural machinery 119, 198, 238, 240
agricultural performance 226-32
agricultural products 134, 168, 187-8, 190; compulsory deliveries of 27, 248 note 1
agricultural producer co-operatives 58, 225, 231, 236-7, 244-5; and central government 232-6; chairmen of 243-4; insolvency of 242-3; numbers of 241-2; production figures 229, 230; subcontracting to 118
agriculture 19, 30, 86, 120, 129-30, 134, 135, 185-6, 225-50; collectivisation of 27; 'first' and 'second' economy in 57; small-scale 48, 225, 231, 244-7
Aluminium Tröszt 116
Anker 113
associations 8-9; *see also* trusts
Austria 128
Austro-Hungarian monarchy 134
automobiles 165, 169

balance of payments 201, 216, 220; deterioration in 15, 94, 293; and exchange rate 171-2; and forint convertibility 153; and planning 88; *see also* foreign trade *and* terms of trade
Balázsy, S. 72-4
bankruptcy 113, 208
banks 91, 99, 134, 162-3, 208, 213; *see also* specific banks
Barone 24
Bauer 96-7
bonuses 4, 15, 73-4, 76; dissatisfaction with 1968 system of 15; in traditional planning 9-10
Bowcan 113
branch ministries: and CMEA trade 34; continued power of 31-2, 78, 103, 162; diminished power of 14, 35; direct bargaining of 14; and EWIC 112, 115-16; and innovation 18; and investment 32, 90; and planning 34-5, 148
Brus, W. 23
Bulgaria 24, 128, 191, 232
Burgert, R. 236
bus production 116, 119, 122, 198

CMEA, *see* Council for Mutual Economic Assistance

Canada 232
capital charges 67, 91, 93, 178, 213; abolition of in 1980 91, 197
Central Development Programmes 116, 122, 141, 147, 150; since 1979 116, 122
centralised planning: behaviour patterns 20; dismantling of 16, 137; dynamic of 24-5; economic indicators under 12; economic management under 4-5; and innovation 134-6; and misinformation 6; and multi-coloured markets 34-5; objectives in the 1950s 135-6; and prices 9
centrally planned economies 24, 83
chemicals 135, 179, 191, 192-3
China, *see* People's Republic of China
'closed production systems' 19, 225, 236-40; and Western machinery 240; history of 236-8; legal basis of 238; problems of 239-40; yields in 238
Common Agricultural Policy 190
Communist Party, *see* Hungarian Socialist Workers' Party
'complex brigades' 244, 249, note 5
computers 122
construction: private sector in 35, 49, 56, 79
consumer goods 94-5, 165-6, 178
consumption 182-4, 195-6, 209; consumption-accumulation trade-off 62, 69
convertible currency: balance 18, 197; deficit 161, 181-2, 184-95; exports 112, 193-5, 215-17; imports 149; markets 7; payments 113, 201-2; solutions to debt 194-9; trade in 161-2, 180; *see also* credits, foreign exchange *and* Hungarian National Bank
Council for Mutual Economic Assistance 7-8, 23, 109, 161, 164, 194; agricultural yields 231; and 'average coefficient' 209; and bilateral agreements 166; co-operation 112, 123, 146; consumer prices 169, 172-4; and convertible currency deficits 186-9; and exchange rate 213, 214-15; exports to 218; foreign trade multipliers 29; and forint convertibility 175-7; internal trade prices 184; joint projects 162, 182; market 7, 123, 178; orientation towards 34, 192, 194; planning 29; prices 202,